ALLIED HAMBRO
CAPITAL TAXES
AND ESTATE PLANNING GUIDE

ALLIED  HAMBRO
CAPITAL TAXES
AND ESTATE PLANNING GUIDE

By

W I Sinclair, FCA,

A partner in Kidsons

and

P D Silke, B Phil, M Soc Sc, *Solicitor* with *Herbert*

Oppenheimer Nathan and Vandyk

Oyez Longman

Published in 1984 by
Oyez Longman Publishing Limited,
21-27 Lamb's Conduit Street,
London WC1N 3NJ

ISBN 0 85120 894 0

First published 1982
Second edition 1984

© 1984 Fiscal Services Limited

Printed in Great Britain by
Biddles Ltd, Guildford and King's Lynn

Introduction

This is the second edition of a book which was originally published as the *Hambro Capital Taxes and Estate Planning Guide* in 1982. It has now been revised to reflect the many changes to the legislation which have taken place in the fields of capital taxes, trusts and estates. We are most grateful to those who have written to us with kind and helpful comments regarding the first edition, some of which have been taken into account in the preparation of this volume.

As a broad generalisation, tax planning covers two main areas. The first concerns taxes on income and the second taxes on capital. This book is concerned with the area of capital taxation and gives both a guide to the actual taxes as well as planning points. In addition, separate chapters outline the law involved in such matters as drawing up your will and forming trusts; also administering trusts and the estates of deceased persons. In other words, the book takes a comprehensive look at the taxes on capital and practical ways in which savings are possible, with an eye on the most important legal aspects of estate and trust planning and administration.

The book does not deal with the field of taxes on income. Naturally, you should always bear in mind that specific transactions may involve taxes on both income and capital. However, there is a logical dividing line in most cases. What is certain is that capital taxes often inter-relate one with another, which is one reason for including within a single book capital gains tax, capital transfer tax, development land tax and stamp duty.

Another reason for grouping together within one volume the various taxes on capital is that changes to the legislation sometimes cover more than one capital tax at the same time. Perhaps more important, a relief from one capital tax may raise planning considerations concerning another. For example, if you avail yourself of the capital gains tax rollover rules regarding certain gifts, you may well still be liable to capital transfer tax in that respect.

The present Government has stated its intention to carry out widespread reforms in the field of capital taxation. Some of these have already been made, including the highly important capital gains and capital transfer tax indexation rules, bristling with planning implications. It is our intention to bring out further editions to reflect major changes to the legislation although not necessarily on a regular annual basis. This second edition is based on the law as at 1 October 1984, including the Finance Act 1984 and the Capital Transfer Tax Act 1984.

Now, just a word about the way in which the book is organised. Each of the taxation chapters explains the basic rules, sometimes illustrating these with examples. Planning points are given where appropriate in the text. These will be found in contrasting italic type. A comprehensive table of contents at the front of the book makes it easy to refer to the appropriate subject matter and hence any related planning points. (In addition, an index is provided at the back of the book). A further feature is a section called *Tax planning signposts* which will help you locate tax planning points regarding selected situations.

This book is a companion volume to the *Allied Hambro Tax Guide*, like which it has been designed as a general guide for both the professional and non-professional user. Because the book concisely covers a very wide field, it has been necessary to omit some of the exemptions and qualifications with which the law abounds. This does have the positive advantage of increased clarity. However, if a particular problem is not solved by this book, the time has come to look at one of the multi-volume text books or consult a specialist. Certainly reference to a solicitor will normally be necessary in matters concerning wills and trusts.

We acknowledge with thanks the very valuable assistance given to us in connection with this edition by our respective colleagues, including Messrs E B Lipkin, LLB, FCA, ATII and K G S Stockings, ATII of Kidsons; and by Messrs A N Homburger, BCom, FCA, ACMA, (of Blick, Rothenburg and Noble) and P C Howe, LLB, Barrister, V J Jerrard, LLB, Solicitor, M S Lipworth, BCom, LLB, Barbara Lock, BA, Solicitor, W W Dobbin, BA, Barrister, P J Matthams, MA, Barrister and D C Vessey, BSc (all of Hambro Life Assurance PLC). Our special thanks are extended to K A Bulgin, MA, FCII, ATII, Barrister for contributing the original chapter on capital taxes and life assurance, and to V Jerrard for updating it.

1 October 1984   W I Sinclair

                                                                     P D Silke

Contents

1 The basis of liability to capital taxes

2 Capital gains tax — general

Contents

3 Capital gains tax — Shares and securities

4 Capital gains tax — Special reliefs

5 Capital gains tax — Trusts, estates and companies

6 Development land tax

7 Capital transfer tax

Contents

8 Capital transfer tax — Trusts

9 Drawing up your will

10 Administering the estate

Contents

11   Income tax — Trusts and estates

12   The legal aspects of trusts

13 Capital taxes and life assurance
by Ken Bulgin

Contents

14 Stamp Duty

15   Capital tax planning signposts

Abbreviations

AEA	Administration of Estates Act 1925
AJA	Administration of Justice Act 1982
CAA	Capital Allowances Act 1968
CGT	Capital gains tax
CGTA	Capital Gains Tax Act 1979
CTT	Capital transfer tax
CTTA	Capital Transfer Tax Act 1984
DLT	Development land tax
DLTA	Development Land Tax Act 1976
FA	Finance Act
F2A	Finance (No 2) Act
FLRA	Family Law Reform Act 1969
FPA	Family Provisions Act 1966
IEA	Intestates' Estates Act 1952
IPFDA	Inheritance (Provision for Family and Dependants) Act 1975
JTA	Judicial Trustee Act 1896
MFPA	Matrimonial and Family Proceedings Act 1984
NCPR	Non-Contentious Probate Rules
PA	Partnership Act 1890
PTA	Public Trustees Act 1906
S	Section (of Income and Corporation Taxes Act 1970 unless otherwise stated)
Sch	Schedule (of Income and Corporation Taxes Act 1970 unless otherwise stated)
TA	Trustee Act 1925
TIA	Trustee Investments Act 1961
TMA	Taxes Management Act 1970
WA	Wills Act 1968
WA 1837	Wills Act 1837
WSSA	Wills (Soldiers and Sailors) Act 1918

1 The basis of liability to capital taxes

Who pays capital taxes?

Tax on capital gains arising in the United Kingdom is payable by individuals, partnerships, estates, trusts, companies and certain other organisations which are resident and/or ordinarily resident here (p 5). They are also liable to tax on capital gains arising abroad, subject to the rules outlined later in this book (p 28). Non-resident individuals etc, may be liable to capital gains tax on assets realised in the United Kingdom in certain circumstances, for example if they were used in a trade here (p 28).

Development land tax applies to individuals, partnerships, estates, trusts and companies etc, whether or not they are UK resident for tax purposes (p 5). All that is needed is that the land is situated in the UK and there is a real or deemed realisation of development value (p 62) in excess of the exemptions.

Capital transfer tax normally only applies to individuals and trusts (occasionally close companies). UK domiciled individuals (p 4) are liable on their worldwide assets but, in general, those not domiciled (or deemed domiciled — p 69) in the UK are only liable on their assets situated in the UK.

In general, stamp duty is charged on documents (instruments) and may be payable by any of those listed earlier. However, if the instruments are executed overseas and relate to foreign property, no UK stamp duty is likely to be due. Reference should be made to the more detailed treatment of this subject in Chapter 14 (p 200).

What capital taxes are payable?

In certain circumstances (see below) income tax may be chargeable on capital profits but this book is concerned chiefly with capital taxes. In particular, four main taxes apply in the UK to capital realisations and transfers. These are capital gains tax, development land tax, capital transfer tax and stamp duty.

Capital gains tax at 30% applies to chargeable gains (p 10). In the case of companies, corporation tax is charged on the gains but the effective rate is still 30%.

Development land tax (p 60) is charged at 60% on realised development value, subject to the detailed rules.

The percentage rates at which stamp duty applies vary but are seldom more than 1%. Thus, in percentage terms, this tax is not likely to be as important as the others but could be highly significant in large cases.

One feature of the capital taxes listed above is that they are not mutually exclusive. In fact they could all apply at once. For example, if a father sold to his son a valuable property with substantial development value, for less than its full value, he could be assessed to capital gains tax, development land tax and capital transfer tax. Also, the son may need to pay stamp duty. Thus it is necessary to keep in mind all the capital taxes in appropriate situations.

Income tax on capital transactions

As mentioned earlier, income tax might be charged on capital transactions, instead of capital gains tax. In the case of a company, corporation tax would be charged as if the gains were revenue profits. This would normally happen in one of two ways: either certain anti-avoidance legislation would take effect, or the taxpayer would be treated as trading in the assets concerned.

In general, the tax on capital gains is likely to be no more than on trading and in many cases less. It is therefore normally desirable to have purchases and sales of assets treated as *capital* rather than *trading*, if possible.

As well as your regular business, certain other activities might constitute *trading*, depending on the circumstances. The following are some general guidelines:

(1)   Regular buying and selling normally constitutes trading, although this does not usually apply to share dealings by an individual.
(2)   An isolated transaction might still be held to be trading if it is by its very nature commercial. For instance, a single purchase and sale of unmatured whisky would normally be treated as a trading transaction, because unmatured whisky is mainly owned for commercial purposes.
(3)   Isolated purchases and sales of works of art are not normally trading. Here, the items are owned to be admired, rather than for commercial purposes. Capital gains tax, however, might be payable on sales of works of art for over £3,000 each (p 43).
(4)   Isolated transactions in income-producing assets are not usually treated as trading. Capital gains tax would normally apply.
(5)   What you do to something that you purchase before selling it could indicate that you are trading. For example, if you buy a ship, convert it and then sell it you will be treated as trading.

(6)   Repetition of the same transaction is evidence of trading.
(7)   Dealing in property is likely to be treated as trading.
(8)   The possession of expert business knowledge regarding a transaction that you carry out will increase the chances of this being treated as trading.

Anti-avoidance legislation

Certain provisions counter the avoidance of capital gains tax itself. These impose capital gains tax and are considered later (p 27).

Certain other provisions impose income tax on otherwise capital transactions. The main ones are Sections 460 and 488 Taxes Act 1970. Section 460 deals with the avoidance of taxes on income by means of transactions in securities, Section 488 with so-called artificial transactions in land and applies to land in the UK owned by residents or non-residents. There are procedures for applying to the Revenue for clearance for both sections.

Another section of the Taxes Act 1970 which could result in such transactions as making and repaying loans giving rise to income tax is Section 451, which relates to trusts (p 154).

In general, the above provisions are beyond the scope of this book but Section 460 should be considered particularly in larger cases involving company reconstructions. It is advisable to seek clearance from the Revenue in advance. Note that for the Revenue to invoke Section 460 there must be some avoidance of taxes on income (either income tax or corporation tax), but not only capital gains tax.

● *The main requisite for Section 488 to bite is that a capital gain is realised on land which was purchased or developed with a view to selling at a profit. It helps a lot in contesting an assessment under this section to have documentary evidence, such as minutes of meetings and corres-pondence, to the effect that when you bought the land, you did so for investment purposes, etc, and not for quick sale.*

Domicile and residence

As indicated earlier, the incidence of the main capital taxes is greatly affected by the domicile and residence of the potential taxpayer. The rest of this chapter therefore deals with this important subject. The position is summarised in the following table and dealt with in more detail on the next pages. (Domicile is defined on p 4 and residence on p 5).

Table 1: The effect of domicile and residence on capital taxes

Tax	Situation of assets	Tax treatment depending on taxpayers' residence and domicile		
		Taxed on arising basis	Taxed on remittance basis (p 29)	Tax free
Capital gains tax	UK or Abroad	UK domiciled and resident or ordinarily resident	Non-domiciled but resident or ordinarily resident (assets abroad)	Neither resident nor ordinarily resident
Capital transfer tax (residence is normally immaterial)	UK	UK domiciled or non-domiciled		
	Abroad	UK domiciled or deemed domiciled (p 69)		Non-domiciled
Development Land tax	UK	All		
	Abroad			All

Domicile

Your domicile is the country which you regard as your natural home. It is your place of abode to which you intend to return in the event of your going abroad. For most people it is their country of birth. Everyone has one domicile only. Unlike dual nationality, it is not possible to have two domiciles under English law. There are three main categories of domicile:

(a)   Domicile of origin.
(b)   Domicile of choice.
(c)   Domicile of dependency.

You receive a *domicile of origin* at birth; it is normally that of your father at the date of your birth. In the case, however, of an illegitimate child or one born after the death of his father his domicile of origin is that of his mother. Your domicile of origin can be abandoned and you can take on a domicile of choice (see below). You will quickly revert to your domicile of origin, however, if you take up permanent residence again in that country.

If you abandon your domicile of origin and go and live in another country with the intention of permanently living there, the new country will become your *domicile of choice*. You will normally have to abandon most of your links with your original country of domicile (p 8). If you lose or abandon your domicile of choice, your domicile of origin automatically applies once again, unless you establish a new domicile of choice.

Certain dependent individuals are deemed incapable of choosing a new domicile. They have a *domicile of dependency* which is always fixed by the operation of the law. Dependants for this purpose include minors, married women before 1 January 1974 and mental patients. A child under 16 years of age automatically has the domicile of his father if he is legitimate, and otherwise that of his mother. If, however, a girl of under 16 marries then she takes on her husband's domicile. (Prior to 1 January 1974 the relevant age was 18.) In Scotland a boy has an independent domicile from age 14 and a girl from age 12.

Prior to 1 January 1974, a wife assumed the domicile of her husband while they were married. After the end of the marriage (by death or divorce) the woman kept her former husband's domicile unless she took on a fresh domicile of choice. Since 1 January 1974, however, a wife's domicile is independent of that of her husband. If married before that date, the husband's domicile at 1 January 1974 remains as the wife's deemed domicile of choice until displaced by positive action.

Residence

Your residence for tax purposes is something which is fixed by your circumstances from year to year and you may sometimes be treated as being resident in more than one country at the same time.

Residence depends on the facts of each case and is determined by the individual's presence in a country, his objects in being there and his future intentions regarding his length of stay. The main criterion is the length of time spent in the country during each tax year. Another point is whether a 'place of abode' is kept in the country (p 7).

If you have always lived in this country you are treated as being *ordinarily resident* here. Ordinary residence means that the residence is not casual and uncertain but that the individual who resides in a particular country does so in the ordinary course of his life. It implies residence with some degree of continuity, according to the way a man's life is usually ordered.

If you come to this country with the intention of taking up permanent residence here, it is Revenue practice to regard you as being both resident and ordinarily resident in the UK from your date of arrival. If, however, you originally did not intend to take up permanent residence here, you would not be considered ordinarily resident on arrival. You would normally become ordinarily resident from the time when you have been here for two complete tax years, or earlier, if you keep a place to live in this country.

Individuals
(Ss49-51)

If a person visits this country for some temporary purpose only, and not with the intention of establishing his residence here, he is not normally treated as being a UK resident unless he spends at least six months here during the tax year.

An overseas visitor, however, might be treated as acquiring UK residence if he pays habitual substantial visits to this country. This normally means coming here for at least four consecutive years and staying for an average of at least three months each year. If you wish to remain non-resident you must avoid habitual visits.

If you pay only short casual visits abroad you will not lose your UK residence, but if an entire tax year is included in any continuous period spent abroad you will normally be treated as being non-resident for at least the intervening tax year (p 7).

Companies
(S482 & FA 1984 S84)

A company is deemed to be resident where its central control and management are carried out. This is not necessarily where the company is registered, although normally the central control and management would be exercised in the country in which the company is registered. If, however, a company simply has its registered office here but carries on all its business from offices abroad and holds its board meetings abroad, it is non-resident.

If a company registered abroad transacts some of its business in this country, it will not normally be treated as being UK resident provided its management and control are exercised abroad, which includes all board meetings being held abroad.

S482 contains penal provisions to prevent a UK company from becoming non-resident without Treasury consent being obtained. Such consent is also required to transfer part or all of its business to a non-resident and these sections are still in force despite the abolition of exchange control. However, new legislation, postponed from 1982, is possible at some future time, to repeal S482 and change the company residence rules.

Partnerships
(S153)

Where any trade or business is carried on by a partnership and the control and management of the trade are situated abroad, the partnership is deemed to be resident abroad. This applies even if some of the partners are resident in this country and some of the trade is carried on here.

Trusts

A trust is generally treated for capital gains tax purposes as being resident and ordinarily resident in the UK unless its general administration is ordinarily carried on outside this country and a majority of the trustees are neither resident nor ordinarily resident here.

Place of abode in the UK
(S50)

If you maintain a house or flat in this country available for your occupation this will usually be a factor towards deciding that you are resident here. You will normally be treated as resident here for any tax year during which you set foot in the UK. Your residence position will, however, be decided without regard to any place of abode maintained for your use in the UK in the following circumstances:

(a)   You work full-time in a trade, profession or vocation no part of which is carried on in this country.
(b)   You work full-time in an office or employment, all the duties of which (ignoring merely incidental duties) are performed outside the UK.

Visits abroad
(S49)

If you are a British subject or a citizen of the Republic of Ireland and your ordinary residence has been in the UK you are still charged to income tax if you have left this country if it is for the purpose of only occasional residence abroad.

In order to obtain non-residence for UK tax purposes your overseas residence must be more than merely occasional — it must have a strong element of permanency. The normal Revenue requirements are as follows:

(a)   A definite intention to establish a permanent residence abroad.
(b)   The actual fulfilment of such an intention.
(c)   Normally a full tax year should be spent outside this country before you are considered non-resident (although short periods in the UK may be allowed by the Revenue). Thus if you leave the country permanently on 30 September 1983 and have some evidence of this (eg, having sold your house and set up house abroad), you will be provisionally treated as being non-resident; but this will only be confirmed after 5 April 1985. If you leave the UK and are treated on departure as being no longer resident nor ordinarily resident, by Revenue concession you will not be charged to capital gains tax on any disposals after your departure.

Changing your domicile and residence

As has been indicated already domicile and residence normally run together but domicile is much more difficult to change.

The way in which to change your residence is summarised above. You simply establish a permanent residence abroad and remain out of this country for a complete tax year. (In certain circumstances short visits to the UK are allowed.) After that you must avoid returning to this country for as much as six months in any one tax year, averaging less than three months here every year. If, however, you have a place of abode available for you in the UK you are regarded as being resident here for any tax year during which you pay a visit (no matter how short), unless your residence abroad is for the purpose of an overseas trade or employment.

In order to change your domicile to a new domicile of choice, you should take as many steps as possible to show that you regard your new country as your permanent home.

The following points are relevant to establishing a particular country as your new domicile:

(1)   Develop a long period of residence in the new country.
(2)   Purchase or lease a home.
(3)   Marry a native of that country.
(4)   Develop business interests there.
(5)   Make arrangements to be buried there.
(6)   Draw up your will according to the law of the country.
(7)   Exercise political rights in your new country of domicile.
(8)   Arrange to be naturalised (not vital).
(9)   Have your children educated in the new country.
(10) Resign from all clubs and associations in your former country of domicile and join clubs, etc in your new country.
(11) Any religious affiliations that you have with your old domicile should be terminated and new ones established in your new domicile.
(12) Arrange for your family to be with you in your new country.

The above are some of the factors to be considered and the more of these circumstances that can be shown to prevail, the sooner you will be accepted as having changed your domicile.

● *Reference to the table earlier in this chapter (p 4) will illustrate the importance of residence and domicile in ascertaining whether or not an individual is liable to capital gains tax and capital transfer tax. If you are able to become non-resident for tax purposes you will avoid liability to UK income tax on many classes of income and if you are also not ordinarily resident here you will not be liable for any UK capital gains tax on sales of assets here or abroad.*

If you become neither domiciled nor deemed domiciled (p 69) in this country you will only be liable for UK capital transfer tax on assets situated here.

● *A very effective way of avoiding liability to UK taxes is to emigrate and take all of your assets out of this country. Once your have ceased to be resident and are no longer domiciled nor deemed domiciled here you will be outside the UK tax net regarding all income and assets arising and situated abroad. (You should note that if you have shares in a UK company with its registered office here, the shares are treated for capital transfer tax purposes as located in this country unless they are bearer securities – p 86.)*

● *If you have a large potential capital gain you should defer taking this until you cease to be resident and ordinarily resident here; in this way you will avoid capital gains tax. (If you wish you may then return to this country in the following tax year.)*

● *As a pure tax-saving exercise, you should only consider emigrating if you are a very wealthy person; and even then you should only go to a country where you feel that you will be happy. If, however, you wish to spend your retirement abroad, then in choosing to which country you should go, you should take into account the tax which you would have to pay there. Once you have established your foreign residence and domicile, in order to preserve this situation, you must avoid paying regular visits to the UK (p 6).*

2 Capital gains tax — general

Subject to the specific rules that are summarised in the following pages, you will be charged to capital gains tax in respect of any chargeable gains that accrue to you on the disposal of assets during a given tax year. You deduct from your capital gains any allowable capital losses (p 20). The basic rate of capital gains tax is 30%. An annual exemption of £5,600 applies from 6 April 1984 for individuals and broadly £2,800 for trusts (p 50). Companies (p 54) pay corporation tax at an effective rate of 30% on their capital gains, subject to special rules for authorised investment trusts and unit trusts (p 36).

Most references throughout this chapter are to the Capital Gains Tax Act 1979 which consolidates the relevant legislation from Finance Act 1965 onwards. (Although a short term capital tax had briefly existed earlier, capital gains tax as we now know it was introduced by FA 1965.)

Chargeable gains
(CGTA S28)

A chargeable gain is a gain which accrues after 6 April 1965 to a taxpayer (including a company, trust, partnership, individual, etc), such gain being computed in accordance with the provisions of the relevant legislation. There must, however, be a disposal of assets in order that there should be a chargeable gain. Disposals include sales, gifts, etc (p 16).

Liability
(CGTA Ss2, 12 & 14)

Any company, trust, partnership, individual or other taxpayer is chargeable to capital gains tax on any chargeable gains accruing to him in a year of assessment during any part of which he is either resident (p 5) or ordinarily resident (p 5) in this country.

Also, a non-resident taxpayer who carries on a trade in the UK through a branch or agency is generally liable to capital gains tax accruing on the disposal of: (a) assets in this country used in his trade, or (b) assets held here and used for the branch or agency.

If you are resident or ordinarily resident here during a tax year your world-wide realisations of assets will be liable to capital gains tax. However, if you are not domiciled in this country (p 4) you are only charged to capital gains tax on your overseas realisations of assets to the extent that such gains are remitted here (p 29).

Annual reliefs

The first £5,600 of your net gains for 1984–85 is exempted from capital gains tax (p 12). Exemptions for previous years are shown in the following table. (Prior to 6 April 1980 different rules applied as below.)

Table 2   Annual exemptions

	1980–81 1981–82	1982–83	1983–84	1984–85
	£	£	£	£
Individuals	3,000	5,000	5,300	5,600
Personal representatives (p12)	3,000	5,000	5,300	5,600
Trustees for mentally handicapped and those receiving attendance allowance	3,000	5,000	5,300	5,600
Other trusts (p12)	1,500	2,500	2,650	2,800

Alternative basis of charge before 6 April 1978
(FA 1965 S21; & FA 1976 S52)

In calculating your capital gains tax liability for 1977–78 or any earlier tax year, instead of paying the basic 30% rate you paid a lower amount in the circumstances described below:

(a)   If your capital gains were not more than £5,000 then your tax was restricted to the amount payable if you applied your top income tax rates (including investment income surcharge) to one half of your capital gains (less capital losses) for the tax year.

(b)   If your capital gains exceeded £5,000 then your tax was restricted to the amount payable if you applied your top income tax rates to £2,500 plus the amount by which your net capital gains for the tax year exceeded £5,000.

(c)   For the above purposes you deducted from one half of your capital gains (or £2,500 plus the excess over £5,000) any unused personal reliefs, but not life assurance relief nor charges on income.

Relief for gains totalling under £9,500 before 6 April 1980
(CGTA S5 & Sch 1)

For 1977–78, 1978–79 and 1979–80 your net capital gains (including those of your wife unless you were separated) were taxed at less than 30% as follows:

(a)   If your chargeable gains were no more than £1,000, no tax was charged.

(b)   The excess over £1,000 was taxed at 15%, provided your total net gains were no more than £5,000.

(c)   If your total net gains were in the band from £5,000 to £9,500, your tax was £600 (£4,000 at 15%) plus half of the excess over £5,000. Thus on total gains of £8,000 you paid £600 + (8,000–5,000)/2 = £2,100.

(d)   The old alternative basis (see above) applied for 1977–78 only, provided it produced a lower charge.

(e)   Any set-off for losses from previous years (p 19) was restricted to leave £1,000 of gains to be taxed at the nil rate. All losses for the same year were deducted, however, in arriving at the net gains.

(f)   These rules applied to personal representatives for the tax year of death and the following two years.

(g)   The rules also applied to trusts for the mentally disabled and for those receiving attendance allowance. For any other trusts set up before 7 June 1978 a lower limit of £500 applied for complete capital gains tax exemption, with marginal relief limiting the tax to one half of the excess over £500 (p 50).

Annual exemptions from 6 April 1980

(CGTA S5 & Sch 1; FA 1980 Ss77 & 78; & FA 1982 S80)

The annual exemption system was changed from 6 April 1980. The following rules apply (the rates shown are for 1984–85):

(a)   The first £5,600 of your net gains is exempted from capital gains tax. This applies no matter how high are your total gains for the year and includes any gains of your wife (unless you are separated).

(b)   Any set-off for losses from previous years (p 19) is restricted to leave £5,600 of gains to be exempted. In this way your exemption is protected and you have more losses to carry forward. All losses for the same year must be deducted, however, in arriving at the net gains.

(c)   These rules apply to personal representatives for the tax year of death and the next two years.

(d)   The rules also apply to trusts for the mentally disabled and for those receiving attendance allowance.

(e)   For other trusts set up before 7 June 1978 the first £2,800 of net capital gains each year is exempt (p 50).

(f)   Trusts set up after 6 June 1978 by the same settlor each have an exemption of £2,800 divided by the number of such trusts. Thus if you have set up four trusts since that date, they each have an exemption of £700. In any event each trust obtains an exemption of at least £560.

(g)   Any set off for trust losses from previous years is restricted so that the appropriate exemption (£2,800 etc) is not wasted.

(h) The above figures apply for future years subject to indexation. Unless Parliament otherwise directs, the exemptions will be increased in line with the increase in the Retail Price Index for the December before the year of assessment compared with the previous one.

(i) The annual exemptions from 1980–81 to 1984–85 are detailed in Table 2 (p11).

£5,600 net gains exemption

● *Make the best use of this relief. If your sales of chargeable assets produce net gains which are not normally far in excess of £5,600 in any tax year, try to spread your realisations so that your net gains are no more than £5,600 each year – you will then pay no capital gains tax.*

● *Remember that each of your minor children (but not your wife) can also realise up to £5,600 of net gains each year and pay no capital gains tax. It is thus a good idea to spread your share dealings, etc throughout your family. This is made easier by the generous capital gains tax relief which now applies to gifts between individuals, etc, subject to the necessary election (p 46).*

● *If your net gains are less than £5,600 in any tax year, realise further profits. In this way, you will be able to make better use of the exempt band.*

● *Should your net gains be rather more than £5,600 for a tax year, sell assets to create capital losses to bring the net total for the year below £5,600. If you wish to buy back quoted shares which you have sold in this way, remember to do so in the next stock exchange account (p 20). It is no longer in order to buy back the next day (bed and breakfast) since your sale and repurchase will be matched against each other and the required capital gain or loss will not be created.*

Example 1: Capital Gains Tax — £5,600 exemption

Mr A has losses carried forward from 1983–84 of £2,400. He has made no realisation previously in 1984–85 and now wishes to realise £22,000 from share sales in a tax-effective manner. His holdings are as follows and he intends to follow his broker's advice to keep his shares in B Ltd. Ignoring the effects of indexation allowance (p 18), how should he proceed?

Details	Cost (Post-1965) £	Current Value £
Shares in A Ltd	3,000	7,000
Shares in B Ltd	10,000	6,000
Shares in C Ltd	3,000	9,000
Shares in D Ltd	5,000	15,000

Shares in E Ltd	7,000	6,000
Government Stock	10,000 (May 1984)	8,000

It is suggested that Mr A sells all his shares in A Ltd and D Ltd realising £22,000, at the same time selling his shares in B Ltd and buying them back in the next stock exchange account (p 20). Since the Government Stock has been owned for less than one year this yields an allowable loss on sale provided it is not repurchased within one month. Thus Mr A should sell his Government Stock and repurchase it after one month. As a result of these transactions, Mr A will realise £22,000 without any capital gains tax liability, as follows:

Details	Cost	Proceeds	Gain (Loss)	
	£	£	£	
Shares in A Ltd	3,000	7,000	4,000	
Shares in B Ltd	10,000	6,000	(4,000)	Repurchased in
Shares in D Ltd	5,000	15,000	10,000	next account
Government Stock	10,000	8,000	(2,000)	Repurchased after
				one month
			8,000	
	Losses B/fwd		(2,400)	
	Annual exemption		(5,600)	
	Taxable		Nil	

Liable assets
(CGTA Ss19–21)

Subject to various exemptions (see below) all forms of property are treated as 'assets' for capital gains tax purposes including:

(a)   Investments, land and buildings, jewellery, antiques, etc.
(b)   Options and 'debts on a security' (p 15)
(c)   Any currency other than sterling.
(d)   Any form of property created by the person disposing of it or otherwise coming to be owned without being acquired. (This would cover any article which you made or work of art created by you.)
(e)   Foreign currency including that held in bank accounts unless for the personal expenditure of you and your dependants (including a residence) outside the UK.

Exempted assets
(CGTA — see opposite)

The classes of assets listed in Table 3 are exempted from charge to capital gains tax, subject to the relevant rules.

Table 3: Assets exempted from capital gains tax

(1) Private motor vehicles (S130).
(2) Gifts to an individual prior to 6 April 1984 of no more than £100 total value during the tax year (S6). A general gifts election now applies (p46).
(3) Your main private residence (p 42).
(4) National Savings Certificates, Defence Bonds, Development Bonds, Save-as-you earn investments, etc (S71).
(5) Any foreign currency which you obtained for personal expenditure abroad (S133).
(6) Decorations for gallantry (unless purchased) (S131).
(7) Betting winnings including pools, lotteries and premium bonds (S19(4)).
(8) Compensation or damages for any wrong or injury suffered to your person or in connection with your profession or vocation (S19(5)).
(9) British Government securities which you have held for one year or more or which passed to you on somebody's death or out of a settlement (S67).
(10) Certain corporate bonds (p 31) issued after 13 March 1984 which you hold for more than 12 months (or which passed to you from a settlement or on death).
(11) Life assurance policies and deferred annuities provided that you are the original owner or they were given to you. If you bought the rights to a policy from its original owner you may be liable to capital gains tax on the surrender, maturity or sale of the policy, or death of the life assured (S143).
(12) Chattels sold for £3,000 or less (p 43).
(13) Assets gifted to charity (p 49).
(14) The gift to the nation of any assets (eg paintings) deemed to be of national, scientific or historic interest; also land, etc, given to the National Trust (S147).
(15) The gift of historic houses and certain other property of interest to the public, provided they are given access — also funds settled for its upkeep (Ss147–148).
(16) Tangible movable property which is a wasting asset (ie, with a predictable life of 50 years or less). This includes boats, animals, etc, but not land and buildings (S127).
(17) Disposals by a close company of assets on trust for the benefit of its employees (S149).
(18) The disposal of a debt is exempt provided you are the original creditor and the debt is not a 'debt on a security' (a debenture, etc). Otherwise capital gains tax applies. The 'debt on a security' requirement does not apply, however, to certain business loans (excluding those from associated companies) made after 11 April 1978. Loss relief may be available on such debts and also on certain business guarantees made after that date (S134).
(19) Land transferred after 5 April 1983 from one local constituency to another as a result of the Parliamentary boundaries being redrawn (F2A 1983 S7).

Disposals

(CGTA Ss19–26)

The following are examples of circumstances in which you will be treated as making a disposal or a part disposal of an asset:

(a)   The outright sale of the whole asset or part of it.
(b)   The gift of the asset or a part of it — the asset must be valued at the date of gift and this valuation is treated as the proceeds. An election for holding-over the gain is sometimes possible (p 46).
(c)   The destruction of an asset eg, by fire.
(d)   The sale of any right in an asset, eg, by granting a lease, is a part disposal although if you obtain a fair rent there is normally no capital gains tax liability.
(e)   If any capital sum is received in return for the surrender or forfeiture of any rights, this is a disposal. For example, you may receive a sum of money for not renewing a lease in accordance with a renewal option which you possessed.
(f)   If you die, you are deemed to dispose of all of your assets at your date of death but no capital gains tax is payable. Whoever inherits your assets does so at their market value at your death.

The following are not treated as disposals of assets for capital gains tax purposes:

(a)   The sale or gift of an asset to your husband or wife (see below).
(b)   If you transfer an asset merely as security for a debt but retain the ownership this is not a capital gains tax disposal. This would apply, for example, if you mortgaged your house.
(c)   If you transfer an asset to somebody else to hold it as your nominee, this is not a disposal provided that you remain the beneficial owner.
(d)   Gifts of assets to charities are not treated as disposals (p 49).

Husband and wife

If you give or sell an asset to your wife this is not treated as a capital gains tax disposal, provided she is living with you during the relevant tax year. In that case your wife is charged to capital gains tax on any subsequent disposal that she makes of the asset as if she had bought it when you originally acquired it at the actual cost to yourself.

● *As mentioned above, sales and gifts of assets between yourself and your wife are not normally liable to capital gains tax. This enables you to redistribute your assets for capital transfer tax purposes without paying any capital gains tax. (Some stamp duty – (p 200) may be payable, however.) Your wife and yourself will then both be able to use your full capital transfer tax annual exemptions and nil-rate band if you have sufficient spare assets. If a wealth tax is introduced at some future time, it may help to have your assets split between you if husband and wife are separately taxed.*

Computation of chargeable gains
(CGTA Ss28–36; & FA 1982 Ss 86–89 & Sch 13)

The following general rules should be followed:

(1)   If the asset sold was originally acquired before 7 April 1965, special rules apply (p 23).

(2)   Special rules also apply in the case of leases and other wasting assets (p 25).

(3)   Ascertain the consideration for each of your disposals during the tax year — this will normally be the sale proceeds but in the following cases it will be the *open market value* of the assets (p 22):

    (a)   Gifts of assets during the tax year.

    (b)   Transfers of assets (by gift or sale) to persons 'connected' with you including close relations other than your wife and also business partners ('connected persons' is defined in CGTA S63 and the same definition applies for DLT — p 61). This also applies to other disposals of assets not at arm's length. (After 9 March 1981, anti-avoidance rules operate to prevent losses being manufactured artificially in this way.)

    (c)   Transactions in which the sale proceeds cannot be valued, or where an asset is given as compensation for loss of office, etc to an employee. (For example, if you give your friend a valuable picture on condition that he paints your house regularly for the next 10 years, then since this service cannot be accurately valued you are treated as disposing of your picture for its market value.)

(4)   Deduct from the disposal consideration in respect of each asset its original cost (or value at acquisition) together with any incidental expenses in connection with your original acquisition and your disposal of each asset. Also deduct any 'enhancement' expenditure, ie, the cost of any capital improvements to the assets not including any expenses of a 'revenue nature'.

(5)   Your incidental costs of acquisition and disposal (see (4) above) include surveyors', valuers' and solicitors' fees, stamp duty and commission in connection with the purchase and sale; also the cost of advertising to find a buyer and accountants' charges in connection with the acquisition or disposal. No expenses are deductible, however, if they have already been allowed in computing your taxable revenue profits.

(6)   If applicable, deduct indexation allowance (see below), based on the original cost (or other base value) of the asset.

Indexation allowance

(FA 1982 Ss86–89 & Sch 13)

If your disposal is after 5 April 1982 (31 March 1982 for companies) the original cost and enhancement expenditure may be increased by *indexation*. The expenditure is scaled up in proportion to the increase in the *Retail Price Index* between March 1982 and the month of disposal for assets held before April 1981. Otherwise the Index increase is taken between a year after acquisition and the month of disposal. In any event, you must hold the asset for at least one year before indexation starts to run. Recent Retail Price Index figures are as follows:

Table 4: Retail Price Index			
	1982	*1983*	*1984*
January	310.6	325.9	342.6
February	310.7	327.3	344.0
March	313.4	327.9	345.1
April	319.7	332.5	349.7
May	322.0	333.9	351.0
June	322.9	334.7	351.9
July	323.0	336.5	
August	323.1	338.0	
September	322.9	339.5	
October	324.5	340.7	
November	326.1	341.9	
December	325.5	342.8	

Indexation does not operate to create or increase a capital loss (p 20). Special rules apply regarding assets held on 6 April 1965 (p 23) and shares (p 31). The provisions regarding shares should particularly be noted since they give rise to useful planning opportunities.

Transactions between husband and wife do not normally give rise to capital gains tax (p 16). Thus if you acquire an asset from your wife, your deemed acquisition cost is taken to be hers, augmented by any indexation allowance attaching to it at the transfer date. When you sell the asset, you obtain full indexation allowance on your deemed acquisition cost, from the date you took over the asset from your wife (assuming your wife's period of ownership exceeded one year). Similar treatment applies to company intra-group transfers and certain reconstructions. Also, legatees are deemed to acquire assets at the death of the deceased and so obtain indexation allowance as if that was their actual date of acquisition.

Example 2: Computation of chargeable gain

Mr A sells a block of flats in June 1984 for £400,000. The flats were bought during 1970–71 for £100,000 and susequent capital expenditure in 1975 amounted to £20,000. Also £10,000 had been spent on decorations and maintenance. The legal costs on purchase were £2,500 and stamp duty was £1,000. Surveyors' fees prior to purchase amounted to £500. £500 was spent in advertising the sale and agents' commission amounted to £12,000. Legal costs on sale were £3,500. Assuming that Mr A's profit will be taxed as a capital gain, and that his £5,600 annual exemption has already been used, what tax will he pay on it?

Cost of block of flats		£100,000
Add:		
Enhancement expenditure		20,000
(decorations and maintenance not relevant)		
Legal costs on purchase		2,500
Stamp duty on purchase		1,000
Surveyors' fees on purchase		500
Total cost		£124,000
Proceeds		£400,000
Less:		
Cost as above	£124,000	
Advertising	500	
Agents' commission	12,000	
Legal fees on sale	3,500	
		140,000
		£260,000
Less: indexation allowance		
£124,000 × (351.9–313.4)/313.4		15,233
Chargeable gain		£244,767
Capital gains tax at 30%		£73,430.10

Part disposals
(CGTA S35)

Where part of an asset is disposed of (including part of a 'pool' holding of shares in a particular company — p 31) it is necessary to compute the cost applicable to the part sold. This is done by multiplying the original cost by the fraction A/(A + B) where A is the consideration for the part disposed of and B is the market value of the remaining property at the date of the part disposal. This calculation is made before working out the indexation allowance, if relevant (p 18). Indexation is only taken on the cost applicable to the part sold. When the remainder is sold, a different indexation factor will probably apply.

A series of disposals
(CGTA S151)

If you make a series of disposals of assets to connected persons (p 17) they are valued together in arriving at your total proceeds figure, if this gives more than taking the assets separately. This is particularly important if, for example, you sell parts of a controlling share interest to your children.

Capital Losses
(CGTA S29)

If your capital gains tax computation in respect of any disposal during the tax year produces a loss, such a loss is deductible from chargeable gains arising during the year. If after relieving any gains for the tax year there remains a surplus of losses these should be offset against any net capital gains of your spouse. Any remaining surplus of losses is then available to be carried forward and set off against future capital gains of your spouse and yourself. Any capital loss which you make on an asset transferred to a connected person (p 17) can only be relieved against gains made on transfers to the same person.

Your net capital gains are reduced by losses brought forward down to the tax free amount of £5,600 (£5,300 for 1983–84, etc) and any balance of the losses is carried forward (S5(4)).

'Bed and breakfast' transactions

● *Remember that, if necessary, you may be able to create capital losses by 'bed and breakfast' transactions. These involve selling shares on the stock exchange at a loss and buying them back no earlier than the following account (p 33). The costs of such a transaction must be taken into account, however, and will include 1% stamp duty, commission and jobber's turn. The repurchase can be within the same account if a different class of shares in the same company to those sold is acquired (eg, sell ordinary and buy back A ordinary). Alternatively shares in a different company in the same industry might be purchased. (Prior to 6 April 1982 bed and breakfast transactions were effective if the shares were repurchased the next day.)*

● *When bed and breakfasting, take account of the different base values you will be establishing for indexation relief and also the one year period without indexation relief which applies to the new acquisitions.*

● *Note that gilt edge securities and qualifying corporate bonds (p 31) are difficult to use for 'bed and breakfast' transactions. First, they carry no capital gains or losses once you have owned them for a year. Second, the 'buy back' must be no sooner than one month after the sale, otherwise the hoped-for capital loss is not created. However, if you have no suitable shares to sell and buy back, it is possible to realise a capital loss on gilt edge securities and buy back a different but broadly similar stock.*

Assessment and payment of capital gains tax

(TMA S29; CGTA Ss7–9 & 40; FA 1980 S61; & FA 1984 s63)

Your capital gains tax assessments will be raised on you in respect of each tax year as soon thereafter as the Revenue obtain the necessary information. In the case of a company, however, its gains are included in its corporation tax assessment which is due for payment according to the special company rules (p 54).

Your capital gains tax assessment is due for payment on 1 December following the tax year in which the respective gains are made, or 30 days after the assessment is issued, if later. Thus the tax on gains made in 1984–85 would be payable on 1 December 1985 (provided assessed by 1 November 1985). For 1979–80 and previous years the due date was three months after the end of the tax year in which the gains arose; or 30 days after the assessment was issued if this was later.

Interest is normally payable on overdue tax from the earlier of 1 June following the end of the year after the year of assessment or the date when the tax becomes due and payable. However, in no event does interest run from a date earlier than 30 days after the issue of the assessment. The interest is not deductible for tax purposes and the rate is 8% from 6 December 1982 (12% before that date and 9% before 1 January 1980).

Capital gains are treated as arising on the actual date of sale or gift, etc. In the case of a transaction in which a sales contract is used, such as the sale of shares or property, it is the date of the contract which applies. It is not the completion date if this is different. Similar considerations apply to fixing the date of acquisition for capital gains tax purposes.

Regarding certain disposals by gift, etc, from 11 April 1972 to 5 April 1984 of land and buildings, non-quoted shares, or assets used exclusively in your business, you have the option of paying capital gains tax in eight yearly or 16 half-yearly instalments. If you pay by instalments you must pay interest at the appropriate rate on the overdue tax (8% etc — see above). For disposals after 5 April 1984, the instalment basis no longer applies, although relief may be available if the *consideration* is paid in instalments (see below).

After 26 March 1974 controlling interests in companies are included (even if quoted). Disposals of any of the specified assets (except for land and investment companies, etc) qualify for relief from interest on the instalments unless they are overdue or the total market value of the assets exceeds £250,000.

Normally, even if the sales consideration is paid to you by instalments over a number of years the gain is assessed for the tax year of the disposal. If, however, you can satisfy the Revenue that you would otherwise suffer undue hardship, payment of the tax can be spread over the period of the instalments (maximum eight years).

Timing

● *Timing your sales of shares or other chargeable assets can have an important bearing on your capital gains tax liability. If you postpone a sale until after 5 April it means that you delay the payment of your tax for one year. Also, if you know that you will be incurring a capital loss during the next tax year you should defer making any potential capital profits until that year because, although capital losses can be carried forward, they cannot be set off against capital profits in earlier tax years. A further point to bear in mind is that the longer you hold an asset, the higher your indexation allowance (p 18) is likely to be on its sales.*

● *Similarly, if you have already made a lot of capital profits during the current tax year you should consider incurring capital losses during the same year which can then be offset. You should not normally sell investments unless it is sound to do so from a commercial point of view. A loss may be established on a shareholding, however, even if you buy it back later, but the repurchase should not be within the same stock exchange account (p 20). Such transactions may be taxable, however, if done by companies (p 56).*

● *If you have a substantial capital gain on a shareholding which you wish to realise, split it between two tax years by selling part before and part after 5 April. In this way you will be able to offset your annual exemptions (p11) for two years.*

Valuations
(CGTA S150 and Sch 6)

The values of assets must be found for capital gains tax purposes in various circumstances. These include gifts, transactions between connected persons, acquisitions on death and valuations at 6 April 1965. The general rule is that you must take the 'market value' of the assets at the relevant time. 'Market value' means the price which the assets might reasonably be expected to fetch on a sale in the open market.

You need value only the assets actually being disposed of even though they form part of a larger whole. This is particularly important regarding the shares in a non-quoted company. Suppose you hold 90% of the shares in such a company which are together worth £90,000. If you gift 10% of the company's shares to your son you might assume that their value is £10,000. This would, however, probably not be true since your 90% holding carried with it full control of the company whereas 10% of the company's shares is a minority holding which would be normally worth considerably less than £10,000 in the circumstances mentioned.

The 90% holding would be worth nearly 90% of the total value of the company, but the true market valuation of the gifted 10% holding might only be £1,000 depending on the profits of the company and dividends paid. Note that different valuation rules apply for capital transfer tax purposes (p 80).

Unquoted share valuations must take account of all information which a prudent arm's-length purchaser would obtain (CGTA S152). As mentioned above, the size of the holding will be relevant, as will the profits, dividends, net assets and record of the company.

Particular rules relate to the valuation of quoted securities such as shares and debenture stocks. In this case you must normally take:

(a)   the lower of the two prices shown in the Stock Exchange Official Daily List plus one quarter of the difference between them, *or*
(b)   halfway between the highest and lowest prices at which bargains (other than at special prices) were recorded in the shares or securities for the relevant day.

In valuing quoted shares at 6 April 1965 (p 36) however, you must take the *higher* of:

(a)   midway between the two prices shown in the Stock Exchange Official Daily List (ie the middle market price), and
(b)   halfway between the highest and lowest prices at which bargains (other than at special prices) were recorded in the shares or securities for 6 April 1965.

Apart from quoted shares other valuations will normally need to be agreed with the Revenue valuation officers such as the district valuers who are concerned with valuing land and buildings.

The valuation of gifted agricultural property is effectively subject to the same reduction as applies for capital transfer tax (p 89–90).

Relief on sales of assets owned on 6 April 1965
(CGTA Sch 5)

The present system of capital gains tax only operates regarding sales after 6 April 1965. Rules were, therefore, introduced with the purpose of relieving so much of your capital gains as can be related to the period before 7 April 1965. The general rule is that you assume that your asset increased in value at a uniform rate and you are relieved from capital gains tax on such proportion of the gain as arose on a time basis prior to 7 April 1965. This is known as the 'time apportionment' method.

For example, if your total gain is G and you held an asset for A months prior to 6 April 1965 and B months after that date until the date of sale your taxable chargeable gain is $G \times B/(A+B)$. Note that time apportionment is now calculated on gains net of any available indexation allowance (p 18). Your time apportionment benefit is limited to 20 years prior to 6 April 1965. Thus if you acquired an asset before 6 April 1945 you are treated as having acquired it on that date.

Instead of using 'time apportionment' you have the option of substituting for the cost of the asset its market value at 6 April 1965 (Sch 5 (11)). In order to do this you must make an election to this effect to the Revenue within two years of the end of the tax year in which you make the disposal. (In the case of a company the election must be made within two years of the end of the accounting period in which the disposal is made.) Once you make an election it is irrevocable, even if it results in your paying more tax than on a 'time apportionment' basis.

The 'time apportionment' basis *does not* apply to quoted shares and securities (p 31). Nor does it apply to land with development value when sold (or which has been materially developed after 17 December 1973). Such land is normally automatically dealt with on the 6 April 1965 valuation basis.

In the same way that your gain is reduced by 'time apportionment' so any loss that you make on a disposal of an asset that you owned at 6 April 1965 is also reduced in this way. Thus if you bought an asset for £5,000 on 6 April 1946 and sold it for £1,000 on 6 April 1984 your total loss is £4,000 of which only £2,000 (£4,000 × 19/38) is an allowable capital loss. An election for 6 April 1965 valuation is not effective to increase a capital loss and if it converts a gain into a loss, you are treated as having no gain and no loss on the transaction.

Example 3: Relief on sales of assets owned on 6 April 1965

Mr A bought a property for £50,000 on 6 April 1946 and sold it for £200,000 (net of expenses) on 6 April 1984. He considers that at 6 April 1965 the market value of the property was £160,000. Assuming a 10% increase in the Retail Price Index between March 1982 and April 1984, what is Mr A's chargeable gain?

Proceeds 6 April 1984		£200,000
Less: cost 6 April 1946	£50,000	
indexation allowance (p 18) 10%	5,000	55,000
Gain		£145,000
Period 6 April 1946 to 6 April 1965		19 years
Period 6 April 1965 to 6 April 1984		19 years
Total period of ownership		38 years

Chargeable gain on 'time apportionment' basis

$$\frac{19}{38} \times £145,000 = \qquad £72,500$$

Proceeds 6 April 1984		£200,000
Less: market value 6 April 1965	£160,000	
indexation allowance 10%	16,000	176,000

Chargeable gain on election for valuation at
6 April 1965   £24,000

Note: Provided that Mr A is reasonably certain that he can substantiate a valuation of the property of £160,000 at 6 April 1965 he should make the required election and his chargeable gain will be less. If, however, as a result of negotiations with the Revenue or District Valuer the valuation is agreed at a figure below about £116,000, or failing agreement fixed by the Commissioners below this figure, then Mr A will pay more capital gains tax by making the irrevocable election.

Leases and other wasting assets
(CGTA Ss127, 129 & Sch 3)

A 'wasting asset' is defined as an asset with a predictable life not exceeding 50 years, excluding freehold land and buildings, etc. Leases with no more than 50 years still to run are a special kind of wasting asset and have separate rules for capital gains tax (see below).

'Wasting assets' which are also movable property (chattels) are normally exempted from capital gains tax. (This exemption does not generally apply to plant and machinery qualifying for capital allowances.) In the case of other wasting assets apart from leases, you must reduce their original costs on a straight line time basis over the respective lives of the assets. Thus suppose you buy a wasting asset for £10,000 with an unexpired life of 40 years. If you sell it after 20 years for £20,000, assuming the residual value after 40 years would have been nil, your allowable cost is £10,000 × 20/40 = £5,000; thus your chargeable gain is £20,000–£5,000 = £15,000. This assumes no indexation allowance (p 18). Any such allowance available would be calculated on the adjusted cost of £5,000.

In the case of a lease of land with no more than 50 years of its original term to run (including leases for shorter terms) the original cost must be written off according to a special table under which the rate of wastage accelerates as the end of the term of the lease is reached. If you sell such an interest in a property and lease back the premises at a lower rent for less than 15 years, you may be taxed on all or part of the proceeds either as a trading receipt or under Schedule D Case VI.

The exact computaton of the reduced value of the cost of a lease involves using the following table of percentages according to the number of years still to run. The table below gives an appropriate percentage for each year up to 50 (which is 100%).

Table 5: Leases of land — restriction of allowable expenditure

Years	%	Years	%	Years	%
50 (or more)	100	33	90·280	16	64·116
49	99·657	32	89·354	15	61·617
48	99·289	31	88·371	14	58·971
47	98·902	30	87·330	13	56·167
46	98·490	29	86·226	12	53·191
45	98·059	28	85·053	11	50·038
44	97·595	27	83·816	10	46·695
43	97·107	26	82·496	9	43·154
42	96·593	25	81·100	8	39·399
41	96·041	24	79·622	7	35·414
40	95·457	23	78·055	6	31·195
39	94·842	22	76·399	5	26·722
38	94·189	21	74·635	4	21·983
37	93·497	20	72·770	3	16·959
36	92·761	19	70·791	2	11·629
35	91·981	18	68·697	1	5·983
34	91·156	17	66·470	0	0

If the duration of the lease is not an exact number of years the percentage is that for the whole number of years plus one twelfth of the difference between that and the percentage for the next higher number of years for each odd month, counting an odd 14 days or more as one month.

Thus suppose you bought a twenty year lease for £40,000 in 1974 and sell it in 1984, when it has exactly ten years to run, for £50,000. Your base cost of £40,000 must be reduced in the ratio of the relevant percentages at ten and twenty years (ie, 46·695 : 72·770). The capital gain (ignoring indexation allowance) is:

Proceeds	£50,000
Remainder of cost £40,000 × 46·695/72·770	£25,667
Chargeable Gain	£24,333

● *When buying a lease in a company, it can prove beneficial to do so through a newly formed subsidiary. Thus if you are buying the lease of premises for £100,000, create a new subsidiary with share capital of £100,000 and buy the lease. Then when your company wishes to dispose of the premises, by selling the subsidiary the base value remains at £100,000. However, if the lease had been sold out of the subsidiary, only a reduced base cost would have been available, in line with the table (p 26).*

Partnership capital gains
(CGTA S60)

When a partnership asset is sold in such circumstances that, if owned by an individual, capital gains tax would have been payable, this tax is assessed on the partners according to their shares in the partnership asset. Thus if a capital gain of £4,000 is made from the sale of a partnership asset on 1 January 1985 and A, B, C and D share equally in the partnership assets, a capital gain of £1,000 each must be added to the capital gains tax assessments for 1984–85 of A, B, C and D respectively (p 21).

Where a share in a partnership changes hands, a share in all of the partnership assets is treated for capital gains tax purposes as changing ownership and this might give rise to capital gains or capital losses regarding the partner who is disposing of his share. Thus if A, B, and C are equal partners and A sells his share to D, A is treated for capital gains tax purposes as disposing of a one-third share in each of the partnership assets to D. The Revenue operate a concessional treatment regarding certain capital gains which arise in normal commercial partnership operations, including, for example, changes in profit shares.

Anti-avoidance
(CGTA Ss25, 26, 87 & 88; & FA 1981 Ss86 & 87)

With a tax as complicated as capital gains tax, it is not surprising that various loopholes have been exploited. To counter this a number of anti-avoidance provisions have been introduced. Those concerning non-resident companies are dealt with elsewhere (p 59), as are the capital gains tax avoidance rules concerning overseas trusts. In addition, various decisions of the Courts have rendered contrived artificial capital gains tax saving schemes virtually obsolete (eg, *Ramsay* v *IRC* and *Furniss* v *Dawson*).

Rules exist to counter any advantage which you may derive from 'value shifting' schemes. These involve the artificial creation of an allowable capital loss by moving value out of one asset and possibly into another. There are also anti-avoidance rules concerning capital gains tax relief resulting from company reconstructions, takeovers and amalgamations. The rules do not apply if you can show that the arrangements were all carried out for commercial and not tax-saving purposes. A clearance procedure exists under which you may supply full details to the Inland Revenue. They will then, within 30 days, let you know whether or not clearance is granted. Alternatively the Revenue may request further information.

There are provisions in the 1981 Finance Act to prevent the artificial inflation of the capital gains tax acquisition values of your assets. Otherwise, if you sold for true market value, a capital loss would be created. The artificial effect sometimes resulted from the rule that transactions between connected persons are treated as being at market value (p 17); sometimes it arose through reorganisations of share capital (p 34). After 9 March 1981 your capital gains tax cost is only increased to the extent that the capital gains tax position is affected of the person who transferred the asset to you.

Overseas aspects

(CGTA Ss10–18;FA 1981 Ss79–85 & S88; & FA 1984 S66)

As already mentioned (p 10), provided you are resident and/or ordinarily resident in this country you are liable on capital gains anywhere in the world.

Even if neither resident nor ordinarily resident in the UK, a trader (whether an individual, partnership or company) who carries on a trade here through a branch or agency is generally liable to capital gains tax on the disposal of assets (a) used in this country in his trade, or (b) held here and used by the branch or agency. However, this does not apply to land on which timber is grown, even if the latter is taxed under Schedule D Case I. The term 'branch or agency' includes any factorship, agency, receivership, branch or management. Note that it does not include general commission agents and brokers. Also note that double tax relief (p 30) may be available.

● *If you know you will be realising a substantial capital gain in the future and your personal circumstances will allow it, go abroad so that you are neither resident nor ordinarily resident in the UK (p 5) at the time you make the gain. This will normally involve establishing your non-residence to run from the beginning of the year in which you realise the gain. However, the Revenue concessionally treat you as non-resident from the time you leave the UK if you are leaving to work abroad. Of course, you must make sure not to go to a country which will itself tax you on the gain.*

The *market value* rule (p 17) applies in general to gifts and other dispositions for less than full consideration involving non-resident and non-ordinarily resident persons after 5 April 1983 (FA 1984 S66.) From 10 March 1981 until 5 April 1983, however, if you obtain an asset from such a person, your base cost is restricted to the actual consideration, if any (CGTA S29A).

If you are non-domiciled in the UK, you are only liable to capital gains tax on *overseas gains* to the extent that they are *remitted* here. Thus it is important to determine the location of your assets. For these purposes, from 6 April 1984 if you are non-domiciled and have a non-sterling bank account, this is treated as located outside the UK unless both the account is held at a UK branch and you are UK–resident (FA 1984 S69). If you are UK domiciled, the Revenue have powers to apportion to you the capital gains of certain overseas trusts (p 52) and companies. From 10 March 1981 this extends to overseas companies owned by foreign trusts.

The remittance basis

Under the remittance basis you are only liable to capital gains tax on the amount of gain you actually bring into this country in the tax year. Remember, however, that this only applies if you are not domiciled in the UK. Remittances can be made in cash or kind (see below).

If you make no remittances you will have no liability to UK tax on your overseas capital gains taxable on the remittance basis, no matter how high they are in any year, although you might well suffer foreign tax.

Classes of remittance
(S122)

As well as cash and cheques, any property imported or value arising here from property not imported will be classed as remittances. Thus if you buy a car abroad out of your overseas gains and bring it into this country this is a remittance (although strictly speaking the second-hand value of the car at the time of importation should be used instead of the cost of the car). Similarly, if you hire an asset abroad out of unremitted overseas gains, any use that you get from the asset in this country should be valued and treated as a remittance.

If you borrow money against sums owing to you for overseas gains and bring the former into this country, this is a remittance. Similarly, if you borrow money here and repay it abroad out of overseas gains, this is known as a 'constructive remittance' and is taxable. Other forms of 'constructive remittances' include the payment out of overseas capital gains of interest owing in this country, and the repayment out of such gains of money borrowed overseas which was made available to you in this country.

If you use non-remitted capital gains to buy shares in UK companies this is normally treated as a remittance unless you do so through a third party abroad who actually acts as the principal in the transaction.

You are able to use non-remitted overseas gains to cover the cost of overseas visits (including holidays) and provided you bring none of the money back to this country there is no taxable remittance. For this purpose the Revenue allow you to receive traveller's cheques in this country provided they are not cashed here.

● *If you are taxable on a remittance basis in respect of overseas capital gains then isolate the proceeds in a separate bank account, reinvesting money abroad as required. Any money which you remit back to the UK should be from a clearly defined separate bank account so that you can prove you have not in fact remitted any of your proceeds, including overseas capital gains and it comes from a completely different source.*

Double tax relief

(CGTA Ss10 & 11)

Your chargeable gains may be liable to tax both in the UK and another country. In that case, relief will be available in the following ways:

(1)   Under a bilateral double tax agreement with the other country, which covers capital gains, if you are UK resident you may be exempted from overseas tax on gains from non-business assets apart from land and buildings. A list of the countries having comprehensive agreements with the UK covering capital gains appears below. Rules vary from country to country and the actual agreements should be examined as necessary (in some cases you are only given unilateral relief — see below).

(2)   If there is no bilateral agreement or the agreement does not give you exemption, unilateral relief enables you to set off overseas tax on your gain against the UK capital gains tax on it.

(3)   Should neither of the above apply, then the overseas tax on your gain can be deducted in the UK computation as if it was an expense.

Table 6: Double tax relief — countries with general agreements with the UK covering capital gains tax

Australia	Gambia	Korea	Singapore
Austria	Germany	Luxembourg	South Africa
Bangladesh	Ghana	Malaysia	Spain
Barbados	Greece	Mauritius	Sri Lanka
Belgium	Hungary	Netherlands	Sudan
Canada	India	Netherlands	Swaziland
China	Indonesia	Antilles	Sweden
Denmark	Ireland	New Zealand	Switzerland
Egypt	Israel	Norway	Thailand
Faroe Islands	Italy	Philippines	USA
Fiji	Jamaica	Poland	Yugoslavia
Finland	Japan	Portugal	Zambia
France	Kenya	Romania	Zimbabwe

3 Capital gains tax — shares and securities

Quoted shares and securities
(CGTA Ss64–76)

Government securities

The general rules (p 33) do not apply to UK government securities which are exempt from capital gains tax if sold more than a year after purchase. If you sell any such 'gilt edge' securities within a year of purchase you are liable to capital gains tax on your chargeable gain. Also, any compensation stock received on a nationalisation after 6 April 1976 will give rise to a gain or loss when sold. This consists of the gain or loss on your original shares up to the date of issue of the compensation stock, together with the gain or loss on this stock if it is held for less than 12 months before sale (CGTA S84).

● *As a general rule you should defer selling 'gilts' until you have held them for more than a year. In this way, any profit on sale will be tax free. However, should you have losses on certain gilts, these should be sold within a year of purchase so as to make the losses available against your chargeable gains, unless you wish to hold the securities for long-term investment. Should you wish to buy short-dated 'gilts' these should have at least a year to run; otherwise you are likely to have chargeable gains on their redemption. (For 'bed and breakfasting' see p 20.)*

Exemption for corporate bonds
(FA 1984 S64 & Sch 13)

The exemption for capital gains tax for gilt edge securities which you have held for one year or more has been extended to *qualifying corporate bonds* satisfying the following conditions:

(1) The bonds are issued after 13 March 1984 or if issued before that date, are acquired after it otherwise than through an excluded disposal (broadly, one deemed to give rise to neither gain nor loss, or involving a held-over gain, if before the disposal the bond is not yet a qualifying one).
(2) They are debentures, loan stocks or similar securities, not necessarily secured but 'debts on security'.
(3) They are normal commercial loans, expressed in and redeemable in sterling.
(4) At least some of the shares or debentures of the issuing company are quoted.
(5) The bonds are capable of being marketed but are not issued by a company to another company in the same group.

In a takeover or reorganisation; etc, the 'paper for paper' holdover reliefs (p34) only apply if both your old and new bonds are qualifying bonds.

● *Similar planning points apply to qualifying corporate bonds as to 'gilts' (see above).*

'Pooling'

All shares of the same company and class that you held prior to 6 April 1982 (1 April for companies) were put into a 'pool'. With the introduction of indexation allowance (p 18), however, pooling no longer applies to new purchases. The 'pool' was considered indistinguishable regarding the various numbers of shares that it comprised. Thus if you bought 100 ordinary shares in A Limited on 1 May 1966 for £200 and another 200 ordinary shares in A Limited on 30 September 1970 for £1,000 your total pool cost was £1,200 (ie £4 per share). If you then sold 100 shares they were not treated as being the original ones which you bought for £200; they were treated as coming from your 'pool' at the average pool cost of £4 per share giving a cost of £400.

'Pooling' does not apply to shares purchased on or before 6 April 1965 unless you elect for all your shares to be valued at that date (p 36). In the absence of this election, you allocated any sales prior to 6 April 1982 first against your holdings at 6 April 1965 on a 'first in first out' basis. After these shares were eliminated you then went to the 'pool'. Thus if you bought 100 shares in A Limited for £100 on 1 October 1960 and a further 100 shares for £200 on 1 February 1963 followed by 100 shares for £300 on 1 June 1969; if you sold 150 shares in June 1979 and 150 shares in June 1980 your disposals in 1979–80 were allocated as follows:

	Number	*Cost*
Purchased 1 October 1960	100	£100
Purchased 1 February 1963	50	100
	150	£200

Your disposals in 1980–81 were allocated as follows:

Purchased 1 February 1963	50	£100
Purchased 1 June 1969	100	300
	150	£400

The above assumes that you had not elected for the application of 6 April 1965 valuation to your shares. If you had made such election and supposing the value of the shares was £1·50 each at 6 April 1965 then the 'pool' became 200 at £1·50 (= £300) + £300 = £600, ie £2 per share.

Each separate purchase or sale of shares of the same company and class resulted in adjustments to the 'pool' except that if you bought and sold shares on the same day the respective sale and purchase were first matched against each other. Any surplus or deficit was then added to or deducted from your 'pool'. This rule ceased to apply for transactions from 6 April 1982 (1 April for companies).

Identification — Sales from April 1982
(FA 1982 Ss88–89)

For disposals of quoted shares and securities after 5 April 1982 (31 March 1982 for companies), new identification rules apply. Similarly, shares purchased after those dates are no longer pooled. Each of your existing share pools is treated as a separate asset with its own pool cost at 6 April 1982, and, in general, treated for indexation purposes as if acquired one year earlier (but see below). For companies, there is a special 'parallel pooling' election (p55).

Disposals after 5 April 1982 must be taken in order and identified first against purchases in the previous year taking the earliest first. Then, you must look at previous purchases, taking the latest first. Note, however, that purchases and sales in the same Stock Exchange account (for settlement on the same day) must be matched against each other.

● *For effective bed and breakfast transactions (p 20) the repurchase should normally be in the next stock exchange account, at the earliest. However, the shares could be repurchased several days earlier by means of new time buying for the next account.*

As mentioned above, your 'pool' holdings are to be treated as separate entities, so if you purchased 1,000 shares in company A from, say, 1970 to 1978 at an average cost of £5, the sale now of 500 would be taken to cost 500 × £5 = £2,500. However, an exception applies where certain dealings in the shares take place in 1981–82 (year to 31 March 1982 for companies). If a holding increases in cost during that year, you effectively treat part as being acquired for indexation purposes in 1981–82, by matching the 1981–82 sales against the purchases in that year. The earliest sales in 1981–82 are matched against the latest purchases (even if later than respective sales). Any unmatched purchases in 1981–82 only qualify for indexation after holding for one year.

Example 4: Share identification

Mr A carried out the following transactions in the ordinary shares of B Ltd, a quoted company:

		Date	Number	Cost
Purchases:				
	(a)	15.6.75	1,000	£1,200
	(b)	15.1.78	1,000	1,400
	(c)	8.4.82	1,000	2,000
	(d)	20.7.82	1,000	2,200
	(e)	*10.3.84	1,000	2,300
Sales:				*Proceeds*
	(f)	*14.3.84	1,000	£2,400
	(g)	20.3.84	1,000	2,500
	(h)	25.3.84	1,000	2,500
	(i)	31.3.84	1,000	2,600
	(j)	30.6.84	1,000	4,000

*Assumed within the same Stock Exchange account.

The share sales allocated as follows:

(f)	1,000 shares — proceeds		£2,400
(e) (same account)	cost		2,300
	gain		£100
(g)	1,000 shares — proceeds		£2,500
(c) (previous year taking earliest first)	cost		2,000
	gain		£500
(h)	1,000 shares — proceeds		£2,500
(d) (previous year taking earliest first)	cost		2,200
	gain		£300
(i)	1,000 shares — proceeds		£2,600
(pool cost £2,600)	cost (part of pool)		1,300
	gain (subject to indexation)		£1,300
(j)	1,000 shares — proceeds		£4,000
(pool cost £2,600)	cost (remainder of pool)		1,300
	gain (subject to indexation)		£2,700

Bonus issues, take-overs and company reorganisations

(CGTA Ss77–91; FA 1981 S87; & FA 1982 Sch 13)

If you receive a free scrip (or bonus) issue of shares of the same class as those that you already hold, you must treat the additional shares as having been bought when your original shares were bought. Thus if you bought 1,000 shares in A Ltd for £2 each in 1975 and you now receive a bonus issue of 1,000 shares you will have 2,000 shares at a cost of £1 each which are all treated as having been bought in 1975. Note, however, that scrip dividend options are normally taxed as income, whether taken in cash or shares.

A company in which you own shares may have a capital reorganisation, in the course of which you receive shares of a different class either instead of or in addition to your original shares. You are not normally charged to capital gains tax on any old shares in the company which you exchange for new ones. Any capital gains tax is only payable when you sell your new holding. The rules for reorganisations including bonus issues hold good under the new 'indexation' system unless new consideration is given.

Previously, if you took up 'rights' to subscribe for additional shares in a company of which you are a shareholder, your rights shares were treated as having been acquired when your original shares were purchased and the cost of the rights shares was added to the original cost of your holding. If you sold your 'rights' on the market without taking up the shares this was considered to be a 'part disposal' of your holding which accordingly was charged to capital gains tax (p 19). (If the proceeds are small in relation to your holding, however, you may elect not to pay tax now but set off the proceeds against the original cost of your holding.) Under the new identification rules which now apply (p 33) any new consideration (for rights shares, etc) is treated effectively as a new acquisition so that indexation starts twelve months later on that cost element.

Anti-avoidance rules act to prevent you from obtaining capital loss relief artificially from reorganisations taking place after 9 March 1981. Any increase in the capital gains tax acquisition value of the shares which you obtain through the reorganisation is limited to the actual increase in value.

In the case of a take-over you may receive cash for your shares in which case this is taxed as an ordinary disposal. If, however, you receive shares or loan stock, etc in the acquiring company, you will not normally be liable to pay capital gains tax until you actually sell your new shares or loan stock, subject to certain conditions and anti-avoidance laws (p 27). One of the conditions is that the acquiring company already held, or obtains as a result of the take-over, over 25% of the ordinary share capital of the other company. (For shares or debentures issued before 20 April 1977 this percentage was 50%.) All of the above rules concerning bonus issues, take-overs and company reorganisations apply equally to unquoted shares (p 39).

● *As a general rule, reorganisations should only be carried out with commercial rather than tax-saving motives. Where possible, it is advisable for the directors to obtain for the company Inland Revenue* clearance both in respect of the capital gains tax anti-avoidance provisions and Section 460 (p 3).

Investment trusts and unit trusts
(CGTA Ss92–98; & FA 1980 S81)

Special rules apply regarding disposals both of shares owned *by* the trusts and of shares and units *in* the trusts by their shareholders and unit holders.

After 31 March 1980 authorised unit and investment trusts are exempt from tax on their capital gains. However, from 6 April 1980 any disposals which you make of units and investment trust shares carry full capital gains tax (30%) with no credit.

Prior to 1 April 1980 authorised unit trusts and investment trusts paid capital gains tax at 10% (previously 17%) on their investment gains instead of the normal tax rate of 52% that other companies paid on 15/26ths of their gains. Prior to 6 April 1980 when the ordinary shareholders of investment trusts sold their shares they were allowed to deduct 10% from the capital gains tax rate that they paid on their investment trust ordinary shares. (For 1978–79 the deduction was 17%.) Thus if you paid the maximum 30% rate on your gains for 1979–80 your rate was only 20% on capital gains arising on the sale of ordinary shares in investment trusts. The same applied to any unit trust units that you disposed of during the tax year.

Note that it was the rate of capital gains tax on your units, etc which was reduced, not the actual amount of the gain or loss. This meant that any capital loss (p 20) which you had from selling other assets was less valuable, if used against gains on unit trusts, since the latter would otherwise only bear a low rate of tax.

Holdings at 6 April 1965
(CGTA Sch 5)

'Time apportionment' (p 23) does not apply to quoted shares. Instead you must consider the mid-market price at 6 April 1965 (p 23). Subject to the election described below, your gain on any sales after 6 April 1965 of shares held at that date is the difference between the proceeds and the higher of the cost of the shares and their value at 6 April 1965. Similarly, any allowable capital loss on such share sales is the difference between the proceeds and the lower of the cost of the shares and their value at 6 April 1965. If the price at which you sell shares held at 6 April 1965 is between their value at that date and their cost then you are treated as having no gain and no loss for capital gains tax purposes (subject to the election described below).

Disposals after 5 April 1982 may entitle you to indexation allowance (p 18). If you have elected for a 6 April 1965 valuation; your indexaton allowance will be based on that amount. Otherwise, for quoted shares and securities, it will be based on the cost, subject to the rules (p 18).

As regards disposals of quoted shares and securities which you held at 6 April 1965, you have the right to elect that any capital gains or losses on such disposals shall be calculated by substituting the 6 April 1965 values for the original costs in all cases. The following rules apply:

(1)   The election for each category must be made within two years of the end of the tax year (or accounting year for a company) in which the first sale after 19 March 1968 is made. *Thus in many cases elections will either have been made or are now out of time.*

(2)   Separate elections must be made for you and your wife — your respective holdings are separately considered for these purposes.

(3)   Separate elections are required for ordinary shares and fixed interest securities (such as loan stock and preference shares).

(4)   You and your wife have the option of electing or not in respect of each category.

(5)   Companies, trusts, estates, etc must make separate elections.

(6)   Once made, the elections are irrevocable.

Making the election is particularly beneficial regarding shares whose cost was lower than their value at 6 April 1965 but which have now dropped below the latter value. An election would increase the available capital loss on sale. A further advantage arises if the original costs cannot be ascertained in which case, on election, the 6 April 1965 values are used. Otherwise the Revenue would not normally allow any capital losses on the disposal of such shares. The election was originally a most important tax planning tool and is still available in some cases (see above); the following example is therefore given concerning its operation.

Example 5: Quoted shares held on 6 April 1965

Mr A sold no shares from 1967–68 to 1983–84. In 1984–85 he sold all of the ordinary shares that he had held at 6 April 1965 as follows:

Shares held	Company	Cost	Market values 6.4.65	Proceeds
1,000	B Ltd	£2,000	£5,000	£3,000
2,000	C Ltd	£1,000	£2,000	£8,000
4,000	D Ltd	£5,000	£4,000	£3,000

Ignoring indexation, what is Mr A's capital gains tax assessment for 1984–85 (1) on the basis of no election and (2) on the basis that he elects for valuation at 6 April 1965?

(1) No election

	(a) Cost	(b) Market value 6.4.65	(c) Proceeds	(d) Gain (Loss)	Basis
1,000 Shares B Ltd	£2,000	£5,000	£3,000	NIL	No gain No Loss
2,000 Shares C Ltd	£1,000	£2,000	£8,000	£6,000	(c)–(b)
4,000 Shares D Ltd	£5,000	£4,000	£3,000	(1,000)	(b)–(c)
				£5,000	

Capital gains tax assessment 1984–85

(2) Election (cost ignored)

	6.4.65	Proceeds	Gain (Loss)
1,000 Shares B Ltd	£5,000	£3,000	(2,000)
2,000 Shares C Ltd	£2,000	£8,000	£6,000
4,000 Shares D Ltd	£4,000	£3,000	(1,000)
Capital gains tax assessment 1984–85			£3,000

Note: The election must be made to the Revenue before 5 April 1987 and will result in a reduction of £2,000 in the 1984–85 capital gains tax assessment. In fact, if Mr A had no other gains the £5,600 annual exemption for 1984–85 would then cover his liability.

Planning

● *Basic capital gains tax planning regarding quoted shares, etc, should include the following*

(1)   Use your annual exemption (£5,600) to enhance the base cost of your shares. This will also increase your indexation allowance for future sales.

(2)   Unless you have to sell for commercial reasons, hold shares for more than a year, so as to obtain indexation allowance.

(3)   If you have realised gains in the current tax year in excess of £5,600, realise losses to cover such excess, possibly by means of 'bed and breakfast' transactions (p 20).

(4)   In order to maximise the annual exemptions available, split share purchases between yourself and your adult children.

(5)   If you hold qualifying corporate bonds (p31) which show a profit, keep them for more than one year to obtain the exemption. However, if they show a loss, it is necessary to sell within the year to obtain relief.

(6)   Always weigh carefully any potential tax savings against investment criteria.

Traded options
(FA 1980 S84 & FA 1984 S65)

Options to buy or sell quoted shares are dealt with on the Stock Exchange. Prior to 6 April 1980 they were treated as wasting assets (p 26), but from that date they are no longer so regarded which means that the entire cost is deductible on a sale. Also from 6 April 1980 the abandonment of a traded option is treated as a disposal so that its cost is an allowable loss. From 6 April 1984, this treatment also applies to all traded options quoted on recognised stock exchanges or the London International Financial Futures Exchange.

Unquoted shares
(CGTA S152 & Sch 5; FA 1981 S64; & FA 1982 S51)

Many of the above points regarding quoted shares and securities apply also to unquoted shares but the following special rules should be noted:

(1)   Regarding holdings of shares at 6 April 1965 the 'time apportionment' rule normally applies to sales after that date subject to the right of election for valuation at 6 April 1965 (p 23). This is not a 'blanket' election for all your non-quoted shares as is the case for quoted shares. If you have elected for a 6 April 1965 valuation, your indexation allowance will be based on that amount. Otherwise, time apportionment applies to the gain *net* of indexation allowance. Thus indexation may affect the desirability of an election.

(2)   If after 6 April 1965 there is a capital reorganisation or takeover regarding a non-quoted company in which you have shares, 'time apportionment' normally stops at that time and on any future sales you have a time apportioned gain or loss to the date of reorganisation or takeover and the full gain or loss after that time.

(3)   If a reorganisation or take-over as in (2) above occurred before 6 April 1965 any shares still held at that date must automatically be valued at 6 April 1965 and time apportionment does not apply. You still consider, however, the cost of your original holding when computing any capital gain or loss on a future sale.

(4)   Prior to 6 April 1982 (1 April for companies) the 'pooling' rules (p 32) applied to shares acquired after 6 April 1965 but not to acquisitions before that time which must be separately considered on a 'first in first out' basis.

(5)   The new indexing rules (p 18) apply to non-quoted shares as for quoted ones. The rule in (4) above regarding shares held at 6 April 1965 is modified, however, so that the 'last in first out' basis applies.

(6)   Any relief which you obtain against your income, from the new business start up scheme (below) is not also available to create a

capital loss. Thus if you eventually sell the shares at a profit, you will obtain full relief for the cost in calculating your capital gain, but not in a loss situation.

Losses on unquoted shares in trading companies
(FA 1980 S37; & FA 1981 S36)

Special rules apply to disposals after 5 April 1980 of shares in 'qualifying trading companies'. Provided you or your wife was the original subscriber, you can elect to obtain income tax relief for any loss on a full priced arm's-length sale, liquidation, etc. The election is required within two years after the tax year in which the relief is applied.

A 'qualifying trading company' is, broadly, one which has always been UK resident but never quoted and has traded for at least six years, or from within a year of incorporation if less. The company is permitted to have stopped trading within the previous three years provided it has not become an investment company in the meantime. 'Trading' excludes dealing mainly in shares, land or commodity futures. The relief originally applied only to individuals, but has now been extended to certain investment companies regarding disposals of shares held in 'qualifying trading companies' after 31 March 1981.

● *This relief is interesting because it allows you income tax relief for what otherwise would be a capital loss. If you are able to realise the loss in a year when your income tax top rate is particularly high, so much the better. An even more direct way of obtaining income tax relief from a capital transaction is through the business expansion scheme (see below).*

Business Expansion Scheme
(FA 1981 Ss52–67; FA 1982 Ss51 & 52; FA 1983 S26 & Sch 5; F2A 1983 S5 & Sch 1; & FA 1984 S37)

Since 1981–82, first the Business Start-Up Scheme and then the Business Expansion scheme have operated to give you the opportunity of obtaining income tax relief on subscriptions for shares in certain companies.

The Business Start-Up Scheme operated for 1981–82 and 1982–83. During that period you obtained relief from income tax including investment income surcharge in respect of amounts subscribed in a year of assessment for shares in a qualifying company. (From 1982–83 certain wholly owned subsidiaries of qualifying companies are also included.) A *qualifying company* exists to carry on one or more *qualifying trades* — broadly, manufacturing, wholesale and retail business but not leasing and financial activities, etc. Also, your subscription in the company needed to be during the first five years of its trade.

The amount required to be invested was at least £500 in any year and relief was restricted to £10,000 for 1981–82 and £20,000 for 1982–83. Any unused relief for 1981–82 could be used in 1982–83. To obtain the relief you could not own more than 30% of the company (shares or votes or shares and loan), also not more than 50% of the shares, etc, could qualify for relief under the scheme, no matter how many investors were involved.

The scope of the Business Start-Up Scheme was considerably widened regarding shares issued from 6 April 1983 and it is now known as the *Business Expansion Scheme*. Particular features include the following:

(1)   The life of the scheme has been extended to 5 April 1987.

(2)   As well as covering investment in new companies, shares issued by established unquoted trading companies satisfying certain conditions are now included.

(3)   As before, the scheme excludes employees. paid directors and 30% + shareholders.

(4)   The annual total investment limit has been doubled to £40,000 but the minimum remains at £500 unless made through approved investment funds. The 50% restriction has been removed so that any quantity of shares may be included.

(5)   Shares on which relief is claimed must in general be held for at least 5 years.

(6)   Claims for relief can now be made once the company has carried on its qualifying trade for 4 months; and normally must be made within two years after the end of the year of assessment to which the claim relates.

(7)   The relief does not normally reduce the cost for capital gains tax purposes.

(8)   The *qualifying trade* rules are similar to those for the Business Expansion Scheme (see above) with some modifications. For example, in respect of shares issued after 13 March 1984, farming is no longer a qualifying trade.

(9)   In general, a trade whose income is mainly from royalties and license fees does not qualify, but an exception now applies for film producing companies.

4 Capital gains tax — Special reliefs

Main private residence exemption
(CGTA Ss101–105; FA 1980 S80 & FA 1984 S63)

The house or flat where you live is normally exempt from capital gains tax when you sell it, subject to the following rules:

(1) The house must have been your only or main residence during the time that you owned it subject to various allowable absence periods (see below). You ignore all periods before 6 April 1965 for these purposes.

(2) The following periods of absence will not entail the loss of your exemption:
   (a) The last 24 months of ownership.
   (b) Periods of absence totalling three years.
   (c) Any period throughout which you work abroad.
   (d) Any periods up to four years in aggregate when you are prevented from living in your house due to your employment being elsewhere.
   (e) Any period during which you live in job-related accommodation from 31 July 1978, but intend to return to your main residence.

   Provided you have no other residence which you claim to be exempt during the above periods they are taken cumulatively and so you could have a long period of absence and still not lose your exemption. You must, however, return to your main residence at the end of periods (b), (c) and (d) above or else you will lose part of your relief.

(3) Any periods of absence subsequent to 6 April 1965 in excess of those allowed (see above) result in the relevant proportion of your sale profit being charged to capital gains tax. For example, if you bought your house in June 1977 and sell it in June 1984 at a profit of £7,000 having lived elsewhere for reasons unconnected with your employment for the middle five years, your chargeable gain is £7,000 × 1/7 = £1,000. (You are only allowed three years of absence and the last two in any event, leaving one year taxable.)

(4) If a specific part of your house is set aside for business purposes then that proportion of your profits on sale of the house will be taxable. Thus if you have eight rooms of which two are wholly used for business purposes you would normally claim 25% of your house expenses against your business profits and when you sell your house you will pay capital gains tax on 25% of your total gain (arising after 6 April 1965). If, however, you use no rooms exclusively for business purposes you will not normally be liable for any capital gains tax if you sell your house even though you claim part of your house expenses against your business profits.

(5)   Regarding disposals before 6 April 1980 if part of your main residence was let, your capital gain on that part was not covered by the exemption. However, if your disposal is on or after that date and part has been let for residential purposes, you obtain further exemption, which is related to the gain on that part. However, the extra amount is not to exceed the exemption on the part occupied by you, or £20,000 if smaller. (Before 6 April 1983, this figure was £10,000.)

(6)   If you have two residences you can give written notice to the Revenue within two years of acquiring your second residence to elect which of the two should be treated as your main private residence and thereby be exempted from capital gains tax. Should you not elect within two years, you can still do so, but it will then only apply to the period commencing two years before the date of your election. If you do not elect then the Revenue will decide in the light of the time that you spend at each of your residences which of these is your main private residence.

(7)   For the purposes of the exemption your main residence is taken to include land of up to one acre (including the site of the house). If the house is large and its character requires a larger garden than one acre, this will normally be allowed.

You also obtain capital gains tax exemption on no more than one residence owned by you and occupied by a dependent relative (not able to keep him or herself — also the widowed or separated mother of either your spouse or yourself).

● *Ensure that you gain the maximum benefit from the private residence exemption. If you have two residences, claim within two years of the date of purchase of your second abode which should be treated as your main private residence to be free of capital gains tax. You have a free choice in this matter and so should select the house or flat likely to increase in value the most.*

● *Remember that the election could apply to a residence which you rent, as well as one which you own. Thus, if you have one of each, you should elect that the freehold (or long-leasehold) home is your main residence.*

● *Also, if you use part of your house for business, if possible do not claim specific rooms for income tax but merely make a general claim for expenses (see (4) above).*

Chattels
(CGTA S128; & FA 1982 S81)

A chattel is an asset which is tangible movable property such as a chair, a picture, or a pair of candlesticks. For these purposes a set is treated as one chattel. If you dispose of a chattel for no more than £3,000 you pay no capital gains tax and if your proceeds exceed £3,000 your capital gain is restricted to five-thirds of the excess. Thus if you sell a set of antique chairs for £3,300 (original cost £500) your capital gain is restricted to $5/3 \times$ (£3,300–£3,000) = £500.

If you buy a chattel for more than £3,000, and sell it for less than £3,000, your allowable loss is restricted to the excess of the cost over £3,000.

A £2,000 exemption limit applied from 1978–79 to 1981–82. Before 1978–79, the limit was £1,000 and the capital gains tax was limited to half the excess over £1,000.

● *Planning your sales of chattels to take full advantage of the relief can save considerable tax. For example, you may have a valuable brooch whose real worth lies in four diamonds. By selling the stones separately for less than £3,000 the chattels exemption would apply. However, the brooch as a whole would raise, say, £10,000 so that no relief would be obtained. Similarly if you have a set of valuable objects whose value as a set is not much enhanced then sell them separately to different buyers so as to secure relief which you would not otherwise obtain.*

● *The chattels exemption should be borne in mind when you build up a collection of, say, antiques or pictures. By choosing items in a moderate price bracket, you stand a good chance of being able to sell them within the £3,000 exemption, or whatever it is at the time.*

Replacement of business assets
(CGTA Ss115–121)

You are liable for capital gains tax in respect of gains realised on sales of assets used in your business. Similarly a company is liable regarding its sales of business assets. If further business assets are purchased within one year preceding and three years after the sale, 'roll-over' relief is obtained as a result of which the gain on the disposal is deducted from the cost of the new business assets. Thus, the gain is 'rolled over' and no tax is paid until the new business assets are sold, unless the latter are in turn replaced. (Furnished holiday lettings are treated as a trade for the purposes of 'roll-over' relief—FA 1984 Sch 11.)

In order for the relief to be obtained the old and new assets must be 'qualifying'. This means that they must be within the following categories:

(a)   Land and buildings (but not trading stock).
(b)   Fixed plant and machinery not forming part of a building.
(c)   Ships, aircraft and hovercraft.
(d)   Goodwill.

Since plant and machinery only qualifies if it is fixed, items such as motor vans, fork lift trucks and movable machines are excluded.

To get the relief you must use the old and new assets in the same business. However, if you carry on several trades, they are treated as one for this purpose. (This applies, by concession, if there is a gap of no more than 3 years between one trade ceasing and the other starting). Also, roll-over relief applies regarding purchases and sales by you of personally owned assets used in your 'family company' (p 47). Note that to obtain total relief, the entire proceeds must be invested, otherwise you pay tax on your capital gain up to the extent of the shortfall.

If the new business asset is a wasting asset (p 25), unless it is replaced by a non-wasting asset within 10 years, the rolled-over gain becomes chargeable. This also applies to assets which will become 'wasting' within 10 years, such as a lease with 59 years to run.

'Roll-over' relief is applicable to companies (p 54). Also a special extension of the rules covers 'gilts' obtained by companies in exchange for group companies in the aircraft and shipping industries on compulsory acquisition through nationalisation. An election is required within four years of the exchange and then the normal new compensation stock rules do not apply.

● *Always remember that to obtain full roll-over relief you must reinvest the full proceeds within the next three years (or the previous year), This will be a strong argument in favour of, say, buying the freehold of a new factory rather than leasing one, finances permitting.*

Roll-over relief on compulsory purchase
(CGTA Ss 111 A & B)

From 6 April 1982 a form of roll-over relief, similar to that available on business assets (above) applies to certain property which is sold to local authorities. The property must either be compulsorily bought from you or the purchasing local authority must have compulsory acquisition powers. The relief is not available if your replacement property qualifies for main residence relief (p 42).

Transfer of a business to a company
(CGTA S123)

You will obtain this form of roll-over relief if you transfer your business as a going concern to a company, wholly or partly in exchange for shares in that company. You must transfer all of the assets of your business except for its cash, which you need not pass over to the company. The relief equally applies to the transfer to a company of a partnership business but not one already carried on by a company.

If you obtain nothing but shares as your consideration, your entire gain is rolled-over and you will pay no tax until you sell some or all of the shares. However, if you receive part of your consideration in other form, such as cash or even a debt owing to you, you will immediately be liable for the capital gains tax attributable to that part of the consideration (subject to your annual exemption of £5,600). Thus if your total gain is £4,000 and your consideration is shares worth £4,000 and cash of £12,000, you will pay tax now on £4,000 $\times$ 12,000/16,000 = £3,000; the remaining £1,000 being rolled-over.

● *The decision of whether to take part of the consideration in cash or other taxable form provides an opportunity for tax planning. If you take all shares, your entire gain will be rolled over. However, if you have not used all your annual exemption (£5,600) it will be beneficial to take enough of the consideration in cash, etc, to cover it.*

Gifts of business assets
(CGTA S126 & Sch 4)

A form of 'hold-over' relief applied to certain transfers of assets, other than bargains at arm's length, made after 11 April 1978. The assets covered were any used in your trade or 'family company' (p 47); also shares in such a company. A claim was required from both the recipient and yourself, similar in effect to that for general gifts (see below). A more general relief applies for indiviuals after 5 April 1980 and for settlements after 5 April 1981 (see below). The old relief still applies for gifts to companies, however.

General relief for gifts
(FA 1980 S79; & FA 1981 Ss78 & 79; & FA 1982 S82)

In general, transfers of assets which you make after 5 April 1980, other than bargains at arm's length, are covered by 'hold-over' rules. Only UK resident or ordinarily resident *individuals* (p 5) were covered up to 5 April 1981. However after that date gifts *to trusts* are included and from 6 April 1982 gifts *from* trusts are covered.

A claim is required from you both, whereupon your gain is reduced to nil and the recipient deducts your original capital gain from his acquisition value for the asset. (If your gift is to the trustees of a settlement, you alone need elect.) Should you receive some consideration the claim covers only the gift element, if this is less than your total gain. If you are entitled to retirement relief (below) this reduces the held-over gain. If any capital transfer tax (p 68) is payable on the transaction, to the extent that this is no more than the original gain, the acquisition value is increased for the recipient.

If you have received a gift after 5 April 1981 and made the election, then the held-over gain is assessed on you, subject to certain exceptions, should you become neither resident nor ordinarily resident in the UK before having sold the asset. The exceptions are:

(1)   Returning within 3 years and becoming UK resident or ordinarily resident once again.

(2)   Working wholly abroad being the reason for you having become non-resident.

(3)   Not becoming non-resident until at least 6 years after the gift.

● *If you are making gifts subject to a 'hold-over' election, consider having some payment so as to enable you to use up your own £5,600 annual exemption if you have not already done so; also retirement relief (see below) if applicable. Thus if you wish to give your son some shares which cost you, say, £5,000 and are now worth £20,600, sell them to him for £10,600 so that your capital gain of £5,600 is covered by the annual exemption. Effectively, your son obtains a base cost of £10,600 because the gain of £10,000 is 'held over'. (If necessary, you could gift £10,600 to your son to cover the cash element if he did not have the necessary funds.) With larger gifts, capital transfer tax will need to be considered (p 68).*

Business retirement relief
(CGTA Ss124 & 125 & FA 1984 S63)

If you are over 65 and dispose by gift or sale of the whole or part of a business which you have owned for the past 10 years, you are exempted from capital gains tax on the first £100,000 of any gain arising in respect of the 'chargeable business assets' of the business. If you have several businesses your total relief is restricted to £100,000. (For disposals before 6 April 1983, this figure was £50,000, with £20,000 before 12 April 1978 and £10,000 before 3 July 1974.)

'Chargeable business assets' include assets used for the trade, etc, of the business, and also goodwill. Assets held as investments, including shares in subsidiary companies, are not classified as chargeable business assets, however. Also excluded are assets where there could be no capital gains tax liability if you sold them; for example, trading stock (part of your trading profit) or cash (exempt).

The above relief also covers any disposal of shares in a trading company which has been your 'family company' for at least the last 10 years during which time you have been a full-time director of the company. A 'family company' is one in which you have 25% of the voting rights or your immediate family has at least 51% including 5% held by yourself. (Before

12 April 1978 the last two percentages were 75% and 10%.) Only the proportion of the gain on the shares attributable to the 'chargeable business assets' of the company compared with its total chargeable assets qualifies for the relief.

The relief also applies (by extra-statutory concession D11) if you personally dispose of an asset used rent-free by your 'family company' in its trade. To obtain this relief, you must have been a full-time working director of the company throughout your period of ownership of the asset. Limited relief is available if you receive less than a market rent. Similar rules apply concerning assets owned by partners and used in the partnership business.

If your age is between 60 and 65 your relief as above is limited to £20,000 (£10,000 before 6 April 1983, £4,000 before 12 April 1978 and £2,000 before 3 July 1974) for each year by which your age exceeds 60. (Add a corresponding fraction of £20,000 for the odd months.) Thus if you are $63\frac{1}{2}$ your relief is restricted to £20,000 $\times$ ($63\frac{1}{2}$ – 60) = £70,000. If your wife complies with the above requirements, she too will be eligible for the relief if she sells her business or shares in a 'family company'.

Concerning disposals after 11 April 1978, of the whole or part of a business which you have owned for less than 10 years, you obtain 10% of the full relief if you owned the assets for at least one year prior to disposal, 20% relief for at least two years of ownership and so on, adding a further 10% for each year up to ten.

● *If you have a family business or company and are at least 60 years of age, use the capital gains tax retirement relief (maximum £100,000) to its best advantage (p 47). This may mean waiting until you reach the age of 65 before selling your business and also continuing to work in it until that time. Remember that, subject to the rules, your wife can also get the relief if she works in the business and owns part of it.*

● *Note the importance of the proportion of chargeable business assets in your company. In particular, remember that shares held in subsidiaries are not chargeable business assets and would thus reduce your retirement relief when you dispose of shares in the holding company. This should be considered when structuring your business. If necessary, consider transferring the business of a subsidiary company up to the parent company to increase the chargeable business assets of the latter.*

Example 6: Business retirement and gifts relief

Mr A is 63 and holds all of the share capital in B Ltd, of which company he is a full-time director. His shares are worth £150,000, on which a capital gain of £100,000 would arise on disposal. Assume that all the value represents chargeable business assets and Mr A has owned the shares for eight years; also that he has used none of his £5,600 exemption for 1984–85. How should Mr A gift or sell his shares to his son, C, in the most tax-efficient way, ignoring capital gains indexation allowance and capital transfer tax?

Disposal proceeds of shares in B Ltd		£150,000
Chargeable gain before reliefs		100,000
Retirement relief — maximum	£100,000	
available for ownership period 8/10ths	(80,000)	
available at age 63 3/5ths	48,000	
Annual exemption	5,600	53,600
		£46,400
Capital gains tax on gift without election at 30%		£13,920

If both A and C make a gift hold-over election, then A will not be assessed to the capital gains tax but the base value of the shares for C will be reduced by the gain *before* the annual exemption, becoming £150,000 − £52,000 = £98,000. C's base cost could be increased to £103,600 without A paying any capital gains tax if C buys the shares for £103,600. This will leave A with a gain of £5,600, covered by his annual exemption. (C could borrow the money from A to purchase the shares.) The transaction would also involve a gift element of £46,400 for which a gift election should be made. Also some capital transfer tax (p68) might be involved if the exemptions and nil rate band are exceeded.

Charities
(CGTA Ss145 & 146)

Charities are exempted from capital gains tax in respect of any gains on the disposal of assets provided that such gains are applied to charitable purposes.

If you make a gift of an asset to a charity you pay no capital gains tax on this disposal.

● *Thus if you wish to make a generous gift to a charity of a capital amount (rather than recurring annual amounts under deed of covenant) you will save yourself future capital gains tax if you gift a chargeable asset on which you have a large potential profit. For example, if you wish to give £20,000 to a charity and own shares in A Ltd which cost £4,000 in 1968 and are now worth £20,000 you should gift those shares. (If you sold the shares and donated cash they would only produce £15,200 net of 30% capital gains tax, assuming your £5,600 exemption has already been used.)*

5 Capital gains tax — trusts, estates and companies

This chapter deals with capital gains tax (CGT) as it applies to trusts, estates and companies. Other taxation matters relating to trusts and estates are covered in Chapter 11 (p 151). The legal aspects of trusts are dealt with in Chapter 12 (p 158) and the administration period of estates is considered from a legal point of view in Chapter 10 (p 127).

Trusts

(CGTA Ss51–58 & 126 & Sch 4; FA 1980 S78; FA 1981 S78, Ss86–87 & 89; & FA 1982 Ss80, 82 & 84)

Annual exemptions

Trusts are charged to CGT at 30% on all gains from the sales of chargeable assets (less capital losses) during each tax year. For 1984–85 the £5,600 annual exemption (p 12) applies to trusts for the mentally disabled and those receiving attendance allowance. Other trusts formed before 7 June 1978 obtain a straight annual exemption of £2,800 no matter how high their gains. Regarding trusts formed from that date, the exemption of £2,800 must be split between all those with the same settlor. Thus if you have settled four such trusts they each have an annual exemption of £700. If there are more than five, however, they each still have an exemption of £560. For future years, these figures will be increased with the retail price index (unless the Treasury order otherwise), rounding up to the nearest £100 as necessary.

For 1980–81 and 1981–82 the £3,000 annual exemption (p 12) applied to trusts for the mentally disabled and those receiving attendance allowance. (From 6 April 1981 only broadly half the property and income need be applied to the disabled.) Other trusts formed before 7 June 1978 obtained a straight annual exemption of £1,500 no matter how high their gains. Regarding trusts formed from that date the exemption of £1,500 was split between all those with the same settlor. Thus if you have settled four such trusts they each had an annual exemption of £375. If there are more than five, however, they each still had an exemption of £300. For 1982–83 the exemptions were £5,000 (instead of £3,000) and £2,500 (£1,500). The minimum exemption was £500 (£300). Similarly, for 1983–84, these figures were £5,300, £2,650 and £530 (see Table 2—p11).

Prior to 1978–79, the half-income rule which then applied for individuals did not apply to trusts. The £1,000 net gains exemption and marginal relief up to £9,500 (p 11), however, applied to trusts for the mentally disabled and those receiving attendance allowance for 1977–78, 1978–79 and 1979–80. Other trusts formed before 7 June 1978 obtained exemption if their net annual gains for those three years were no more than £500. Up to £1,250, the tax was limited to 50% of the excess over £500 (p 11).

Assets settled

When any chargeable assets are introduced into the trust by the settlor this is a realisation by him on which he pays capital gains tax if applicable. For example, if A bought 1,000 shares in B Ltd for £1,000 in May 1968 and gifts them in June 1984 to a settlement that he created, the shares must be valued at that time. If the shares are then worth £2,000 (ignoring indexation allowance) he has a chargeable gain of £1,000 for 1984–85. If, however, the shares are worth only £600 at that time, he has an allowable loss of £400 (£1,000–£600), which he can only set off against any capital gains resulting from other transactions between A and his trust. This is because they are treated as being 'connected persons' (p 17).

Any capital loss arising on property transferred to a beneficiary, which cannot be used by the trust in that tax year becomes available for use by the beneficiary in that and subsequent years against general gains.

Gifts relief

Between 11 April 1978 and 6 April 1981, where business assets, including shares in 'family companies' were settled, the trustees and settlor could jointly claim for any gain on the assets to be rolled over (p 44). The effect was that the settlor had no CGT to pay on the settled business assets, etc, and the acquisition value for the trustees was correspondingly reduced. The general gifts relief (p 46) applies to all kinds of gifts to trusts after 5 April 1981, but gifts by trusts are only covered if made after 5 April 1982. Prior to this the business assets gifts relief applied.

Disposals, etc

The disposal of an interest in a trust by one of the original beneficiaries is normally exempt from CGT. However, after 9 March 1981 this does not apply to non-resident settlements.

Where a capital asset of a trust is distributed to a beneficiary this is a chargeable event which can give rise to a capital gain in the trust. (This even applies for minors, etc, who are not yet able to legally own the property.) Thus if a trust bought 1,000 shares in B Ltd for £2,000 in April 1970 and it distributes them to beneficiary C in July 1984 when their market value is £3,000 the trust will have a capital gain of £1,000 (£3,000–£2,000), which is assessable for 1984–85 subject to the annual exemption and indexation allowance. (An exception to this rule is where a beneficiary under a will receives his entitlement — p 54.)

Prior to 6 April 1982, where a *life interest* ended in a discretionary settlement, CGT could arise on the excess of its value over the base cost. This did not apply on a death, however. From 6 April 1982 this charge is removed, provided the property remains in trust. However, on a subsequent disposal the original base value must be used. (FA 1982 S84.)

● *CGT planning for trusts is similar in many ways to that for individuals. Thus, for example, the £2,800 annual exemption should be used where appropriate and losses created (p20) to cover gains made in the tax year.*

Foreign trusts
(CGTA S17; FA 1981 Ss80–85 & 88 & FA 1984 Ss66, 70–71 & Sch 14)

A trust is generally treated as being resident abroad for capital gains tax purposes if a majority of the trustees are so resident and its administration and management is carried out overseas. Such a trust is exempt from CGT on realisations of assets in the UK and elsewhere. There are, however, rules under which the Revenue can sometimes assess UK resident beneficiaries with their shares of any capital gains (provided that the settlor is UK domiciled and resident or ordinarily resident either when he made the settlement or when the capital gain is made). Prior to 6 April 1981, this applied whether or not the beneficiaries received any part of the gains. However, tax assessed prior to 6 April 1984 in respect of gains arising before 6 April 1981 can now be deferred until the benefit passes, provided the tax was unpaid at 29 March 1983. After 5 April 1981, however, UK beneficiaries are only charged to tax to the extent that they receive capital payments attributable to such gains.

A different system applies regarding the gains after 5 April 1981 of overseas settlements (settlor UK domiciled and resident or ordinarily resident). Where the capital gains by the overseas trust and capital payments to UK beneficiaries are in different tax years, the beneficiaries are taxed in the later one. There are rules to prevent CGT being avoided by transfers between settlements and by a trust changing its residence. From 1984–85, for the purposes of the rules, the term 'settlement' is enlarged to include dispositions, arrangements and agreements. Similarly 'settlor' takes in those making reciprocal arrangements or undertaking to provide funds indirectly.

If you are a beneficiary of a foreign trust and obtain an asset from it after 5 April 1983, as a general rule, your base value is taken to be the market value of the asset. (From 10 March 1981 to 5 April 1984, except in certain cases where the trust was liable for UK capital gains tax, your base value was limited to the amount of any consideration which you actually gave for the asset—normally nothing.)

● *In an overseas discretionary settlement with some resident and some non-resident beneficiaries, UK CGT can be saved by distributing the gains to overseas beneficiaries in one tax year and then making capital distributions to UK beneficiaries in the next. (If all the beneficiaries had received distributions in the same tax year, those resident in the UK would have been assessed on their shares of the capital gain.)*

Estates of deceased persons

The CGT liability of the deceased
(TMA Ss40, 74 & 77)

When a person dies, CGT must be settled on all his capital gains up to the date of his death. Any of this tax that is not paid during his lifetime must be settled by his executors or administrators out of his estate.

If the deceased has not been assessed to tax on all his capital gains prior to his death, the Revenue are allowed to make assessments on such gains within three years after the end of the tax year in which death occurred. In the case of fraud, wilful default or neglect by the deceased, however, the Revenue may make assessments in respect of any tax years ending within six years before the date of death, but no earlier years can be assessed.

The administration period
(Ss426–433)

The administration period of an estate is the period from the date of death of the deceased until the assets are distributed to the beneficiaries according to the will of the deceased or according to the rules of intestacy. Where, however, a trust is set up under a will the administration period normally lasts only until the trust takes over the residue of the estate. (See Chapter 10 (p 127) for details.)

Capital gains tax during the administration period
(CGTA Ss5 & 49 & Sch 1)

No capital gains tax liability accrues to the estate of the deceased on the passing of his assets at death. The executors or administrators of the estate are regarded as acquiring the assets at their market value at the date of death and if they later sell any of the assets during the administration period the estate is assessed to capital gains tax on any surplus. Thus suppose part of the estate of A, deceased, consisted of 1,000 shares in B Ltd whose value at his death on, say, 30 June 1980 was £2,000. If those shares are sold on 1 November 1984 for £3,000 (in order to pay capital transfer tax, for example), the estate is assessed to capital gains tax on £1,000 (£3,000–£2,000) for 1984–85. (This ignores indexation allowance.)

In computing the capital gains the executors or administrators are allowed to deduct their costs of establishing title. For gross estates not exceeding £400,000 the Revenue allow the use of a scale now extending from ·75% to 1·5% of the probate value of the asset sold. Also selling costs are, of course, deductible.

Transfers of assets to beneficiaries

No CGT is charged on the estate on unconditional transfers of its assets to beneficiaries, in settlement of their entitlements under the will of the deceased. Instead, each beneficiary is treated for capital gains tax purposes as if he had acquired the assets at the same time as the personal representatives acquired them and at the same value.

Thus in the example mentioned above, if instead of selling the 1,000 shares in B Ltd for £3,000 on 1 November 1984 the executors gave them to C on that day in satisfaction of a legacy provided by the will of A, deceased, C is treated as having acquired the shares on 30 June 1980 for £2,000 only. (The value of £2,000 was the probate value of the shares at the date of death.) Thus no CGT is payable by the estate in respect of the transfer. If, however, C were to sell the shares on 1 December 1984 for £3,500 his chargeable gain will be £1,500 (£3,500–£2,000), although the shares have only gone up in value by £500 since he received them. This is because his entitlement to the legacy is considered for capital gains tax purposes to extend back to the date of death. Note that any indexation allowance for C would also relate back to that time, subject to the rules (p 18).

Annual exemption

For the year of assessment in which death occurs and the next two years, the first £5,600, etc of net gains is exempted (depending on the annual exemption for that year), as for an individual. (Prior to 1980–81 the special reliefs for aggregate net gains not exceeding £9,500 applied (p 11).)

Deeds of family arrangement

If the terms of the will are varied by means of a deed of family arrangement (p 84) within two years of death, no CGT results at that time. Furthermore, new beneficiaries receive their legacies without the estate incurring any chargeable gains, but on future disposals their base value will be the probate value.

● *Make use of the annual exemption (£5,600 etc) where practicable in the year of death and next two years. This will probably save CGT for the beneficiaries. Assets with high capital gains which have arisen since death should be transferred direct to respective beneficiaries to avoid crystallising any capital gain. If it is agreed that certain members of the family should have particular assets, this could be facilitated by a deed of family arrangement (see above).*

Companies

(Ss265–281; FA 1972 S93; FA 1974 S10 & FA 1984 S18)

For any accounting period ending before 1 April 1983, 15/26ths of the chargeable gains of a company, computed according to the normal CGT rules (p 17), are added to the assessable profits of the company and charged to corporation tax at 52%. Even if the lower rate (38%) applied to the company's profits, 15/26ths of the capital gains were still subjected to the 52% rate. This produces an effective rate of 30%, as for individuals, etc.

With the recent cuts in the rates of corporation tax, the taxable fractions of capital gains have been adjusted to keep the effective rate at 30% (even if the small companies rate of now 30% applies). Details are:

Year to 31 March	Tax rate	Taxable fraction of capital gains
1984	50%	3/5
1985	45%	2/3
1986	40%	3/4
1987	35%	6/7

Companies pay tax on their gains at the same time as the rest of their corporation tax liabilities. The due date is normally nine months after the year-end in the case of companies which started trading after March 1965. However, if a company traded before April 1965, it retains the same interval between its accounting date and tax due date even if this exceeds nine months. If the corporation tax assessment is issued later than the date given above, the due date becomes 30 days after the date of issue of the assessment (unless there is an appeal).

Asset ownership

● *An important tax planning point to consider when buying a valuable asset for use in your company's business is whether you should own the asset personally or whether your company should be the purchaser. For example, the company which you control could buy a new building or you could buy it and let it to the company. If the company buys the asset and sells it later, making a capital gain, the company will pay tax on it (subject to possible roll-over relief—see p 44). Should you then liquidate the company you will probably incur CGT on any increase in the value of your shares. The double CGT effect is an argument for holding the asset direct, but this could be over-ridden by commercial considerations. Also, consider the possible loss of retirement relief, particularly where you let the asset to your company (p 48). Note, however, the benefits of a wasting asset, such as a lease, being held by a company (p 26).*

Parallel pooling
(FA 1983 S34 & Sch 6 & FA 1984 S67)

The parallel pooling provisions apply only to companies. A formal and irrevocable election is needed which then covers all disposals, after 31 March 1982 of 'qualifying securities' (excluding gilts, shares in non-qualifying offshore funds and 6 April 1965 holdings for which no market value election had been made). The election is required within two years of the end of the accounting period in which the first such disposal occurs.

Disposals must first be matched against acquisitions within the previous twelve months, taking the earliest first. Then, the pooled shares are regarded as being disposed of and finally non-pooled 6 April 1965 holdings. Two pools of costs are required, one indexed and one not. The costs of disposals are calculated in proportion to the shares sold, using the indexed pool. The indexation factor is reduced or eliminated to avoid producing a loss.

Capital losses

Chargeable gains can be relieved by means of capital losses in the same period or those brought forward from previous periods. Trading losses can be set off against gains of the same period or the previous period. Gains can also be off-set by group loss relief claims (below). Note that the chargeable gains are first reduced to the appropriate fraction (p 55) and the trading losses are deducted from the remainder. Trading losses brought forward from previous periods, however, can only be set off against future trading profits and not against future chargeable gains.

Capital losses (p 20) incurred by a company can only be set off against any capital gains of the company in the same accounting period or a future accounting period. They cannot be set against trading profits, as a general rule, for any year. Unused capital losses can be carried forward to future years even if the company has ceased trading whereas a cessation prevents trading losses from being carried forward.

Unlike individuals, rules apply to prevent a company from manufacturing capital losses by sales from large holdings (2% upwards) of another company's shares and buying them back within a month if quoted and six months otherwise (F2A 1975 S58).

Groups of companies
(Ss256–264 & 272–280; FA 1973 S28; & FA 1984 Ss46 & 47)

Special rules concerning CGT relate to groups of companies (broadly, parent and subsidiaries). A subsidiary company is classified according to the percentage of its ordinary capital owned (directly or indirectly) by its parent. Thus a 51% subsidiary is over 50% owned by its parent; and a 75% subsidiary is not less than 75% owned by its parent.

Some of the main rules affecting chargeable gains in groups of companies are as follows:

(1)   Group loss relief is available in respect of a parent company and its

75% subsidiaries subject to various rules. This enables a capital gain in one group company to be relieved by a trading loss surrendered from another company in the same group.

(2)   Subject to certain rules, group relief also applies to a consortium of companies which own a substantial part of another. Up to 26 July, a consortium was limited to five companies which had to own at least 90% of the ordinary shares. After that date, only 75% need be owned in total, with each consortium company having at least 5% of the ordinary shares.

(3)   Transfers of assets within a group consisting of a parent and its 75% subsidiaries (all resident in the UK) do not give rise to CGT. When the asset leaves the group, however, CGT is paid on the entire chargeable gain on the asset whilst it was owned by any of the companies within the group.

(4)   For the purposes of CGT 'roll-over relief' (p 44) in a UK group consisting of a parent company and 75% subsidiaries, the gain on an asset sold by one trading company may be 'rolled over' against the purchase of an asset by another trading company in the group. Property holding companies are also included, where they hold assets used for their trades by trading companies in the group.

● *In a group situation, you should be alert to the advantages sometimes to be obtained from transferring an asset into another group company before selling it. For example, company A might be carrying forward a capital loss of £500,000 with no immediate prospect of gains to set against it. If company B in the same group as A is planning to sell an asset, making a capital gain of £600,000, it is advisable to transfer the asset into A. Then A will sell the asset, thus realising the capital gain and offsetting the £500,000 loss, leaving a net assessable balance of £100,000.*

● *If a capital loss is carried forward in a company it remains available even if its trade ceases. Thus such a company in a group should not be liquidated until the loss is used. Alternatively it may be possible to sell the company to a group or single company which could transfer its own asset into it before selling the asset at a gain and offsetting the old loss.*

● *Note that the Revenue may try to involve the Ramsay, Burmah Oil or Furniss v Dawson decisions to counter partly artificial group CGT schemes. However, commercial arrangements with no artificial tax-saving links should be safe.*

Demergers
(FA 1980 Sch 18)

Sometimes it is wished, for commercial reasons, to split a group into two or more separate parts. Rules now operate which make it easier for two or more trading businesses to 'demerge' where they are carried on by a single company or a group. In demergers, subject to the detailed provisions:

(1)   Where a company distributes shares in a 75% subsidiary (p 56) to its shareholders this is not treated as a distribution and no advance corporation tax or income tax arises for the company or its shareholders.

(2)   Relief also applies where one company transfers a trade to a second company which in turn distributes its shares to the shareholders of the first.

(3)   CGT relief applies to any distribution which you receive in the above circumstances until you sell the actual shares.

(4)   There is also certain relief from development land tax and stamp duty in demergers.

(5)   The new provisions only apply to the genuine splitting off of trades or trading subsidiaries. There are anti-avoidance provisions to counter, for example the extraction of tax-free cash from companies subject to an advance clearance procedure.

(6)   To obtain clearance from the Revenue, full particulars should be sent and the Revenue must then either signify their approval or require further details within 30 days.

Unquoted company purchasing its own shares
(FA 1982 Ss53–56 & Sch 9)

The 1981 Companies Act has now enabled companies to purchase their own shares and issue redeemable equity shares. If the proceeds exceed the original cost, the excess would be treated as a distribution under existing law and taxed in the same way as a dividend. (Thus the company would pay ACT at 3/7th on the excess and an individual receiving the payment would pay higher rate tax on the grossed up excess less a tax credit.) In order to remove the disincentive of this heavy taxation, relief is provided in certain circumstances so that the company pays no ACT and the shareholder's liability is restricted to CGT (unless he is a share-dealer, in which case the gain is treated as his income).

Thus the relief in general involves reducing taxes on income and normally substituting taxes on capital at often lower rates. Because of the importance of unquoted companies repurchasing their own shares as a tax planning tool, the basic conditions for relief are given below:

(1)   The company must not be quoted nor be the subsidiary of a quoted company. (Shares dealt with on the Unlisted Securities Market are not treated as quoted.)

(2)   The company must be a trading company or the holding company of a trading group.

(3)   The purchase or redemption of the shares must be mainly to benefit a trade of the company or its 75% subsidiary.

(4)   The shareholder must be UK resident and ordinarily resident, having normally owned the shares for at least five years.

(5)   If the shares were inherited, the shareholder is required to have normally owned the shares for at least three years, including ownership by the deceased.

(6)   If the payment is used for capital transfer tax within two years after a death, (4) and (5) above do not apply and relief is due, provided that to pay the tax out of other funds would have caused undue hardship.

(7)   If the shareholder keeps part of his shareholding in the company (or its group) his shareholding must be substantially reduced. Broadly, this means reducing his interest by at least 25% and not being 'connected' (ie, holding 30% of the shares, etc).

(8)   The relieving provisions apply to payments after 5 April 1982 and advance clearance application may be made to the Revenue.

(9)   As indicated, the above rules do not apply where a company buys back its shares from a dealer. Instead, the company remains liable for ACT on the excess of the proceeds over the original cost and the dealer is taxed under Schedule D Case I or II (p 2), receiving no tax credit.

Overseas companies

(CGTA S15; & FA 1981 S85)

Any UK resident and domiciled shareholders of an overseas company can have its capital gains apportioned to them if the company would have been close if UK resident. The gain is apportioned between the shareholders according to their entitlement on liquidation and any with less than 5% avoid assessment. After 9 March 1981 this rule is extended to cover overseas trusts with shares in such companies. The effect is that UK beneficiaries of the trusts could then be taxed on capital payments to them.

● *S15 does not apply if the gain is distributed within 2 years. Thus UK capital gains tax can be saved if the gain is distributed to non-domiciled shareholders, who are neither resident nor ordinarily resident in the UK.*

6 Development land tax

Introduction

Over recent years, a very severe system of taxation on capital profits has evolved. Capital gains tax applies to such capital profits, subject to possible tax on development value. For example, development gains tax applied broadly before 1 August 1976 to any part which is a development gain. The charge was, broadly, at your top income tax rate.

Any realised development value after 31 July 1976 will normally suffer development land tax (DLT), instead of development gains tax. An exception is where a property was transferred from one spouse to another before that date; development gains tax will still apply to a subsequent disposal to a third party. As a further complication, the Revenue have powers to tax the profits from so called 'artificial transactions in land' (p 3), as if they were income.

DLT is charged on real and deemed realisations of development value after 31 July 1976 subject to certain exceptions. The start of a project of material development (p 63) is a deemed realisation for these purposes.

DLT is also charged on part disposals which involve the realisation of development value, including the grant of a lease. In this case the disposal proceeds are the aggregate of the market value of the right to receive the rent together with any premiums or other consideration.

Scope of DLT

The scope of the tax is wider than development gains tax, which it replaced, since, for example, pension funds are included, as well as individuals, partnerships, companies, trusts, estates, etc. The tax applies to both UK residents and non-residents, but relates to land in the UK only. The legislation is very detailed and the following is only a brief outline.

● *You should always be aware of the possibility of DLT applying in connection with land transactions. Even if you sell land with only the hope of planning consent, the price you obtain may reflect development value and give rise to DLT.*

Time of disposal

Realisations for DLT purposes normally take place on sales. For a sale, the disposal is treated as taking place at the time an unconditional contract is made and not on completion.

● *Careful timing of your DLT disposals can result in valuable tax savings. For example, if you have already used your £75,000 exemption this year and can postpone an impending sale contract until after 31 March, you will then have the benefit of next year's £75,000 relief.*

Rate of DLT

(DLTA Ss1, 12 & 13; FA 1978 S76; F2A 1979 S24 & Sch 4 & FA 1984 S118)

The rate of the tax is 60% for all taxpayers, whether individuals, partnerships, trusts or companies. The first £75,000 of realised development value is normally free of tax, however, for each year ended 31 March. For each year from 1 April 1979 to 31 March 1984, the annual exemption was £50,000.

For the year ended 31 March 1979 and earlier years, the first £10,000 of realised development value was normally free of tax with the next £150,000 being taxed at 66⅔% and the remainder at 80% each year. These two rates were replaced by the single 60% rate for realisations of development value made on or after 12 June 1979.

For the period from 1 April 1979 until 11 June 1979 inclusive, no more than £10,000 of the £50,000 annual exemption was available (leaving the balance for the rest of the year) and the next £150,000 was taxed at 66⅔%.

Note that you and your wife are taxed separately for the purposes of the tax. Thus you each have the £75,000 exemption. If you obtain a property from your spouse, however, you must wait a year before disposing of it or else you will not get the exemption when you sell or realise development value. This rule applies equally to all persons *connected* with you. Connected persons are as defined for CGT purposes and *include* husband and wife, each of their parents, grandparents, brothers, sisters, children, grandchildren; together with their respective spouses. Trustees are connected with the settlor, etc, and companies are connected if under common control or one controls the other (CGTA S63).

For disposals other than by individuals the *one year rule* is extended to *six years* in certain circumstances. This now applies particularly to disposals made of land which formed part of the original holding of a 'connected person'.

● *With this in mind, 'fragmentation' of land held by one company in a group among its fellow group companies is not practicable unless done initially by each company purchasing a part. Failing this, eventually it may be advisable to sell the land-owning company, thus avoiding crystallising any DLT. When the sale of land is likely to give rise to DLT, consider staging its disposal by selling separate plots in consecutive DLT years (to*

31 March). In this way, you may obtain the use of more than one £75,000 exemption. Similarly, if you are starting a project of material development (p 63) try to phase the development so as to start separate projects on separate plots in different DLT years.

● *A partnership is a separate DLT entity from the individual partners. Thus if you are in partnership with your wife you can obtain between you 3 separate £75,000 exemptions in any year, one for the partnership, one for you and one for your wife.*

Realised development value
(DLTA S4)

The DLT which you pay is based on your realised development value. This is the surplus of your net proceeds over your incidental costs (stamp duty, legal costs, etc) and relevant base value (see below).

Relevant base value
(DLTA S5; FA 1980 S102; & FA 1981 S129)

Relevant base value is the highest of three different amounts computed as follows:

A   Cost+
     expenditure on 'relevant improvements' (p 63)+
     increase in current use value (below) since later of 6 April 1965 or acquisition date+
     special addition (p 63)+
     further addition (p 63)+.
B   *115% of current use value (p 63)+
     expenditure on 'relevant improvements' (p 63).
C   *115% of cost, increased to 150% after 9 March 1981 for residential developments on land held as trading stock+
     *115% of expenditure on 'improvements' (increased to 150% as above).
(*110% for disposals before 26 March 1980.)

There are no hard and fast rules as to whether A, B or C above will give the highest value and all should be calculated. The recent increase of Base C to 150% of cost and improvements for residential development businesses is likely to make that the highest base in such cases. Note that Base C is not available on the disposal of a short lease (less than 50 years to run).

Where land has been acquired from a 'connected person' (p 17) within 12 months of disposal, Bases A and C are restricted. For Base A, the special and further additions do not apply. For Base C, you must only take the actual cost rather than 115% or 150% of it.

Current use value

(DLTA S7; FA 1980 S116; & FA 1981 S133)

This is the value of your property on the assumption that only development which is not 'material' can be carried out; that is to say, it is considered unlawful to carry out any 'material development'. If, however, at the date of the valuation you already possess planning permission for any development on which work has started, this is included in the current use value of the property. *'Material development'* is defined as the making of any change in the state, nature or use of the land; but there are various exclusions, including the following:

(a) Alterations which do not involve an increase of more than one third in the cubic content of a building or group of buildings. For rebuilding work, the limiting fraction is one tenth. (Prior to 10 March 1981 the fraction was one tenth for alterations including rebuilding.)

(b) The use of land and buildings for agriculture and forestry.

(c) The use of land for advertising purposes.

(d) The change from a temporary use of land to its original use.

(e) The change from one use to another when both are within one of the following classes (if a building is empty you consider its previous use):

Class A– Dwelling house or activities not carried on for profit.

Class B– Office or retail shop.

Class C– Hotel, boarding house, public house, etc.

Class D– Use for activities carried out for profit except those falling within the other classes or agriculture or forestry.

Class E– Manufacturing, processing and warehousing, etc.

Special addition, further addition and improvements

(DLTA S6 & Sch 3; & FA 1977 S55)

The above only relate to a disposal of an interest in land which you acquired before 1 May 1977. They do not normally apply to disposals which occur after the start of a project of material development, unless, for example, the development value was not fully exploited in the first instance. ('Start' includes digging foundations, etc.)

For land acquired before 13 September 1974, the 'special addition' is 15% of the original cost for every year of ownership up to four. Thus the maximum is 60% of cost. For acquisitions after 12 September 1974, the 'special addition' is 10% of the original cost for every year of ownership up to four. Thus the maximum is 40% of cost. For the above purposes a part of a year counts as a year.

The 'further addition' effectively extends the 'special addition' to *'relevant improvements'*. These are amounts spent on enhancing the value of property and defending this, less the increase in current use value brought about by improvements. The 'further addition' is found by multiplying the 'special addition' by the amount of the 'relevant improvements' and dividing by the original cost of the property.

'Improvements' include the cost of prospective works which a landlord agrees to carry out in connection with a lease which he grants. Such works can be taken into account in computing the DLT on the part disposal constituted by the grant of a lease, even though the actual work is done later.

Exemptions

The following are some of the exemptions from DLT:

(a)   Land situated outside the UK (S1).

(b)   Disposals by local authorities, etc (S11) and urban development corporations under the Local Government, Planning and Land Act 1980 (FA 1981 S130).

(c)   The first £75,000 of realised development value each year per person (husband and wife separate) (p 62).

(d)   Gifts (donor's acquisition, cost etc is taken over by recipient (S10)).

(e)   Devolution on death is not a chargeable event (S9).

(f)   Principal private residences (husband and wife can have one each) — also land owned on 12 September 1974 which is developed as a dwelling for your own occupation (Ss14 & 15). For DLT purposes your private residence includes a garden of one acre, or more if in keeping with the house.

- *If you own one house and your wife another, you may be able to occupy them in such a way that one is your wife's main residence and one is your own. For example, you may have a town house which you occupy during the week whilst your wife lives in her house in the country. In this way, both houses will be exempted from DLT.*

(g)   Land held as trading stock with planning permission on 12 September 1974 (S16).

(h)   Deemed disposal of project within three years of acquisition, if you would have obtained no significant amount of realised development value, had you started the development as soon as you obtained the land (S18). After 9 March 1981, you assume for these purposes that the law has not changed between the acquisition of the land and the start of the project (FA 1981 S131).

(i)   Industrial development for your own use (tax charge deferred until sale) (S19).

(j)   Developments begun after 9 March 1981 for your own use and occupation. This is not restricted to industrial development and the tax is deferred until sale. In certain cases ((i) and (j)), the liability is extinguished if not crystallised within 12 years (FA 1984 S119).

(*k*)   Transfers within a group of companies (75% holding — S21). But items acquired *within* the group then disposed of *outside* within six years do not qualify for the £75,000 annual exemption (S12) (unless there was no original fragmentation, when a one year limit applies).

- *In order to maximise the use of the £75,000 exemption, purchases of land by a group can be split between different group companies at the outset.*

(*l*)   Developments by statutory undertakers (such as the electricity board, etc) for their own operations (but there is a charge on sale) (S23).

(*m*)   Disposals of land in enterprise zones (unless more than 10 years after first inclusion) (FA 1980 S110).

(*n*)   Disposals by charities (see below).

(*o*)   Deemed disposals by approved co-operative housing associations and self-build societies (S26); after 12 March 1984, also the Housing Corporation and registered housing associations (FA 1984 S120).

(*p*)   Operations regarding telecommunication cable laying, including housing structures and troughs (F2A 1983 S14 & FA 1984 S122).

Charities
(DLTA Ss24 & 25; FA 1980 S111; & FA 1982 S155)

In general, charities were liable to the tax on disposals before 26 March 1980. If development value was realised from land held at 12 September 1974, however, no DLT was charged on the charity. This exemption was extended to land held continuously by different charities since before that date. If a charity developed land acquired after 12 September 1974 for its own charitable use, any DLT was deferred until a subsequent disposal. However, after 9 March 1982, this deferred liability is extinguished.

After 25 March 1980 charities are exempted from the tax. However, if subsequently a body which made an exempt disposal ceases to be a charity DLT normally becomes payable on amounts previously exempted, unless the assets are insufficient.

Trusts and estates
(FA 1974 Sch 7 & DLTA)

The trustees of settlements and the estates of deceased persons were both liable to income tax on development gains. The rate charged was 50%, being the basic rate at the time when development gains tax normally applied plus the 15% investment income surcharge.

Realisations of development value after 31 July 1976 are in general subject to DLT. This applies to both settlements and the estates of deceased persons.

● *Actual devolutions on death of land with development value are not subject to DLT. Since no CGT is payable either (p 54) there could be circumstances when land with development value should be held until death. This is particularly true because there is no uplift of the relevant base value for DLT (unlike CGT).*

Collection
(DLTA S41 & Sch 8; FA 1980 Ss112–115 & FA 1984 Ss121 & 123)

DLT is payable three months after the date of the chargeable occasion or, if later, 30 days after the issue of a notice of assessment. This is subject to an appeal procedure similar to that for other taxes.

If the consideration for a disposal is rent, or in the case of a deemed disposal, DLT may be spread over a period of up to ten years (eight years for disposals before 6 August 1983). Usually instalments begin two years after the disposal (one year for disposals before 26 March 1980). If the proceeds consist of instalments of capital, the Revenue allow spreading in cases of hardship. Interest (8% from 1 December 1982, previously 12%–6% prior to 1 January 1980) is normally paid on overdue tax unpaid three months after the chargeable occasion. If the tax is payable by instalments, however, the interest will only run from normally the due date of each instalment.

For disposals up to 5 August 1983, there is the option of paying either in half-yearly instalments or annually. Subsequent to that date, however, only annual instalments are provided for.

A local authority to whom you sold a property was empowered to deduct DLT from the price if the disposal was prior to 6 August 1980, but not subsequently.

Should you buy any land from a *non-resident* for more than £75,000, you are normally required to deduct tax at 40% from the price and pay it to the Revenue. Prior to 6 August 1984, the percentage was 50% but it only applied to certain 'development land'. (Before 1 April 1984, the exemption was £50,000.) The deduction process does not normally apply to dwelling houses bought for no more than £150,000.

● *If you are buying from a non-resident, ensure that you do not infringe this rule, because you could be liable to pay the tax to the Revenue in any event.*

Advance assessment
(FA 1980 S114)

You are allowed to give special notice to the Revenue if you plan to begin a *project of material development* (p 63) on any of your land. The effect is that you are assessed to tax by reference to the value of the land, etc, as at the date of the notice. If you subsequently start your project within two years of the notice, in general the liability will remain as previously assessed. Otherwise, you will be repaid the tax, with interest if appropriate.

Note that any notice given is void if it does not disclose all material facts fully and accurately. You are only allowed to give notice once in respect of any particular land. Advance assessments may be paid by instalments (see above), the first of which is payable after one year (not two).

Relief for other taxes
(DLTA S34 & Sch 6)

There are generous but complicated rules concerning the interaction of DLT with other taxes. They cover CGT, corporation tax on capital gains, development gains tax, estate duty, capital transfer tax and income tax and corporation tax on trading gains. As a general rule, the part of the gain which is charged to DLT is not charged to the other taxes.

For example, if you sell a property and make a capital gain of £20,000 and your realised development value is £15,000 you will pay DLT on £15,000 and CGT on only £5,000 (£20,000–£15,000). This assumes that you already had used up your £75,000 DLT exemption for the year (p 61) and your £5,600 CGT exemption (p 12).

The relief is not only given when the disposals are at the same time for the purposes of the different taxes, it also normally applies if there are separate disposals to which DLT and another tax apply. The two disposals must be within a limited period however, which normally is 12 years.

Where you acquire land by way of gift and you later obtain realised development value from it, you are entitled to a credit agsinst your DLT based on the capital transfer tax (if any) paid by the donor.

7   Capital transfer tax

The following is a brief outline of capital transfer tax (CTT) stressing various planning points. This tax is highly complicated, however, and some of its complexities are beyond the scope of this book.

The rules for CTT were originally contained in sections 19 to 52 and Schedules 4 to 11 of the 1975 Finance Act, which received the Royal Assent on 13 March 1975. Substantial changes have been made in subsequent Finance Acts and the legislation has now been consolidated into the Capital Transfer Tax Act 1984 (CTTA). The tax applies to lifetime gifts made after 26 March 1974, transfers on deaths occurring after 12 March 1975 and settled property (see p 101).

Capital transfer tax replaced estate duty which does not apply to deaths occurring after 12 March 1975. Where property passed on deaths after 12 November 1974 and before 13 March 1975, estate duty applied at CTT rates (p 97). Whereas estate duty only arose on death, CTT also applies on transfers made during your lifetime.

● *The essence of CTT planning is the conservation of wealth. Remember that at your death the tax normally bites at a higher rate than on transfers during your life (p 70). Also, bear in mind that a future government could introduce an annual wealth tax.*

Thus in broad terms you should aim to spread assets amongst your family to minimise the effects of these two taxes. Do not make gifts which you cannot afford, however, nor give too much money outright to young or irresponsible children.

Property chargeable
(CTTA Ss 1–6 & 10)

The property which you leave, when you die, will need to be considered (p 83). Also, subject to various exemptions and reliefs (p 74) you will be charged to CTT on the decrease in value of your assets less liabilities which you suffer as a result of any transfer of your assets (chargeable transfer). Normally, arm's length transactions are ignored if they are not intended to convey any gratuitous benefit. Any CGT which you pay is ignored in calculating the decrease.

If you are domiciled (p 4) in the UK or deemed domiciled here, CTT applies to all of your property wherever situated (p 86). Otherwise it only applies to your property in this country.

Deemed domicile
(CTTA S267)

You are deemed to be domiciled in the UK if:

(a)   you were domiciled here on or after 10 December 1974 and within the three years preceding the date of the chargeable transfer; or

(b)   you were resident here on or after 10 December 1974 and in not less than 17 of the 20 years of assessment ending with that in which you made the chargeable transfer.

Change of domicile

● *As already mentioned above, you are only liable to capital transfer tax on your assets situated in the UK, provided you are neither domiciled nor deemed domiciled here. Hence to cease to be liable on your overseas assets, you will need to emigrate and lose your UK domicile and deemed domicile.*

Changing your domicile and residence is discussed in Chapter 1 (p 7). The two concepts are related but for CTT mainly domicile and deemed domicile (see above) are significant. Provided that you establish your domicile there, it is now sufficient if you move to the Channel Islands or the Isle of Man. Wherever you go, you will need to be treated as domiciled abroad for at least 3 years before the exemption applies.

Associated operations
(CTTA S268)

Special rules enable the Revenue to treat two or more transactions related to a certain property as forming one 'chargeable transfer'. Where transactions at different times are treated as associated operations, the chargeable transfer is treated as taking place at the time of the last of these transactions.

● *This is probably the most important anti-avoidance provision for capital transfer tax purposes and can be used to counter many arrangements which otherwise would be successful in avoiding the tax. If you have any plans to save capital transfer tax in a complicated way, you should always have regard to the associated operations rules.*

Rate scale

(CTTA S7 & Sch 1 & 2; FA 1984 S101)

CTT is charged on the cumulative total of all your lifetime transfers after 26 March 1974 together with the property passing on your death. There is now a ten year limitation on cumulation (p 71). There are, however, various exemptions from CTT (p 74). Currently the tax is charged at the progressive rates shown in the following table. A lower scale applies to lifetime gifts and a higher one to property passing on death. If you die within three years of making a chargeable transfer, additional tax is payable to bring the charge on it up to the scale applicable on death.

When making a chargeable transfer, you normally have two options. Either you pay the tax yourself, based on the value of the transfer plus the tax; or the recipient pays your tax, calculated on the transfer value excluding the tax. If you give cash, however, you could deduct the tax, shown by the following table, from the amount given. Thus — suppose that having previously made £120,000 of chargeable transfers, you wish to make an £8,000 cash gift to your son. Tax on the £8,000 is payable at 20% and so you could keep £1,600 for the tax and pay £6,400 to your son. If you want him to get £8,000 net, however, one of you would have to pay the capital transfer tax of *£2,000;* ie 20% × (£8,000 + £2,000).

In general, the current rate scale applies to lifetime transfers and on deaths after 12 March 1984. Previously the rate scales had been modified as from 27 October 1977. Each time the burden was reduced. The full tables appear in the Appendix (p 97). Certain rules apply where the CTT rates change. For example, if you have paid CTT on the old scales, a transfer which you now make is taxed by reference to the new scale.

Table 7: Capital transfer tax rates on lifetime transfers and deaths after 12 March 1984

Slice of cumulative chargeable transfers	Total	Lifetime scale % on slice	Lifetime scale Cumulative total tax	On death % on slice	On death Cumulative total tax
The first					
£64,000	£64,000	Nil	£Nil	Nil	£Nil
The next					
21,000	85,000	15	3,150	30	6,300
31,000	116,000	17.5	8,575	35	17,150
32,000	148,000	20	14,975	40	29,950
37,000	185,000	22.5	23,300	45	46,600
47,000	232,000	25	35,050	50	70,100
53,000	285,000	27.5	49,625	55	99,250
The remainder		30		60	

On a death within three years of chargeable transfers at the old rates, the additional tax is found by taking the difference between the tax already paid and that payable at the new rates applying on death. If the death is after 12 March 1984 and the chargeable transfer is on or before that date, the tax on the new death scale could be less than that already paid, but no refund is made.

Indexation of rate bands

(CTTA S8)

For the year to 5 April 1986, the CTT rates shown in Table 7 (p 70) will apply subject to indexation. The threshold (£64,000) and the various rate-bands will be increased in proportion to the rise in the retail prices index from December 1983 to December 1984 and each new threshold will be rounded up to the nearest £1,000. This applies for 1985-86 and similarly for future years unless the Treasury otherwise direct. Thus the thresholds for 1986-87 would be increased in line with the index increase from December 1984 to December 1985, and so on.

The ten year cumulation period

(CTTA S7)

There is a ten year limitation on cumulations. If you make a chargeable transfer it must now be added to all chargeable transfers which you made in the previous ten years and any made before that time drop out. Since CTT applies after 26 March 1974, the earliest that any transfers may fall out of cumulation is 1984. Thus suppose you gifted £40,000 in May 1974 and then nothing more until June 1984; your CTT on a gift then of £64,000 will be calculated completely ignoring the earlier gift. In fact it would be covered by the nil rate band if the current rates apply.

Gifts within the nil rate band

● *Gifts are one of the main ways of saving CTT. The smaller exempt transfers are dealt with later (p 74), but in considering the ten year cumulation period it is worth remembering that, in addition to the annual £3,000 gift exemption (p 74) and other exempt amounts, £64,000 can be gifted each 10 years within the nil rate band. (This ignores future rate scale changes caused by indexation – p 71.) Thus, every ten years a fresh £64,000 nil rate band will be available. Alternatively you would be able to augment your £3,000 annual exemption with £6,400 (1/10 × £64,000) each year (assuming that you have not otherwise used your nil rate band).*

Now that the rate-band thresholds are indexed, every year that indexation applies, the nil rate band will similarly be increased. Thus, suppose you have previously used your entire £64,000 nil rate band, if indexation is at 10% you will have a further 10% × £64,000 = £6,400, rounded up to £7,000 available for gifts, etc, in 1985-86, as well as the £3,000 annual exemption, etc.

For elderly people with smaller estates it is not necessarily advisable, however, to gift merely the £64,000 nil rate band since this is equally tax free on death and it could be better to retain this sum for contingencies.

Larger gifts

● *If you have a large estate, you should consider making more substantial gifts which will entail the payment of CTT. The rate will be nil for the first £64,000 of chargeable transfers, however (p 70), and effectively more if business property relief (p 87) or agricultural property relief (p 89) applies. After that the lower lifetime gifts scale will apply unless you die within three years of the gift. (This eventuality can be covered by temporary life assurance (p 95) to pay the extra tax.) The new rate scale which applies after 12 March 1984 shows a bigger differential between lifetime rates and those on death than previously. In fact, the former are half the latter throughout the scale. Thus, particularly bearing in mind that cumulation ceases after ten years, so that you will then have the use of fresh nil and lower rate bands, you should be able to make useful capital transfer tax savings by larger gifts.*

Exempt transfers

(CTTA Ss18–27 & Sch 6(2))

Broadly, exempt transfers can be divided between those which apply both on death and during your life and those which are only exempt if the transfers are during your life. The first category includes transfers between your wife and yourself.

Transfers between husband and wife

Transfers between your wife and yourself both during your lives and on death are exempt from CTT. This exemption also applied for estate duty purposes on deaths after 12 November 1974. Similarly gifts *inter vivos* between your wife and yourself prior to 27 March 1974 are outside the CTT net provided the donor survived 12 November 1974.

These exemptions do not apply, however, if the recipient of the property is not domiciled (or deemed domicilied) in this country (p 3) (unless the giver is also non-domiciled at the time). In this case, only the first £55,000 (£50,000 to 9 March 1982 and £25,000 prior to 26 March 1980) transferred to the non-domicilied spouse is exempt.

Under the estate duty rules, if you left property in trust for your wife for life duty was paid when you died; but none was payable on her subsequent death. Where the first death occurs after 12 November 1974, the new relief will apply and so no CTT is payable on property passing to the surviving spouse. For this reason, when the latter dies, full CTT is payable on the trust property. However, if the surviving spouse had property left in trust by a husband or wife who died before 13 November 1974, no CTT arises on that property on the death of the survivor (because estate duty would have been payable on the first death).

Equalisation of assets of husband and wife

- *Provided the recipient is UK domiciled (or deemed domiciled) no CTT is payable on transfers which you make to your wife or she makes to you, either during your lives or on death (above). But do not keep all of your assets until you die and then leave them to your wife because this may ultimately result in high CTT on her death which is more than the combined tax if your estates were equal and you each left your assets to your children.*

- *Thus, suppose you have £232,000 and your wife has nothing. If you die first, leaving it all to her, no tax is then payable. But if she still has £232,000 when she dies and has made no previous chargeable transfers, the CTT at present rates will be £70,100 (p 70). If you had given your wife £116,000 before you died, however, and left your remaining £116,000 to your children, on your death £17,150 would be paid in CTT. Similarly, on your wife's death £17,150 would be paid making a total of £34,300, compared with £70,100 CTT paid if your wife inherits all your wealth. However, make sure that your wife has sufficient to live on.*

- *If your wife otherwise has insufficient funds, giving her assets will also enable her to make exempt gifts to your children; thus you both take advantage of the exemptions. Should there be insufficient funds for your wife if money is left or given to your children, the use of a small discretionary trust (p 107) is useful. From this trust, either created in your lifetime or by your will, your wife could draw income or capital as required. The amount settled would normally be within the nil rate band.*

- *A further point in favour of equalising your estate with your wife's is that wealth tax, if it is ever introduced, would be expected to apply separately to husband and wife at progressive annual rates. Thus less tax is payable on two smaller estates than on one larger estate. Of course, these tax planning considerations must be tempered by practical points such as making sure your wife has sufficient to maintain her, should you die first. Also, a certain mutual trust is necessary. Your planning should also take account of your respective ages and states of health by arranging for a larger share to be in the hands of the one likely to live longer.*

The matrimonial home

● If you are buying a new home, put it into the joint names of your wife and yourself. Since the matrimonial home often comprises the major part of the assets of a married couple, this would be a very useful step towards equalising your respective estates.

● You can own your house jointly with your wife as joint tenants or tenants in common (p 118). Under a joint tenancy the share of the first of you to die passes automatically to the survivor on death. Thus the security of your wife is best served by having the house owned in this way and this is certainly the simplest method, advisable for smaller cases.

● For CTT planning purposes, however, it is likely to be better for your wife and yourself to own the house as tenants in common. In this way you will each have a clearly defined share in the house, normally half each although you could have different fractions. You will then be able to dispose of your share independently, either by lifetime gift or in your will. For example, you could leave your share by your will to your son and express the wish that he allows your widow to live in the house for as long as she wishes. (You will need to trust your son but the executors should be able to exert some influence, if required.) In this way your £64,000 nil rate band will be more or less used at your death, if not already absorbed. Otherwise, in order to use your nil rate band it may have been necessary to gift to your son (or others) liquid assets needed by your wife to live on.

Exempt transfers — Lifetime Gifts

The following transfers are only exempt if made by an individual during his life. They do not apply to transfers made by trustees nor to assets passing on death. In any one fiscal year to 5 April, you can make all of these exempt transfers cumulatively and so can your wife. Note, however, the limitation in (2) below regarding small gifts.

(1) *Transfers each year up to a value of £3,000*
     Prior to 6 April 1981 the limit was £2,000 and before 6 April 1976 it was £1,000 each year. (The period from 27 March 1974 to 5 April 1974 counted as a year for this purpose.) If you do not use up the full £3,000 allowance in one year, you can carry the unused part forward for one year only. If your transfers taken against this exemption reach £3,000 in one year, you have nothing available to carry forward, even though you may have had £3,000 carried forward from the previous year.
     For example, if you made no chargeable transfers in the year to 5 April 1984, you have £6,000 (3,000 + 3,000) available for exempt transfers under this category in the year to 5 April 1985. If,

however, you transferred £1,000 in the year to 5 April 1984 you have £2,000 carried forward and so can transfer £5,000 in the year to 5 April 1985.

(2)   *Small gifts*
Outright gifts to any one person not exceeding £250 for each year to 5 April are exempt. Up to 5 April 1980 the annual amount was £100. This applied in addition to the £2,000 exemption. However, from 6 April 1981 the £250 exemption cannot be used against gifts larger than that amount. Thus you can make an unlimited number of exempt gifts of £250 to different people but any gifts of £251 or more must be set against the £3,000 and other exemptions with the excess being taxable (if the nil rate band has been exhausted).

(3)   *Normal expenditure out of income*
To qualify under this exemption, a transfer must be part of your normal expenditure. This means that there must be an element of regularity. Life assurance premiums (p 94) are particularly suited for this. Further conditions are that the transfer is out of your after-tax income and you are left with enough income to maintain your usual standard of living.

Life policy premium payments will not qualify for this exemption, however, if they are made out of an annuity purchased on your life, unless you can show that the policy and the annuity were effected completely independently of each other. This rule even applies if you make gifts out of your annuity receipts and the donee pays the premiums on the policy on your life.

If you buy an annuity after 12 November 1974, and make transfers from it after 5 April 1975, only the income proportion of the annuity (p 183) is treated as your income for the purposes of the normal expenditure rule; the capital element is not.

● *Where both you and your wife have high incomes, you will be taxed on your wife's investment income and may well pay most of your joint living expenses. This will leave a major part of the income of your wife available to make normal expenditure gifts which she should consider doing.*

(4)   *Gifts in consideration of marriage* made to one of the partners of the marriage or settled on the partners and their children, etc. The limits are £5,000 if the donor is a parent of one of the marriage partners, £2,500 if a grandparent or great-grandparent or one of the parties themselves, or otherwise £1,000. (From 6 April 1981, the relief extends to marriage gifts from settlements where an interest in possession ends.)

● Note that if your son gets married, your wife and yourself can each give £5,000 to him and his bride making £10,000 in all, and the bride's parents could do likewise. If you would like to make more substantial gifts to the couple, these could be found from your annual exemption (p 74) and nil rate band and those of your wife.

(5)   Family maintenance
If you make any of the following gifts during your life, they are not treated as transfers of value (CTTA S11):

(a)   For the maintenance, education, etc of your child, former wife or illegitimate child.

(b)   For the maintenance or education of a child not in his parent's care, who has been in your care during substantial periods of his minority.

(c)   For the care or maintenance of a dependent relative.

Reducing your assets by exempt gifts

● Take advantage of the various exempt transfers (above). By this means you can gift to your children, and others you may wish to benefit, considerable amounts over a period of years free of tax. As seen, gifts to your wife are normally free of CTT (p 72).

● If you have funds surplus to your requirements, you can make gifts totalling £3,000 in any year (p 74). In addition, you can make outright gifts of up to £250 each year to any number of other individuals apart from the recipients of the gifts totalling £3,000. Furthermore, if you have surplus after-tax income you can make normal expenditure gifts out of income (p 75). Do not overlook the reliefs applied to marriage gifts for your children and grandchildren, etc (p 75). By means of all the above transfers you can reduce your estate without incurring any CTT liability. Furthermore, by making the required election (p 46) any CGT will be held over until the recipient's disposal.

● Remember that the above exemptions apply to both your wife and yourself. Also, do not forget that unused portions of the £3,000 limit can be carried forward for one year only. Thus if, say, your wife wishes to give a £12,000 necklace to your daughter, it can be done free of CTT if you each give her £6,000 in cash (covering two years, assuming no gifts last year) and she then buys the necklace from your wife for £12,000. (This could involve a CGT liability, however: see p 10).

Example 7 – Using the annual exemption and nil rate band

Mr A has not used his 1983-84 annual exemption but pays life assurance premiums for the benefit of his daughter, which exhaust his normal expenditure relief. He has not used any of his nil rate band. He wishes to make the maximum possible tax free gifts to his son for 1984-85, 1985-86 and 1986-87. Assuming indexation at 10% and an annual exemption of £3,000, the maximum gifts are:

	1984-85	1985-86	1986-87
	£	£	£
Annual exemption	3,000	3,000	3,000
Annual exemption brought forward	3,000	—	—
Nil rate band	64,000	—	—
Extra nil rate band			
from indexing	—	7,000	8,000
Maximum gifts to son	70,000	10,000	11,000

Exempt transfers — During life and on death

The following transfers are in general exempt, whether made during your life or on death. Similar rules also apply to trusts (p 101).

(1)   *Transfers in the course of trade, etc* are exempt if allowed as deductions in computing the profits for income tax purposes. This applies equally to professions and vocations, as well as allowable deductions from other forms of profits or gains for the purposes of income tax and corporation tax.

(2)   *Gifts for national purposes, etc* made to certain bodies. These include the National Trust, National Heritage Memorial Fund, National Gallery, British Museum and similar organisations including universities and their libraries; also museums and art galleries maintained by local authorities or universities.

(3)   *Gifts for public benefit* of property deemed by the Treasury to be of outstanding scenic, historic, scientific or artistic merit including land, buildings, pictures, books, manuscripts, works of art, etc.

(4)   *Gifts of shares* to an employee trust provided it will then hold at least half of the ordinary shares of the company.

(5)   *Gifts to charities* are exempt without limit if made after 14 March 1983. If made before 15 March 1983 and on or within a year of death, however, the first £250,000 was exempt. The exemption was £200,000 before 9 March 1982 and £100,000 before 26 March 1980. Gifts to settlements for charitable purposes are covered by the exemption, as are gifts to charities from other trusts.

(6)   *Gifts to political parties* are wholly exempt if made more than a year before death, and otherwise there is an exemption of £100,000 in total. For these purposes a 'political party' is one with at least two members sitting in Parliament or one member and not less than 150,000 votes for its candidates at the last General Election.

Gifts to charities, etc

● *As noted above, unlimited gifts to charities are exempt without limit. Exemption also applies to the first £100,000 gifted to political parties within a year of death (otherwise unlimited — see above). Thus you should consider making such gifts during your lifetime and bequests in your will. Both will reduce the value of your estate for CTT purposes, and CGT relief applies concerning charitable dispositions (p 49).*

● *If you have a really large estate and are charitably disposed, then you should consider making large donations to charity during your lifetime, so that no CTT is paid. (A charitable settlement may be appropriate in this connection.) Also, you should not overlook the advantages of making regular payments by deed of covenant (p 154), which will attract useful income tax benefits.*

Excluded property

(CTTA S6)

As well as the various transfers mentioned above being exempt from CTT, certain categories of property must be 'excluded' from your estate for CTT purposes. The following 'excluded property' must be left out of the value of your estate, regarding both lifetime transfers and property passing on death:

(1)   Property outside the UK (p 86), if you are neither domiciled nor deemed domiciled in this country. As already noted (p 69), this has important planning consequences.

(2)   A reversionary interest, unless either you bought it or it relates to the falling in of a lease which was treated as a settlement (p 101). After 9 March 1981 certain anti-avoidance rules apply to prevent misuse.

(3)   Cash options under approved retirement pension schemes, provided an annuity becomes payable to your dependants instead of the cash option itself.

(4)   Certain property in this country belonging to visiting forces and NATO headquarters staff.

(5)   Certain overseas pensions from former colonies, etc, including death payments and returns of contributions.

(6)   Savings such as national savings certificates and premium bonds, if you are domiciled in the Channel Islands or the Isle of Man.

(7)   Those UK government securities on which interest may be paid gross to non-residents, provided you are neither domiciled nor ordinarily resident here (see Table 8 opposite).

● *If you are neither domiciled nor ordinarily resident in the UK but have substantial assets here, sell some of them and reinvest the proceeds in exempt gilts (see above). In this way your UK estate for CTT purposes will be reduced. Also, the income will be exempt from UK income tax.*

Table 8: United Kingdom securities exempt for certain non-residents

3½	War Stock 1952 or after	9%	Treasury Loan, 1994
5½%	Treasury Stock, 2008-12	9%	Treasury Loan, 1992-96
5¾%	Funding Loan, 1987-91	9½%	Treasury Loan, 1999
6%	Funding Loan, 1993	12½%	Treasury Loan, 1993
6½%	Funding Loan, 1985-87	12¾%	Treasury Loan, 1995
6¾%	Treasury Loan, 1995-98	12¾%	Treasury Stock, 1992
7¾%	Treasury Loan, 2012-15	13%	Treasury Stock, 1990
7¾%	Treasury Loan, 1985-88	13¼%	Treasury Loan, 1997
8%	Treasury Loan, 2002-06	13¼%	Exchequer Loan, 1996
8¼%	Treasury Loan, 1987-90	13¾%	Treasury Loan, 1993
8½%	Treasury Loan, 1984-86	14½%	Treasury Loan, 1994
8¾%	Treasury Loan, 1997	15¼%	Treasury Loan, 1996
		15½%	Treasury Loan, 1998

Example 8: Calculation of capital transfer tax — lifetime gifts

Mr A made the following gifts in excess of his normal expenditure:

(1)   3 April 1974 to his son D £21,100 cash*
(2)   10 April 1976 to his son B £3,000 cash
(3)   15 April 1976 to his wife W £20,000 cash
(4)   31 May 1976 to B £10,100 cash* on his marriage
(5)   30 September 1976 to C shares worth £4,600
(6)   1 December 1979 to B £14,100 cash*
(7)   30 June 1981 to D £5,000 cash
(8)   15 August 1981 to B £250 cash
(9)   20 August 1982 to charity £100,000
        *Less CTT Paid by Mr A.
(10)   30 June 1984 to B £16,000

What CTT is payable on the above by Mr A during his lifetime?

Capital transfer tax payable during Mr A's life.

(Gift 3 is exempt, being to his wife, and gifts 2, 7 and 8 are covered by the respective small gifts and annual exemptions including carry forwards. Gift 9 is covered by the exemption for charitable gifts.)

	Amount Charge-able	Rate	Tax Payable
(1) 3 April 1974 to D	£21,100		
Less:			
Small gift exemption £100			

		Amount Chargeable	Rate	Tax Payable
Annual exemption	1,000	£1,100		
		£20,000	£15,000 at Nil	—
			£5,000 at 5%	£250
(4) 31 May 1976 to B on his marriage		£10,100		
Less:				
Small gift exemption	£100			
Marriage exemption	5,000	£5,100 £5,000	£5,000 at 7½%	£375
(5) 30 September 1976 to C shares worth		£4,600		
Less:				
Small gift exemption	100	£4,500 £5,000 (grossed)	£5,000 at 10%	£500
(6) 1 December 1979 to B		£14,100	£5,000 at 7½%	
Less:				
Annual exemption	£2,000			
Annual exemption bought forward	£2,000			
Small gift exemption	100	£4,100 £10,000	£5,000 at 10%	£875
Gift (1) falls out of cumulation on 3 April 1984		(20,000)		
(10) 30 June 1984 to B		£16,000		
Less:				
Annual exemption	£3,000			
Annual exemption	£3,000	6,000 £10,000	Nil	—
Cumulative totals of chargeable gifts and tax		£30,000		£2,000

Valuation
(CTTA Ss 160–170)

For CTT purposes your assets are normally valued at their open market value at the transfer date. If the value of an asset which you keep is affected by the transfer, you will need to value your 'estate' both before and after the transfer in order to calculate the resultant fall on which you are taxed. Your liabilities must be taken into account in valuing your total 'estate'. Any 'excluded property' (p 78) must be left out of the totals, both before and after the transfer.

For further comments on valuation, please refer to Chapter 2 (p 22).

Valuation of related property
(CTTA S161)

Certain property (such as shares in a private company) is worth more valued collectively than if considered as the sum of the individual items. Where the value of any of your property is less than the appropriate portion of the value of the aggregate of that and any 'related property' you must value your own property as the appropriate portion of the value of that aggregate.

'Related property' is property belonging to your wife, or property in a settlement in which you or your wife has an interest in possession. Also included is any property transferred by you or your wife after 15 April 1976 to a charity or charitable trust (unless leaving again more than 5 years ago.

This rule particularly applies to the valuation of unquoted shares. For example if you and your wife each have 40% of the shares of an unquoted company, then the value of 80% of the shares is normally much higher than twice the value of 40% of the shares. This is because an 80% holding carries with it full control of the company. Thus the successful estate duty saving device of splitting a shareholding in a non-quoted company between your wife and yourself, so that neither of you has control, is not effective (so far as the first transfer is concerned) in producing a lower aggregate value for CTT purposes. Similarly, if you gift to your son, say, 2% out of a combined 51% holding, CTT falls on the difference between the controlling 51% and 49% minority holdings —far more than the value of 2% in isolation.

Special relief applies where you sell the related property which you inherited within three years of the death for less than the value on which tax was originally paid. Subject to various conditions including the requirement that the sale is at arm's length for a freely negotiated price, you can claim for the related property in question to be revalued at death on the basis that it was not related to any other property.

● *Concerning gifts of cash, quoted shares or other securities there is normally no valuation problem. However, regarding substantial gifts of other items like land, businesses, antiques, shares in unquoted companies or paintings you would be well advised to obtain professional advice before you make the gift, from an estate agent, surveyor, valuer or accountant. In this way you can decide whether your* likely tax liability would be too high. Also, professional valuers will be able to assist you, your lawyers and accountants in negotiating with the Capital Taxes Office an agreed value on which CTT is paid. Remember that the Revenue will bring in their own valuation experts and so you will need valuation expertise on your side to negotiate as low a value as possible.

Capital transfer tax on death

(CTTA S4)

CTT on your death is charged as if immediately before your death you made a chargeable transfer equal to the *net value* of your estate, subject to certain adjustments and exemptions (p 77) if appropriate.

The *net value* of your estate is determined by making certain deductions (p 83) from the *gross value* of all the property passing on your death.

The general rule is that if you are domiciled (or deemed domiciled — p 69) in the UK at the time of your death, all of your assets, wherever they may be situated, form part of the *gross value* of your estate (p 83).

If you are not domiciled in the UK at your death then CTT is only chargeable on those assets which are situated in the UK (p 86)

The tax payable is calculated from the special rate scale which applies at death (p 70) taking account of your cumulative lifetime gifts after 26 March 1974 (and within 10 years of death) to ascertain the starting level on the scale. Thus suppose your chargeable lifetime transfers totalled £100,000, the first £16,000 of the estate passing on your death would be taxed at 35%, the next £32,000 at 40% and so on.

If you have made any chargeable transfers within three years before your death, then additional CTT will be payable to bring the charge up to what it would have been on your death. The property transferred is aggregated with your estate at death, CTT calculated and any tax already paid on those transfers deducted (p 70).

Wills

(See also Chapter 9)

● *You should think carefully about the preparation of your will and, of course, obtain legal advice. Substantial CTT savings can result from a well drawn will. For example, you should ensure that both your wife and yourself by your separate wills leave at least £64,000 to other people so that you each get the benefit of the £64,000 nil rate band. (This presupposes that the free band has not been exhausted by lifetime gifts and also that you each have adequate funds for your old-age.) Also, avoid leaving too much directly to your children if they are already*

*wealthy; it is more beneficial for tax planning purposes to leave money
in trust for your grandchildren. Such will trusts, might be discretionary,
but more usefully of the accumulation and maintenance variety (p 102).*

- *If you wish to ensure that your widow has sufficient funds to live on, and
at the same time utilise your nil rate band of £64,000, you should
consider creating a trust by your will. This could give the trustees
discretionary powers to advance funds to your wife if she needs them.
Unless your estate is large, the amount comprised in the trust should be
no more than your nil rate band which should ensure no CTT in the trust
unless its funds appreciate (p 104).*

Gross value of estate

(FA 1975 S23)

This includes all your property situated anywhere in the world, such as
land, shares, the goodwill of a business, debts owing to you, etc. Certain
other amounts must also be included in your gross estate, even though
they do not belong to you or only arise after your death, such as the
proceeds of a life policy held by you on your own life, or any death
benefit under a pension scheme which is payable to your estate (rather
than under the more usual discretionary disposal clause contained in
most pension schemes).

Also to be included in your gross estate are various interests in trusts
(p 101). In these cases the trustees may pay the tax appropriate to the
trusts but the rate is calculated by reference to the value of the estate
including the trust interests.

Deductions from gross estate

The more common deductions which are made from the gross value of
your estate in order to arrive at its *net value* are as follows:

(1) Excluded property (p 78) and certain exempt transfers (p 77).
(2) Funeral expenses.
(3) Debts owing by you at the date of death which are payable in the
     UK.
(4) Debts due to persons outside the UK (normally only deductible
     from the value of assets situated outside this country).
(5) Whilst legal and other professional fees owing at the death may be
     deducted as debts, no deduction is given for probate and
     executors' expenses.
(6) Liabilities for income tax and CGT up to the time of death,
     whether or not assessments were made before that time. (No
     deduction can be made for CTT payable on your death, nor tax
     liabilities regarding income and capital gains arising for periods
     subsequent to your death).

Land sold within three years of death

(CTTA Ss190–198)

If land or buildings are sold within three years of a death for less than probate value, the person paying the CTT can claim that the sale proceeds are substituted, and the tax adjusted. There are a number of conditions including the requirement that the shortfall is at least the lower of £1,000 and 5% of the probate value of the land. Relief is extended beyond the three years regarding a compulsory purchase notified before the end of the three years.

● *Only rarely should this rule be allowed to persuade the executors to sell land which otherwise would have been kept. Possible circumstances might be where an unfairly high probate value was fixed, or the market drastically falls but funds are needed. However, if a sale is intended and the price is below probate value then you should ensure that contracts are exchanged within the three year period.*

Quoted securities passing on death

(CTTA Ss178–189)

Where quoted shares or securities or holdings in authorised unit trusts are realised within one year of death, the persons liable to pay CTT can claim that the total of the sale prices should be substituted for the original probate values of the investments. Where, however, the proceeds are re-invested by those persons in the same quoted shares or unit trusts after the death and within two months after the last sale, the above relief may be reduced or lost.

● *This rule should be borne in mind by the executors in dealing with the quoted securities during the administration period (p 147). If the stock market is falling and seems likely to do so for some months, then the executors (in consultation with their stockbrokers) could do well to sell within 12 months of the death. They could then distribute cash to beneficiaries under the will who could reinvest in shares if they wished, without disturbing the CTT relief.*

Deeds of family arrangement

(CTTA S17)

CTT is not charged on certain variations in the destination of property passing on death. Nor is it charged on the disclaimer of title to property passing on death. The variation or disclaimer must be within two years of the death. An election to the Revenue is required within six months of the variation or disclaimer. (See also pp 54, 126). Note that the variation normally has no effect for income tax purposes.

This exemption operates similarly, but without time limit, where a surviving spouse's life interest under an intestacy is redeemed. It also applies if an interest in settled property is disclaimed unless there is some consideration in money or money's worth.

- *Deeds of family arrangement are a valuable CTT planning tool. Transfers free of the tax can be effected in this way so that, for example, if you are one of the legatees, you might arrange for money to go direct to your children (this could result in your bearing income tax on the income if the children are minors). If all the estate has gone to the widow under the will then up to £64,000 of this could be diverted to other members of the family without any CTT arising.*

In large estates, deeds of family arrangement could include large amounts for charities. This would normally substantially reduce the CTT liability at a relatively modest cost to the beneficiaries.

Example 9: Calculation of CTT payable on death

Mr A (see Example 8, p 79) made no further lifetime gifts and died on 30 September 1984 leaving a net estate of £300,000. Of this he left £100,000 to his wife and £50,000 to charity. CTT on the death wil be paid as follows:

	£	£
Net estate		300,000
Less:		
Bequest to wife	100,000	
Charitable bequests*	50,000	
	150,000	
Chargeable to CTT		150,000
Cumulative transfers to date of death (see Example 8)*	30,000	

Tax band (£)	Rate (%)	Chargeable slice (£)	Tax payable (£)
30,000- 64,000	Nil	34,000	Nil
64,000- 85,000	30	21,000	6,300
85,000-116,000	35	31,000	10,850
116,000-148,000	40	32,000	12,800
148,000-180,000	45	32,000	14,400
		£150,000	£44,350

Thus the total CTT at death is £44,350.

*Notes:
(1) The charitable bequests and the gifts within one year of death are within the exemption limit of £250,000 and thus are free of CTT.
(2) The only gifts made within 3 years of death were within the nil rate band and so no adjustment of any tax originally paid on them is required.

Overseas property

If you are neither domiciled nor deemed domiciled in the UK (p 69) it is important to ascertain the situation of your particular property for tax purposes. This is because you will normally only pay CTT on your assets situated here. It is also important with reference to double taxation relief (p 87). The situation of property for capital transfer tax purposes is generally deemed to be as follows:

(1) Cash — its physical location.
(2) Bank accounts — the location of the bank or branch (see also below).
(3) Registered securities — the location of the share register.
(4) Bearer securities — the location of the title documents.
(5) Land and buildings — their actual location.
(6) Business assets — the place where the business is conducted.
(7) Debts — the residence of the debtor.

Foreign currency bank accounts

(FA 1982 S96)

Regarding deaths after 8 March 1982 foreign currency accounts with UK banks will be exempted from CTT if the deceased is not UK domiciled (or deemed domiciled). This also applies if the deceased had an interest in possession (p 101) in a settlement with such an account, unless the settlor was UK domiciled when he made the settlement or the trustees were so domiciled.

● *Should you now be, or later become, neither domiciled nor deemed domiciled in the UK, you will be able to minimise your liability to CTT by careful planning. This need not only consist of taking cash and other assets abroad. If you have land and buildings here, which you wish to keep, you could form an overseas company to acquire the property. Your company and all its assets will be regarded as property outside the UK and thus outside the CTT net, to the extent that you own the shares.*

An overseas-based holding company could also be used for holding UK quoted securities and other assets but the effect of other taxes should always be carefully investigated.

● *You may be neither domiciled nor deemed domiciled in the UK but know that this status will soon change. Before you become UK domiciled, consider gifting assets situated overseas (see above) which you will be able to do free of CTT in this country. Also consider settling overseas assets. This could provide continuing CTT savings, even if you are a beneficiary. Highly specialised advice from a solicitor and/or accountant should be taken, however, since there are both capital and income tax pitfalls.*

Double taxation relief

(CTTA Ss158–159)

Various other countries also operate systems of CTT. The government of the UK is empowered to enter into agreements with them for the avoidance of the double payment of CTT both here and in the other country.

Concerning CTT payable on death, relief is continued for estate duty payable on the same property in other countries if there was a 'double estate duty' agreement with the countries in question as at 12 March 1975. The following countries have agreements with the UK covering estate duty and/or CTT.

France	Pakistan
India	South Africa
Ireland	Sweden
Italy	Switzerland
Netherlands	United States of America

Unilateral double taxation relief is available for overseas tax paid on death or a lifetime transfer. The tax must be of a similar nature to CTT and if the property is situated in the overseas country, a credit is given against the UK tax of the amount of the overseas tax. If the property is either situated *both* in the UK and the overseas country, or in *neither* of those places, the credit against the UK tax is C×A/(A+B). A is the amount of CTT, B is the overseas tax and C is the smaller of A and B.

Relief for business property

(CTTA Ss 103–114)

A reduction is allowed in the values for CTT purposes of 'relevant business property'. This applies both during life and on death.

'Relevant business property' includes a business or part of a business; shares owned by the controller of a company; unquoted minority shareholdings; and land, buildings, plant and machinery used in your partnership or a company which you control. Control of a company for these purposes includes shareholdings which are 'related property' (p 81) in relation to your own shares.

In general, investment company and land or share-dealing company shareholdings do not qualify for the relief. You must normally own the business property, or property which has directly replaced it for at least two years prior to the transfer or else it is not 'relevant business property' and so no relief is due.

After 26 October 1977, rates of relief are available as follows:

(1)   The whole or part of a business — 50%.
(2)   Qualifying company shares to be valued on a control basis — 50%.
(3)   Property transferred by you which is used in a trade by a company controlled by you or partnership in which you are a partner —30%.
(4)   Shares in an unquoted trading company to be valued on a minority basis — 30% (20% prior to 15 March 1983).

Relief applies to certain business assets owned by trusts. After 9 March 1981, the 30% relief category is extended to cover the transfer by a beneficiary with an interest in possession of trust assets (land, buildings, plant or machinery) used in his business.

Broadly a reduction of 30% was given in the valuation of 'relevant business property' transferred during the period from 7 April 1976 to 26 October 1977. Where appropriate the relief applied to both individuals and settlements and was made on a net assets valuation basis.

Protecting family companies

● *The 'related property' valuation rules (p 81) may make it costly for you to transfer valuable holdings in your family company to your children, etc. This is because CTT is payable on the transfers, normally on an assets basis. The charge on the shares on your death would be even higher, however, and so you should plan to transfer shares to your children before they become too valuable, and your wife should do the same. The best time would be on the formation of a new company or early in its development.*

● *Watch out for CGT complications – for example higher valuations resulting from several transfers to connected persons (p 18). However, gifts elections will be effective to 'hold over' the gain (p 46) and should be considered carefully as a means of at least deferring CGT.*

● *Business property relief is very beneficial if you wish to pass part of your business or shares in your family company to your children. For example, if you have a controlling interest so that your shares attract 50% relief you could gift to your son shares worth £128,000. After the relief the value would be £64,000 – below your annual exemption and nil rate band, assuming you have not used these.*

● *Watch carefully the point when your holding in your family company drops below 50% so that you lose overall control (taking your wife's shares into account). The relief rate will go down from 50% to 30% regarding your next transfer of the shares. Therefore try to make the transfer which loses you control a large one, since it attracts 50% relief.*

• If you are planning a new business venture, then do not put it into your main family company. Form a new company whose shares are owned by your children (or others whom you wish to succeed to your business). The new company should be allowed to handle as much business as possible and you may even let your old company run down. In this way the next generation of your family eventually will be left controlling the major company.

• In the case of a partnership, the interest of each partner is valued on the appropriate share of the underlying assets. If, however, the partnership is incorporated into a company, the value of each partner's interest is normally reduced appreciably, if it is a minority holding.

Relief for agricultural property
(CTTA Ss115–124)

The system of agricultural relief was changed as from 10 March 1981. Before that date the relief applied to transfers on death and lifetime transfers by 'working farmers'. To qualify you needed to have been mainly or wholly engaged in agriculture as a farmer, farm worker or student in five of the seven preceding years. The relief applied to land including farmhouses and buildings occupied for farming by you for at least two years before the transfer.

Regarding transfers made after 6 April 1976, the value of agricultural property was reduced by 50%. There was a limit of the most valuable of £250,000 and 1,000 acres, for which rough grazing land was counted as one-sixth of its actual area. This limit does not apply, however, under the new system, which operates after 9 March 1981. The relief only applies to agricultural property in the UK, the Channel Islands or the Isle of Man.

Under the new scheme you must have either occupied the property for the purposes of agriculture for at least 2 years before transferring it, or owned it for 7 years up to that time, with others farming. The rules are relaxed where you inherit the property or where you have replaced one agricultural property by another. Both the present and previous systems extend relief to controlling shareholders in farming companies. For the purposes of the relief, 'agriculture' includes stud farming (FA 1984 S107).

Relief of 50% is now obtained if you enjoy the right to vacant possession or can obtain this within the next 12 months. Otherwise, the relief is normally 30% (20% before 15 March 1983), which applies to tenanted situations, etc. After 9 March 1981, the grant of a tenancy of agricultural property is not to be treated as a transfer of value if it is made for full consideration (FA 1981 S97). If you would have qualified for 50% relief under the old but not the new rules, you still obtain 50% relief regarding property held at 9 March 1981 and transferred after that date, up to the old limit of £250,000 or 1,000 acres if more valuable. The excess is then relieved at 30% only.

● *Agricultural property relief is now generally as beneficial as business property relief and takes priority. For pre-10/3/81 transfers, however, you might seek the latter instead. For example, previously annual and small gifts exemptions, etc (p 74) were deducted before the agricultural relief was calculated. Now, however, the same order is followed as for business property relief so that the exemptions are applied afterwards. In this way, the agricultural relief is maximised.*

Although you only obtain 30% relief if your farmland is tenanted instead of 50%, its value is normally accepted to be much less – possibly less than 50% of its unencumbered worth. Hence the established practice of granting a tenancy to members of your family is still worth considering as a means of saving CTT. However, you should take careful advice since the authorities might argue that a tenancy to people connected with you should be disregarded for valuation purposes.

Woodlands
(CTTA Ss125–30)

The old estate duty relief for growing timber applied in general before 13 March 1975. After that a corresponding but more restricted relief applied to the CTT charge on your death provided you either owned the woodlands for at least five years, or acquired them by gift or inheritance.

Under the current system, provided that within two years of your death the inheritor elects, tax is not charged in respect of the timber on your death. If, however, before the recipient dies, the timber is sold or given away, tax is charged on the proceeds or value of the gift. The tax rate is found by adding such proceeds to the estate at your death. Remember that the relief applies only to the timber and not the land on which it grows.

Where timber is disposed of after 26 October 1977, the new rates prevailing at the date of disposal are applied, even if the death was before they take effect. Furthermore, the disposal value is halved in charging the tax, if the death was after 12 March 1975 and the new business property relief would have been obtained, except that the death was too early.

Administration and collection
(CTTA Ss215–261, etc.)

CTT is under the care and management of the Board of the Inland Revenue. Generally speaking, the rules for administration, appeals and penalties resemble those for income tax.

Chargeable transfers must be reported to the Inland Revenue within 12 months from the end of the month of transfer. As for estate duty, tax chargeable on death must be paid on at least an estimated figure before probate is granted.

Returns of lifetime gifts are not required if these are covered by your exemptions (£3,000 etc). Also, no account need be submitted if the amount of your gift and any other chargeable transfers in the same year to 5 April does not exceed £10,000 and your cumulative total (including the latest gift) is no more than £40,000.

Interest on unpaid tax runs from when the tax is due. The due date is six months after the end of the month in which death occurs. For lifetime transfers it is six months after the end of the month in which the transfer is made. In the case of lifetime transfers between 5 April and 1 October, the due date is 30 April in the following year.

From 1 December 1982, the rate of interest on overdue CTT is 6% for transfers on death and 8% otherwise; whilst from 1 January 1980 the respective rates were 9% and 12%. Previously the respective interest rates were 6% and 9%. This interest is not deductible for income tax purposes. If you overpay CTT you will get tax-free interest at the same rates, up to the date on which the repayment of the excess tax is made.

Payment of tax by instalments
(CTTA Ss227–229)

The option of paying estate duty on certain assets in eight yearly or 16 half-yearly instalments continued for CTT on death. However, for deaths after 14 March 1983, instalments are annual, over a ten year period. This applies to land and buildings, controlling holdings of shares in companies and certain other unquoted shares, as well as business assets.

Instalments paid on time concerning the shares and business assets mentioned above are free of interest. Land and buildings qualify for this relief only if they are held as business assets; otherwise interest is payable at 6% (9% before 1 December 1982 and 6% before 1 January 1980). A limit of £250,000 of assets qualifying for this relief existed before 10 March 1981 but has now been removed completely. After 9 March 1981, tax in respect of property qualifying for the new agricultural relief may be paid in interest free instalments as above.

The above provisions apply to *lifetime transfers,* if the donee bears the tax, and for settled property which is retained in a settlement. If interest is payable it is at 8% (12% before 1 December 1982 and 9% prior to 1 January 1980). The interest free category is extended to include lifetime disposals of timber.

● *The interest rates of 6% or 8% are moderate by current standards and so it is worthwhile considering opting for the instalments basis. When realty comprised in the estate of a deceased person is sold, however, the balance of CTT on that property will become payable.*

Quick succession relief
(CTTA S141)

Quick succession relief reduces the tax payable on death where the deceased himself received chargeable transfers within five years of his death on which CTT was paid. The deduction is, broadly, a proportion of the original tax, being 100%, 80%, 60%, 40% or 20%, depending on whether the period between the transfer and the death is one, two, three, four or five years or less in each case. Similar relief was given where the previous transfer was a death on which estate duty was payable. (Prior to 10 March 1981 the period was only four years and the rates 80%, 60%, 40% and 20% respectively.) Where there are two or more transfers of the same property within five years of each other, special rules apply.

Mutual and voidable transfers
(CTTA Ss148–150)

Complicated rules have been introduced which refer back to periods before the 1976 Finance Act was passed, as well as after. Broadly, the object is to relieve both the giver and receiver from CTT, where the receiver later returns the property, etc, concerned to the original giver. (A similar rule is found in CTTA S150 concerning voidable transfers.)

Thus, if you give money to your brother, paying CTT as a result, and he later returns it to you, subject to the detailed rules, he is not charged to CTT on his transfer of the money to you. (The relievable amount is reduced by 4% for every year which elapses between the original gift and gift-back.) Furthermore, you can reclaim the tax which you first paid (recalculated in line with rate changes after 25 March 1980, between the respective gifts).

From 27 March 1980, anti-avoidance rules operate to prevent CTT being saved by *gifts-back*, where the original gift had obtained business property (p 87) or agricultural property relief (p 89). Those reliefs are ignored in the calculations. Also savings from exploiting the rules for valuing life assurance policies in conjunction with gifts-back have been blocked.

Waivers of dividends and remuneration
(CTTA Ss14 & 15)

In relation to dividends and remuneration there are rules which apply from the inception of CTT. No CTT accrues on the waiver of any dividend to which you have a right, provided you waive the dividend by deed within the 12 months before it is due.

If you waive any remuneration to which you are entitled, this normally does not produce any CTT liability, provided the amount waived would otherwise have been assessable to income tax under Schedule E and your employer obtains no income tax or corporation tax relief for the waived remuneration.

Conditional exemption for certain objects and buildings, etc
(CTTA Ss27, 30–35,78–79 & Schs 4 & 5)

Property similar to that mentioned in (2) and (3) in the exempt transfers list (p 77) is exempt from CTT on death provided the recipient undertakes to keep it in the country, preserve it and allow reasonable access to the public. If it is later sold the tax is payable unless the sale is to an institution such as the British Museum, National Gallery or National Trust.

A similar relief applies to lifetime transfers subject to various conditions. The recipient must give the required undertaking. The relief extends to historical and artistic buildings and objects comprised in settlements. It also applies to settlements set up to maintain historic buildings and objects historically associated with them, together with land of outstanding interest. Such settlements must tie up the capital for at least six years for maintenance purposes only, but after that funds may be withdrawn subject to CTT in certain circumstances.

With effect from 9 March 1982 new rules apply regarding maintenance settlements for approved objects and buildings, etc. Provided the Treasury are satisfied that the trusts and trustees comply with certain requirements, transfers to such a settlement are exempt (p 76) for CTT purposes. In general, the trust funds must be used for the maintenance of approved assets for at least six years; also, certain reasonable improvements. The trustees must be resident in the UK and at least one must be a solicitor, accountant or trust corporation.

Close companies
(CTTA Ss94–102)

Close companies making transfers of value are brought within the CTT net. (This even includes deemed transfers resulting from certain capital alterations.) Broadly, tax is charged on the company as if each of the participators had made a proportionate transfer according to his or her interest in the company. The rules are extended to cover close companies being owned by trusts or being their beneficiaries. Following the introduction of the new provisions regarding discretionary trusts (p 104), the close company rules have been correspondingly modified as from 9 March 1982.

Free loans

(CTTA S29)

From 6 April 1976 to 5 April 1981, subject to certain exemptions, if you allowed someone else the use of money or property at no interest or less than the market rate, you were treated as making a chargeable transfer for each year to 5 April that the arrangement continued. The amount of the chargeable transfer was the shortfall of the interest (less tax), or other benefit which you got, compared with the market rate. These taxing provisions ceased to have effect after 5 April 1981 although interest-free loans for a fixed stated period can still be treated as a chargeable transfer under general principles.

● *Free loans now constitute a valuable part of CTT planning, but be wary of the application of the associated operations rules (p 69) to complicated arrangements. For example, suppose you wish to transfer your £100,000 house to your son without paying any CTT. You could sell it to him for £33,000 which would involve a gift element of £67,000, covered by your £64,000 nil rate band and £3,000 annual exemption. You could then leave the £33,000 owing to you in the form of an interest-free loan. Your son could repay you in future years when he has funds available.*

CTT and life assurance

(See also p 179)

● *If you effect a policy on your life for your own benefit, the proceeds payable on your death will be taxable as part of your net estate.*

● *You may, however, effect a policy in trust for some other person or persons such as for example your wife and children. In this case the policy proceeds will not be paid into your own estate but will be paid to the trustees for the beneficiaries. Each premium payment, however, will constitute a separate chargeable transfer by you on which tax is payable unless an exemption applies such as the £3,000 or £250 reliefs (p 74), or the normal expenditure rule (p 74) or if the policy is for your wife.*

● *If someone else effects a policy on your life and pays the premiums, then the proceeds are not taxable on your death. This is known as a 'life of another' policy. If the person who effects the policy pre-deceases you, however, then the market value of the policy at the date of death of that person is normally included in his taxable estate. Please refer to Chapter 13 (p 179) for further details concerning this subject.*

Providing the funds to pay CTT on death

- You may not be able, or indeed wish, to avoid leaving a large estate when you die. In this case you should ensure that sufficient funds are available for paying the CTT. This avoids forced realisations of assets and, for example, the sale of shares in a family company which it might be desirable to keep.

- Life assurance provides one of the best means of providing money to pay CTT arising on your death, as well as being a very suitable vehicle for exempt gifts. Ensure, however, that the policy proceeds themselves are not subject to the tax, which could happen if the policy were taken out (with no trust provisions) by you on your own life. Consider taking out policies in trust for your children where you leave assets to them; this will put cash into their hands to pay the tax. This should be a 'whole of life' policy, under which a capital sum, with or without profits or one that is unit-linked to combat inflation, is payable when you die.

- If both you and your wife have large estates then you should each insure your respective lives in trust for your children, assuming that you each leave your estates to them. If, however, you each leave assets to the other by your will, then a joint life last survivor policy could be useful, under which a payment is made only on the second death. If the policy is correctly drawn (in trust for the eventual heirs on the second death) and the premiums are within the annual exemptions (p 74), it will not attract CTT. Further, the premium rate for such a policy is usually substantially lower than for two individual policies.

- The policy can be written under a suitable trust for your heirs. Take care that there is at least one trustee other than you so that the proceeds may be claimed without delay on your death.

- Temporary life assurance may be used to cover the three-year period following a gift or settlement on which you have paid tax at the lifetime rate. The amount covered should be the additional tax payable on that transfer should you die within three years.

Annuities

- If you need to increase your income, annuities provide a means of doing this which at the same time immediately reduces the value of your estate. For example, if you buy an annuity for £10,000 which produces, say, £1,400 yearly until your death, no part of your original capital outlay is charged to CTT on your death. You have thus saved potential tax on your death at your top rate band. Do not overlook the effects of inflation, however; an annuity which is sufficient for your present needs soon may be worth too little to maintain you.

- If you do not need the income, you may use the annuity to make gifts to your beneficiaries. For the purposes of the normal expenditure gifts exemption, however, it is only the income element and not the capital portion which is taken into account (p 75).

Appendix — Capital transfer tax rates

Before 27 October 1977

Slice of cumulative chargeable transfers	Total	Lifetime Scale % on slice	Lifetime Scale Cumulative total tax	On death % on slice	On death Cumulative total tax
The first £15,000	£15,000	Nil	£Nil	Nil	£Nil
The next					
5,000	20,000	5	250	10	500
5,000	25,000	7.5	625	15	1,250
5,000	30,000	10	1,125	20	2,250
10,000	40,000	12.5	2,375	25	4,750
10,000	50,000	15	3,875	30	7,750
10,000	60,000	17.5	5,625	35	11,250
20,000	80,000	20	9,625	40	19,250
20,000	100,000	22.5	14,125	45	28,250
20,000	120,000	27.5	19,625	50	38,250
30,000	150,000	35	30,125	55	54,750
50,000	200,000	42.5	51,375	60	84,750
50,000	250,000	50	76,375	60	114,750
50,000	300,000	55	103,875	60	144,750
200,000	500,000	60	223,875	60	264,750
500,000	1,000,000	65	548,875	65	589,750
1,000,000	2,000,000	70	1,248,875	70	1,289,750
The remainder		75		75	

from 28 October 1977 to 25 March 1980

Slice of cumulative chargeable transfers	Total	Lifetime Scale % on slice	Lifetime Scale Cumulative total tax	On death % on slice	On death Cumulative total tax
The first £25,000	£25,000	Nil	£Nil	Nil	£Nil
The next					
5,000	30,000	5	250	10	500
5,000	35,000	7.5	625	15	1,250
5,000	40,000	10	1,125	20	2,250
10,000	50,000	12.5	2,375	25	4,750
10,000	60,000	15	3,875	30	7,750
10,000	70,000	17.5	5,625	35	11,250
20,000	90,000	20	9,625	40	19,250
20,000	110,000	22.5	14,125	45	28,250
20,000	130,000	27.5	19,625	50	38,250
30,000	160,000	35	30,125	55	54,750
50,000	210,000	42.5	51,375	60	84,750
50,000	260,000	50	76,375	60	114,750
50,000	310,000	55	103,875	60	144,750
200,000	510,000	60	223,875	60	264,750
500,000	1,010,000	65	548,875	65	589,750
1,000,000	2,010,000	70	1,248,875	70	1,289,750
The remainder		75		75	

from 26 March 1980 to 9 March 1981

Slice of cumulative chargeable transfers	Total	CTT Payable Lifetime Scale		On death	
		% on slice	Cumulative total tax	% on slice	Cumulative total tax
The first £50,000	£50,000	Nil	£Nil	Nil	£Nil
The next					
10,000	60,000	15	1,500	30	3,000
10,000	70,000	17.5	3,250	35	6,500
20,000	90,000	20	7,250	40	14,500
20,000	110,000	22.5	11,750	45	23,500
20,000	130,000	27.5	17,250	50	33,500
30,000	160,000	35	27,750	55	50,000
50,000	210,000	42.5	49,000	60	80,000
50,000	260,000	50	74,000	60	110,000
50,000	310,000	55	101,500	60	140,000
200,000	510,000	60	221,500	60	260,000
500,000	1,010,000	65	546,500	65	585,000
1,000,000	2,010,000	70	1,246,500	70	1,285,000
The remainder		75		75	

from 10 March 1981 to 8 March 1982

The first £50,000	£50,000	Nil	£Nil	Nil	£Nil
The next					
10,000	60,000	15	1,500	30	3,000
10,000	70,000	17.5	3,250	35	6,500
20,000	90,000	20	7,250	40	14,500
20,000	110,000	22.5	11,750	45	23,500
20,000	130,000	25	16,750	50	33,500
30,000	160,000	30	25,750	55	50,000
350,000	510,000	35	148,250	60	260,000
500,000	1,010,000	40	348,250	65	585,000
1,000,000	2,010,000	45	798,250	70	1,285,000
The remainder		50		75	

from 9 March 1982 to 14 March 1983

Slice of cumulative chargeable transfers	Total	CTT Payable Lifetime Scale		On death	
		% on slice	Cumulative total tax	% or slice	
The first £55,000	£55,000	Nil	£Nil	Nil	£Nil
The next					
20,000	75,000	15	3,000	30	6,000
25,000	100,000	17.5	7,375	35	14,750
30,000	130,000	20	13,375	40	26,750
35,000	165,000	22.5	21,250	45	42,500
35,000	200,000	25	30,000	50	60,000
50,000	250,000	30	45,000	55	87,500
400,000	650,000	35	185,000	60	327,500
600,000	1,250,000	40	425,000	65	717,500
1,250,000	2,500,000	45	987,500	70	1,592,500
The remainder		50		75	

from 15 March 1983 to 12 March 1984

The first £60,000	£60,000	Nil	£Nil	Nil	£Nil
The next					
20,000	80,000	15	3,000	30	6,000
30,000	110,000	17.5	8,250	35	16,500
30,000	140,000	20	14,250	40	28,500
35,000	175,000	22.5	22,125	45	44,250
45,000	220,000	25	33,375	50	66,750
50,000	270,000	30	48,375	55	94,250
430,000	700,000	35	198,875	60	352,250
625,000	1,325,000	40	448,875	65	758,500
1,325,000	2,650,000	45	1,045,125	70	1,686,000
The remainder		50		75	

from 13 March 1984

Slice of cumulative chargeable transfers	Total	CTT Payable			
		Lifetime Scale		On death	
		% on slice	Cumulative total tax	% on slice	Cumulative total tax
The first £64,000	£64,000	Nil	£Nil	Nil	£Nil
The next					
21,000	85,000	15	3,150	30	6,300
31,000	116,000	17.5	8,575	35	17,150
32,000	148,000	20	14,975	40	29,950
37,000	185,000	22.5	23,300	45	46,600
47,000	232,000	25	35,050	50	70,100
53,000	285,000	27.5	49,625	55	99,250
The remainder		30		60	

8   Capital transfer tax — Trusts

Settled property
(CTTA Pt III & FA 1984 Ss102–104)

For further details concerning trusts and settled property reference should be made to Chapter 5 (CGT — p 50), Chapter 11 (income tax — p 151) and Chapter 12 (legal aspects — p 158).

The rules concerning CTT in relation to settled property are most detailed and the following are just a few guidelines:

(1) Broadly, any settlement is subject to the tax (based on the lifetime rate scale — p 70) on its world-wide assets, if at the time it was made the settlor was domiciled in the UK. Otherwise, only assets situated in this country (p 86) are caught.

(2) The settlement of any property after 26 March 1974 is itself treated as a chargeable transfer by the settlor.

(3) If you have an interest in possession in any settled property for the time being (eg, you are entitled to receive any income as of right), the property itself is treated as yours for capital transfer tax purposes. Thus if your interest ends, you will be treated as making a chargeable transfer of the value of the property concerned. The tax is calculated on the basis of your cumulative transfers to that time. Since 5 April 1981, you can deduct your £3,000 annual exemption (p 74) and also marriage gifts allowance if applicable (FA 1981 S94).

(4) No CTT is payable if you obtain an absolute interest in property in which you previously had a life interest (or other interest in possession). Similarly, the tax normally is not payable on the reversion to you in your lifetime (or your spouse during your life and within two years of your death) of property which you previously settled. Regarding discretionary trusts, however, this rule does not normally apply after 8 March 1982.

(5) Special rules apply to trusts where there is no interest in possession — particularly discretionary trusts, etc and accumulation and maintenance settlements (see below).

(6) Quick succession relief is given if an interest in possession comes to an end within five years of a previous chargeable transfer of the settled property. The relief is given against the CTT on the later transfer. It is calculated, broadly, as a percentage of the tax on the *first* transfer. The percentage is 100%, 80%, 60%, 40%, or 20% where the interval is not more than one, two, three, four, or five years respectively. (Prior to 10 March 1981 relief only extended to a four year period and the chargeable value was reduced by 80%, 60%, 40%, and 20% for the respective years.)

(7) Superannuation schemes and charitable trusts are normally exempted from capital transfer tax, as are those for employees, newspapers, certain 'protective trusts' and trusts for the mentally disabled (treated as having a life interest in property settled for

them after 9 March 1981). Where property is held temporarily on such trusts, some relief is now given; the charge to CTT is proportionately reduced on a time basis (FA 1984 S102).

● *Consider making larger gifts in the form of settlements. If these are discretionary, however, the ten year charge (p 105) would normally apply at some future time, as well as the tax which you pay when you make the settlement and further tax when benefits are paid to the beneficiaries (but the rates will not be great at current levels). Accumulation and maintenance settlements (below) are useful for the benefit of your minor children and grandchildren. If the beneficiaries obtain fixed interests (eg, in the income) to which they become entitled when they are no more than 25 years old, then no further CTT is payable, even if the payment of the ultimate capital is deferred to an older age.*

● *Fixed trusts are also of use if you wish your grown-up children to have income but no capital until a stipulated time. Thus, if you settle money on your 20-year-old son giving him an entitlement to the annual income until he is 35 and then the capital, you are immediately divested of the capital and pay CTT on the amount settled. Your son eventually gets the capital at age 35 and no more CTT is payable. Your son is fully taxed on the income, however, and if his other income becomes high as he matures, his income tax burden could be heavy.*

Accumulation and maintenance settlements

Accumulation and maintenance settlements without any interests in possession for one or more beneficiaries up to an age not exceeding 25 are most favourably treated for CTT purposes. Such settlements are not subject to the periodic charge (see below); nor will CTT be charged on the capital distributions to those beneficiaries. This relief covers, for example, a settlement under which your son obtains an interest in possession at the age of 25 and at 35 gets the capital, the income being accumulated up to 25 apart from various payments for his maintenance. No CTT is payable during the currency of the trust, nor when your son becomes entitled to the income at 25 nor the capital at 35.

Special rules apply to settlements made after 15 April 1976. Relief broadly only applies if either not more than 25 years have passed since the original settlement date (or when it first became accumulating); or if all beneficiaries are grandchildren of a common grandparent (or their widows, widowers, etc).

● *Accumulation and maintenance settlements provide a very tax-effective means of passing on capital to your children and grandchildren. If the beneficiaries are your children, however, be careful they do not receive any benefit until age 18 (unless married) or an income tax charge on you is likely to result (p 153). You might also include similar trusts in your will (this is one way of using your nil rate bar ' if most of your remaining estate is left to your husband or wife).*

When you settle any funds a CTT charge may result but may well not bite because of your annual exemption (£3,000) and nil rate band (£64,000). Remember that your spouse will also be able to settle funds in this way and after ten years each of you will have a fresh nil rate band available (p 71).

Discretionary trusts, etc

The following rules apply where there is no interest in possession in *all* or *part* of the *property*. Note that from 9 March 1982 drastically revised provisions operate (p 104).

Rules applying before 9 March 1982

(1)   CTT was charged on distributions of capital to beneficiaries. If the settlement was made before 27 March 1974 it was charged to tax on its distributions as if it were a separate individual but without certain exemptions (p 74) (unless there was an interest in possession — p 101).

(2)   For a settlement made after 26 March 1974, distributions of capital up to the original amount settled were charged at a special rate. This was the rate which would have been paid by the settlor on a gift of the amount of the original settlement at the time that it was made (revised in line with the rate changes on and after 26 March 1980). Excess distributions over and above the original capital fell into higher rate bands as further gifts by the settlor would have done (subject to subsequent rate changes).

(3)   In addition a *periodic charge* was planned to be made. This would usually have fallen on every tenth anniversary of the date of the settlement occurring after 31 March 1983. (The original date was 31 March 1980 but this had been extended.) Where a transfer requiring Court proceedings was made in the year to 31 March 1983, the onset of the periodic charge would have been further delayed until after that date. Basically, the periodic charge remains in the new system but with modifications and all periodic charges will now arise under the new rules: see below.

(4)   If the trustees of the settlement were not UK resident, an annual charge was payable, starting with the anniversary of the settlement falling after 31 December 1975. The amount was 3% of the total CTT which would have been payable on a distribution of the entire trust capital. Previously, if the tenth anniversary fell between 1 January 1976 and 31 March 1980, no annual charge arose until the next anniversary. With the three year extension to 31 March 1983, tenth anniversaries were similarly treated. The annual charge has been removed from the new rules, however; only the periodic charge applies.

(5)   Transitional relief was given for capital distributions before 1 April 1983 out of pre-27 March 1974 settlements. (This has been continued in the new system.) Thus an old settlement could be reorganised to avoid the periodic charge — for example, by creating an interest in possession, or converting it into an accumulation and maintenance trust (p 102). A percentage only of the full tax was charged on such reorganisations or capital distributions, according to the following scale:

Distribution before	1 April 1976	% of full tax	10%
	1 April 1977		12½%
	1 April 1978		15%
	1 April 1979		17½%
	1 April 1983		20%

(The expiry date for transitional relief was originally fixed as 31 March 1980 but was extended until 31 March 1983 — one year later where Court proceedings were required to make the distribution.)

Breaking discretionary settlements

● *In view of the harsher CTT provisions relating to larger discretionary trusts, it was wise to consider either distributing all of the capital or reorganising a trust to avoid the ten year charge (p 105). (This depended upon the trustees having the power to do this.) If the distribution or reorganisation was made before 1 April 1983, no more than 20% of the full tax was payable. Of course, this needed to be carefully weighed against the non-CTT advantages, such as flexibility, in favour of continuing the discretionary trust. Since 1 April 1983, the full CTT exit charge (see below) is payable on breaking a discretionary settlement, and so this is not normally worthwhile for CTT–saving reasons alone.*

Rules applying after 8 March 1982
(CTTA Ss58–85)

The following notes apply to the new system which operates from 9 March 1982. Major changes have been made which, in some cases, have resulted in relaxations and reductions in the CTT payable. The effect of the new rules coming into operation has been that some of the original provisions, such as the periodic charge as first envisaged, have not taken effect at all.

(1)   As before, CTT is charged on *distributions* of capital to beneficiaries. Now, it is also charged on distributions to the settlor or his spouse (see below). Such charges are in anticipation of the next 10 year charge (see below) and are known as 'exit charges'.

(2)   A *charge* is made on the trust property on every *tenth anniversary*

of the creation of the trust, ignoring any such anniversary occuring before 1 April 1983. The rate is, broadly, 30% of normal lifetime rates, adjusted as below.

(3) The annual charge which previously applied to *non-resident trusts* was abolished from 1 January 1982 but they are now liable to the 10 year charge. A credit is given for any annual charges not previously offset.

(4) Previously, tax was charged on the value of the trust property leaving the trust. However, after 8 March 1982 the charge is based on the *reduction in the value* of trust property, which could be greater. Thus, discretionary trusts have been put in the same position as individuals in that respect.

(5) The CTT charges fall on *'relevant property'*. This excludes property held on accumulation and maintenance trusts, employee and newspaper trusts, maintenance funds, charitable trusts, protective trusts and trade compensation funds. Also, relevant property is that in which there is no *qualifying interest in possession*. This, in turn, is broadly defined as an interest to which an individual (or a company, in certain circumstances) is beneficially entitled.

(6) In general, CTT is now calculated on discretionary trusts in isolation from any others. However, *related settlements* must be taken into account. (Related settlements are those with a common settlor which commenced on the same day; but if one or both is exclusively charitable and without limit of time they are not related.)

(7) The *10 year charge* is made on the relevant property comprised in the settlement at the time. The rate of charge is 30% of the tax at lifetime rates on a notional transfer comprising the value of the relevant and other property of the settlement. The latter is taken at its value when introduced into the settlement. Any transfers made by the settlor during the 10 years up to the date of the settlement are cumulated to arrive at the starting point on the rate scale (p 71). If any of the relevant property has been comprised in the trust for less than 10 years, the proportion of the rate attributable to that property is reduced to N40ths. (N is the number of completed three month periods for which the property has been held on discretionary trusts during the current 10 year period).

(8) Where a substantial additional amount has been transferred to the settlement after its original inception, simply using the settlor's cumulative position at the outset could save substantial tax. For that reason, if it gives a higher figure, it is necessary to include in the notional cumulative total the transfers by the settlor in the 10 years prior to the subsequent addition to the settlement.

(9)   *Exit charges* are calculated on the same basis as the previous 10 year charge (see above), using the same rate, adjusted for subsequent additions. Where there has been no previous 10 year charge, the opening position of the trust and subsequent additions are normally used to calculate the rate. The effective CTT rate is calculated as shown and N40ths of this is charged on the relevant property comprised in the distribution. As before, N is the number of completed three month periods for which the property has been held on discretionary trusts during the current 10 year period. Thus, suppose the effective rate is 20% and the trust was formed on 1 January 1980. If the distribution is made on 1 April 1985, the fraction is $\frac{21}{40}$ and so the rate becomes 10.5%.

(10)   Note that in the case of a settlement made before 27 March 1974, special rules apply regarding exit charges. In computing the effective rate, the settlor's chargeable transfers during the 10 years prior to the start of the settlement should be ignored. However, additions to the settlement after 8 March 1982 must be taken into account. Exit charges are thus based on the cumulation of the current distribution from the trust with previous ones (if any) since 27 March 1974.

(11)   *Transitional relief* applied for pre-27 March 1974 trusts regarding distributions prior to 1 April 1983 (or 1 April 1984 where Court proceedings were involved).In those cases, the rate was 20% instead of 30% of the full rate, subject to the various rules mentioned above. However, the reduction to N40ths did not apply.

(12)   An *election* could be made in respect of pre-27 March 1974 trusts to have them dealt with under the old system until 31 March 1983 (or one year later if an application to the Court was required).

(13)   Under the new rules, where settled property *reverts* to the settlor or his wife, this is no longer exempt. However, for pre-27 March 1974 settlements, no CTT applied to any such reversions taking place before 1 April 1983 (one year later where Court proceedings were involved).

(14)   No exit charge applies when trust property becomes held for *charitable purposes*, etc, or by exempt bodies; also exempt maintenance funds, employee trusts, etc. There is a charge, however, when property ceases to be held on *temporary* charitable trusts, etc.

(15)   If property becomes settled under a will or intestacy it is taken to enter the settlement at death. Where the death is after 12 March 1984, any such property which is distributed within two years of death to a charity, employee trust, etc, is treated as if distributed at death; it is thus CTT-free (FA 1984 S103).

(16)   Any property which passes from one discretionary settlement directly into another is treated as remaining in the first, for the purposes of the rules. (After 14 March 1983 this does not apply to certain reversionary interests existing before 10 December 1981 — FA 1984 S104.)

(17)   If the *settlor* or his wife initially has an *interest in possession* in trust property which then ceases, it is treated as a separate discretionary settlement, starting when that interest ceases. (This does not apply to pre-27 March 1974 interests.)

(18)   Where the *settlor* was domiciled (and deemed domiciled) *outside the UK* when the settlement was made, the property is normally treated as excluded (p 78) although non-domicile is also required at the transfer or interest cesser date in situations (16) and (17).

● *Discretionary settlements provide a very valuable estate planning tool in view of their flexibility and comparatively low CTT. (Note that at current rates the maximum is 30% × 30% = 9% on the top slice for any ten year charge). Thus if you are unsure as to the exact distribution of your estate, discretionary settlements are very useful. But beware of future possible rate increases.*

● *Depending upon the exact circumstances, a number of smaller settlements can result in lower CTT than a single larger one, particularly for future years. This is because the property in the smaller settlements is likely to attract lower CTT rates.*

● *It is particularly beneficial if both spouses create smaller settlements since you may each have your nil rate and lower rate bands available.*

Small discretionary settlements

● *Although large discretionary settlements may sometimes be of questionable CTT benefit, smaller trusts are useful. Subject to the cost of setting them up and administering them (p 158), worthwhile CTT savings can be produced.*

You can establish a discretionary trust with up to £64,000 by your will, including your wife as a beneficiary so as to use your nil rate band. Your wife could then receive funds if necessary (p 119).

Alternatively you could establish a discretionary settlement up to the extent of your nil rate band during your life. If your wife is able to benefit during your life you will be liable to income tax on the trust income. However, if she is able to benefit only after your death you will not be so liable.

Provided the discretionary settlement is made within your nil rate band, little or no CTT is likely to arise either from the 10-year charge or on distributions. However, appreciations in the fund in excess of CTT indexation may result in future tax charges. If it is wished to control the situation, whilst providing some protection against inflation, the fund could be invested in index-linked Government Stock.

Example 10: Capital transfer tax on discretionary settlements

Mr A settles property worth £200,000 on wholly discretionary trusts on 1 January 1980, having made £100,000 of chargeable transfers in the previous 10 years.

On 1 August 1985, the trust makes a capital distribution of £50,000. Assuming no more distributions and that the trust property all remains relevant property throughout and using current tax rates, compute:

(1) the exit charge at 1 August 1985; and
(2) the 10-year charge at 1 January 1990, taking the value of the relevant property as £350,000.

(1) *Exit charge at 1 August 1985*

Value of relevant property when settled	£200,000
Chargeable transfers made by settlor in 10 years prior to commencement	£100,000 (A)
	£300,000 (B)

CTT on (B)	
at lifetime rates £285,000 (see Table 7)	£49,625
£15,000 at 30%	£4,500
	£54,125

Less notional CTT on (A)	
£100,000 (see Table 7)	£5,775
	£48,350

$$\text{Effective rate} \quad \frac{48,350}{200,000} \quad = \quad 24.175\%$$

Completed three-month periods prior to distribution	=	22
CTT on capital distribution of £50,000 is thus		
30% × £50,000 × 24.175% × $^{22}/_{40}$	=	£1,994

(2) *10-year charge at 1 January 1990*

Value of relevant property	£350,000

Pre-settlement transfers		£100,000	(A)
		£450,000	(C)

CTT on (C)		
	£285,000	£49,625
	£165,000 at 30%	£49,500
		£99,125
Less notional CTT on (A)		£5,775
		£93,350
10-year charge		
30% × £93,350		£28,005

9   Drawing up your will

Why you should make a will

In England and Wales, unlike many other countries, there is no compulsory share to which a member of your family is entitled on your death. You are therefore completely free as to how you dispose of your estate subject only to the statutory rights which a former spouse, a surviving spouse, children and certain other persons might have if they were dependent on you (p 115). Otherwise, the Courts have no power to interfere with any of the dispositions in your will unless they are called upon to resolve a problem of construction or interpretation (p 125).

It is therefore advantageous for you to make a will, since it is the only means by which you are able to express your wishes with regard to the disposition of all your property on your death. In addition, a will enables you to give directions with regard to your funeral arrangements and the guardianship of your children. Also, depending on the wording of your will, and your personal circumstances, you will be able to take advantage of the various capital transfer tax exemptions and reliefs which are available. Finally, and most important, by making a will you can avoid an intestacy and the application of statute law which would otherwise govern the disposition of your property in that situation (p 147).

If some of your property is of a personal nature, ie, a bank account or stocks and shares, and it is in the joint names of yourself and another, then, unless there is an agreement to the contrary, such property passes automatically to the survivor on your death. You will not be able to dispose of such property under your will.

In the case of immovable property (ie, land) which is acquired in joint names, this will pass on your death according to the manner in which it is held. If you acquired your house jointly with your wife as 'beneficial joint tenants' then on your death the title to the property passes automatically to your wife as surviving joint tenant. However, if your house is held by your wife and yourself as 'tenants in common' then each of you is entitled quite independently to your share of the proceeds of sale. You are therefore free to dispose of your share by will as it does not pass automatically to the survivor (see p 116).

There are, of course, numerous other ways in which you can make provision for your family independently of the provisions of your will. If you are a member of a company pension scheme, its rules may provide for a discretionary lump sum payment by the trustees on your death. Such payments do not form part of your estate and are therefore free of capital transfer tax. You may request that the trustees pay all or part of such a lump sum to your children. This may enable you to leave your entire personal estate to your wife. Another way is for you to declare trusts of any insurance policies on your life for the benefit of your wife or children, although there could be a capital transfer tax charge when the policies are put into trust (see Chapter 13). On your death the trustees will pay the monies directly to the beneficiaries and they will not form part of your estate.

Who can make a will?
(WA S11; WSSA)

You can make a will provided you are over 18 years of age and have what is known as 'testamentary capacity'. This means that:

(1)   you must know what you are doing and be aware of the implications;
(2)   you must be aware of the extent of the property of which you are disposing; *and*
(3)   you must have regard for your legal and moral obligations to particular beneficiaries.

You must know and approve the contents of your will at the time when you sign it, otherwise it may be contested after your death (p 125). If you later have cause to regret any particular provision, this will nevertheless remain valid until your will is revoked or amended by a codicil (p 124).

If you are a soldier on active service or a sailor on maritime service you can make a will even if you are under 18. In such circumstances you can also make a will orally without complying with the formalities for execution (below). You will also be able to revoke your will informally.

The basic requirements for a valid will
(WA S9; AJA S17)

An English will must be in writing. No special form is required provided it is clear that the document was intended to be a will. It is always revocable. You must also comply with the formalities for execution, otherwise your will will be invalid and of no effect. These formalities are:

(1)   you should sign your will at the foot or end of the document, (another person may sign for you provided you are present and direct him to so do). Even if you have not signed your will at the end it will still be valid if it is apparent that you intended by your signature to give effect to the will;
(2)   your signature must be made or acknowledged by you in the presence of two witnesses both present at the same time; *and*
(3)   thereafter both witnesses should sign in your presence although it is no longer strictly necessary for a witness to do so. It is sufficient if he acknowledges his signature in your presence.

Both witnesses must be aware of what is happening and must be in the line of sight of the proceedings. A proper attestation clause is desirable and is incorporated in most wills.

Witnesses
(WA S15; WA 1968)

A beneficiary under your will should not be a witness to it. Such a person would be a competent witness but as an 'interested person' his or her gift would be invalidated unless there were two other independent witnesses. Neither should the husband or wife of a beneficiary witness your will as the gift would be similarly invalidated.

An executor appointed under your will will not lose his appointment by acting as a witness. However, he cannot also take any benefit if he does witness the will and if he is a professional person this would render invalid a professional charging clause in the will.

If a beneficiary under your will subsequently marries one of your witnesses the gift to him will still take effect. If a beneficiary does not witness your will but witnesses a codicil which confirms your will he will still take the gift.

Drafting your will

There are various ways in which a will may be worded. An infinite number and variety of clauses may be inserted, depending on your wishes and your personal circumstances. You should seek your solicitor's advice on the final draft. What follows is an outline of the main points which you should consider and the most important clauses which should be included.

Appointing executors and trustees

You will need to appoint executors to administer your estate. They will make application for a grant of probate, collect in your assets, pay your debts and then distribute the remainder of your estate according to the terms of your will.

Usually two executors are appointed, although you may appoint up to four. One executor is normally a relative or responsible close friend. It is often advisable to appoint a professional person such as your solicitor or family accountant as your second executor. Deciding on your executors requires careful consideration as they will be responsible for all your assets after your death. The welfare of your family may well depend on their judgment.

To guard against one of your executors predeceasing you or for some other reason being unable or unwilling to act, you can appoint a substitute executor.

Once the administration of your estate has been completed, your executors are usually also appointed to act as trustees if property has to be administered for minors or if you have set up a trust by your will. It is not necessary for the same executors and trustees to be appointed to act for your whole estate. You may appoint separate trustees of any part of your estate and this might be the best course where you intend your business to be carried on after your death. If there are to be trusts for your children, you should consider choosing trustees who are relatively young. This may reduce communication problems when your children come of age.

You may appoint a bank or trust company to administer your estate. The advantages of such an appointment are the experience and confidentiality which such organisations can offer. The main disadvantage is the extra cost involved. You may also prefer your estate to be administered by a close friend or relative rather than by a comparatively impersonal institution.

Funeral arrangements

If you wish to be cremated or to be buried in a particular place you can give directions for this in your will. You can also direct that parts of your body be given to a teaching hospital or for grafting or transplantation. If this is your wish it is advisable to leave separate instructions with your family or relatives so that they can give effect to your wishes as soon as possible after your death.

Guardianship of your children

If you have young children or children who are incapable of looking after themselves you will probably wish to appoint someone to look after them after the death of both yourself and your husband or wife. On your death your husband or wife will automatically become the guardian of your children unless you wish to provide otherwise. A close friend or relative may be appointed as guardian together with your husband or wife only in special circumstances.

You should, of course, discuss the question of guardianship at length with your friends and relatives and ensure that the persons you propose to appoint will be prepared to take on such a responsibility.

Legacies

Beneficiaries generally either receive specific gifts of property (legacies) or a share of your residuary estate (p 118).

Legacies may be either specific sums of cash or specific items of your property. You might wish to leave all your personal effects to one of your relatives or close friends. If you own a particularly valuable item, eg, jewellery, you should consider whether it should be included in such a general gift or left to someone who you feel might particularly appreciate it. The item should, of course, be accurately described to avoid any confusion when your estate is being distributed. You can give a specific gift of shares or the proceeds of an insurance policy provided you are the beneficial owner of such a policy.

You may wish to leave one or more of your personal employees specific legacies. If any of them would be entitled to a redundancy payment on your death you would probably wish this to be deducted from the amount of the legacy and, if this is the case, you should make specific provision for it in your will.

If you wish to leave a legacy to your executor you should state whether it is a condition of the gift that he accepts the office or not.

You may, of course, leave property to a charity or a number of charities. The charity should be accurately described. A receipt clause should be included discharging your executors from liability provided they pay the legacy to the treasurer or another officer of similar standing in the charity concerned. Charitable gifts do have substantial capital transfer tax advantages (p 77).

● *In considering legacies you will need to decide whether or not the beneficiary is to pay any capital transfer tax on the gift. There is no tax disadvantage in expressing a legacy to be 'free of capital transfer tax' and it is often the most favoured procedure. Any capital transfer tax payable on such a legacy will be paid out of your residuary estate by your executors.*

Legacies to children

Vested legacies

A vested legacy is payable immediately on your death. If you wish to benefit a number of children there are three forms of gift open to you:

(1)   Individual gifts of a stated amount to named beneficiaries — eg, '£100 to my son David'.
(2)   Individual gifts of a stated amount to each member of a class —eg, '£100 to each of my children (or grandchildren)'.
(3)   You may provide for a specific sum to be divided equally between a class — eg, '£1,000 equally between the children of my sister'.

Which form you choose will depend largely on your own particular family circumstances. Reference to children in a will automatically includes reference to an adopted or illegitimate child even though such a child may have been adopted or legitimated after your death.

Contingent legacies

A contingent legacy is payable only on the happening of a particular event, such as marriage or the attainment of a particular age.

If you give one or more minor children a contingent legacy then, unless you specifically provide to the contrary, the income of such legacy will belong to your residuary beneficiaries. Your residuary beneficiaries will be regarded as having an 'interest in possession' in the legacy, meaning being entitled to the income (p 158). Their life interest will only come to an end when the legacy becomes vested when the children reach the specified age.

● *If you wish to give minor children contingent legacies you should ensure that the clause is properly drawn. You may provide that the legacy be set aside for the beneficiaries, possibly in the hands of separate trustees. The better course would be to stipulate that the legacy carry the intermediate income for the benefit of the beneficiary. This will prevent a capital transfer tax charge on your residuary beneficiaries at the time when the legacy becomes vested.*

You would probably be best advised to make absolute gifts to minors, particularly if you are planning that they should have legacies on attaining 18. Although a minor cannot give your executors a valid receipt for the gift, it is usual practice to provide for your executors to be discharged if they pay the legacy to his or her parent or guardian. If you do not make such provision your executors can only obtain a discharge by appointing two trustees or a trust corporation to hold the legacy on trust for the minor until he or she reaches majority, ie, 18.

Legacies and family provision claims

In considering legacies you will need to have regard not only to your own personal wishes but also to your legal obligations to persons who might have a claim under the family provision legislation (p 145). If you are divorced, your former wife or husband may have a claim for reasonable financial provision out of your net estate. Any other persons who could show that they were financially dependent on you during your lifetime might also have a claim. It would therefore be prudent to consider making provision for a potential claimant, since a substantial pecuniary legacy given by your will may avert the unpleasantness of a claim after your death which may lead to court proceedings.

Conditional gifts

You should not attach any condition to a specific gift which is too harsh or unreasonable. If the Court felt that this were the case the beneficiary would be entitled to the gift free of the condition. Similarly, a condition may be void for uncertainty if it is held to be too vague to be clearly interpreted and implemented. A condition that is onerous or immoral might be held to be contrary to public policy.

The only exceptions to this rule are gifts to named charities which fail or are too vague to be implemented. In such cases the Court may direct that the subject matter of the gift be applied for purposes which are as near as possible to those which you originally intended.

Failure of gifts

Ademption

(WA S24)

If you give a specific legacy and the subject matter of the gift has been sold, destroyed, given away or stolen during your lifetime the gift will be void ('adeemed') and of no effect. This is because your will takes effect from the date of your death. For these purposes, it is construed as if you had signed it on the day you died.

You may, however, show an intention in your will that it be construed at a time other than the date of your death. If you refer in your will to 'my car' or 'my house in which I now live' these words may be interpreted as denoting the present time. If such a clause in your will is treated as taking effect at the time when it was made and the asset in question is sold or stolen, the gift will be adeemed. This will be so even if the asset is replaced by another which satisfies the description you have given in your will. If your will is confirmed by a later codicil (p 124) it will be construed as referring to the new asset.

A specific legacy is also adeemed if the property is subject to a binding contract for sale on your death. Note that if an asset which is the subject of a specific legacy is subject to an option for sale which you have created after execution of your will, the gift will be adeemed by the exercise of the option, even after your death.

Lapse

(WA S33; AJA S19)

If you benefit a person in your will and this person dies in your lifetime the gift will be void and of no effect. If the gift is a specific gift the property in question will fall into, and form part of, your residuary estate (p 118). If the gift which lapses is a share of residue (p 118) it will pass according to the intestacy rules (p 147).

Specific gifts and gifts of residue may both be saved from lapse by the provisions of Section 19 Administration of Justice Act 1982. The Section provides that if you give property by will to your child or other descendant and the donee dies before you, leaving children of his own alive at your death, the gift does not lapse but passes to your deceased child's children regardless of the provisions in his will.

The Section will not apply if you make the gift determinable at or before the death of the donee, nor does it apply to property appointed under a special power of appointment (p 117). In addition, the operation of

Section 19 may be excluded by any contrary intention which you express in your will.

Similarly, if you leave a fund of property to a class of persons (known as a 'class gift'), eg, 'to all or any of my children living at my death', and one of your children dies before you, his potential share will not lapse but will remain in the fund and be divided amongst those of his children who are living at your death. However, if a gift is subject to your children attaining a certain age and one of them survives you but does not reach that age, his share will remain in the fund and be divided among those of your children who do attain a vested interest.

Exercising powers of appointment
(S27 WA)

You may have been given a power of appointment over a trust fund under the will of a relative or friend or under a settlement. Such a power may be either special, eg, in favour of a certain class of persons, or general, eg, in favour of anyone, and will probably be exercisable by will or by deed.

If you are the donee of a special power of appointment you will have to exercise this by means of a separate clause in your will. If you are the donee of a general power its exercise will probably be incorporated in the wording of the bequest of your residuary estate.

Dealing with the family home

If you are the sole owner of your house you can dispose of it under your will either by means of a specific gift or as part of residue.

If you and your wife own your house as 'beneficial joint tenants' your share will pass automatically on your death to your wife as surviving joint tenant. There is therefore no need to provide for a gift of your share in your will as the principle of survivorship operates quite independently of the provisions of any will.

If you both own the house as 'tenants in common' your share will not pass automatically to the survivor. It will fall into your general estate and pass under the terms of your will. You should thus clearly stipulate in your will that your wife should receive your share, or if this is not your wish, that it should pass to another stated person.

● *By owning your house as a joint tenant with your wife her security is enhanced, whereas owning as tenants in common has capital transfer tax advantages (p 74). The gift under the will of the share in the property (or indeed the whole estate if you have left it to the survivor) should be conditional on the survivor surviving for a specified period, usually 30 days. The reason for this is that if you should both die together in a common accident or within a few days of each other the estate of the second to die (in the absence of a 30 day clause) would be substantially increased by the share in the house and attract an unnecessary capital transfer tax charge. Your children's share may well then have to bear the additional tax burden.*

You might wish that your house be retained after your death in order to provide a home for your wife and family. You could give your house to your executors and trustees on trusts permitting your wife to have the use of it during her lifetime provided she makes it her home. On her death or if she ceases to reside there the house will pass absolutely to another named beneficiary, most probably your children.

You may wish to provide for the possibility that the house may be too large or expensive for your wife to run. You could authorise your executors to purchase another house for your wife to live in. You could also extend your executors' powers of investment in relation to your residuary estate by including the purchase or improvement of land in such powers.

The residuary gift

The term 'residuary estate' comprises everything which is not otherwise specifically disposed of by your will. Whatever is left in your estate —'the residue' — can (subject to payment by your executors of your debts, funeral expenses and any capital transfer tax) either be:

(1)   left outright to one person (eg, your wife) or a charity, or divided equally or in varying proportions between a number of persons or charities or both; or

(2)   left in trust for your family or relatives.

Your residuary estate is usually given to your executors on trust for sale. Their primary duty will be to sell all your property but they will be given power to postpone sale. They will also have power to distribute assets forming part of your residuary estate in kind so that individual beneficiaries could take shares or land without your executors having to sell them first.

The wording of the trust for sale clause usually requires your executors to convert all your property into cash and thereafter to pay debts, funeral and testamentary expenses and legacies. Capital transfer tax on your personal property (ie, cash, stocks and shares and personal effects) and on tax-free legacies is payable out of your residuary estate as a testamentary expense. Since F2A 1983 it is clear that this is also true of land in respect of deaths after 26 July 1983, unless you otherwise direct.

A separate clause — called the 'main beneficial clause' — sets out the distribution of residue between the beneficiaries. You may see the word 'trust' used in this clause in your solicitor's draft even though you have no intention of putting your property into trust on your death. The word 'trust' used in this context does not mean that a formal or 'strict' trust will come into being on your death. It is used to show that your executors do not take your property themselves as beneficial owners and that they hold it as trustees for the beneficiaries you have named. The word 'absolutely' is usually inserted after the name of a beneficiary of full age and this shows that he or she is immediately and unreservedly entitled to the gift.

You can, of course, leave shares of residue directly to your children. If any of them is under the age of 18 your executors will administer the funds for them until they are of age. The income of a child's share can be used for its maintenance, education and benefit but otherwise will be accumulated (p 102). As with contingent legacies, you can postpone the date at which your child becomes entitled to the capital of its share beyond 18.

In considering the division of your estate between your wife and children one of your main considerations will be to ensure that your wife is adequately provided for. While you might wish to leave a substantial portion of your estate to your children in order to reduce the capital transfer tax liability on your wife's death, no advantage would be gained if this left her without adequate means. There are a number of factors which you will need to take into account in deciding how much you should leave to your children, namely:

(1)   your own age and that of your wife;
(2)   the size of your estate and the income produced;
(3)   how much your wife will need to live on, bearing inflation in mind; and
(4)   how much tax will be saved by making a gift to your children if you die first.

It is, of course, clear that the higher the amount left to your children, the smaller will be the capital transfer tax liability on your wife's death. However, if this proportion is too high the cost of additional tax on your death could well outweigh the saving on your wife's death.

If you direct an equal division between your wife and children, your children may get less than their full one-half share. This is because your wife's share will be exempt from capital transfer tax and the children's share will therefore have to bear all the tax attributable to it as a non-exempt share of residue. This rule applies despite a contrary intention expressed in the will. (CTTA s41.)

Setting up a trust by will

Your wife's fund

Instead of giving your residuary estate to your wife absolutely you may consider giving her an entitlement only to the income from your residuary estate (or part of it) during her lifetime. After her death the capital will pass to your children then living or to other persons or to charity.

There is no capital transfer tax advantage in giving your wife a life interest as opposed to an absolute interest. Indeed, it could merely produce a deferment of the capital transfer tax liability which would then arise on your wife's death.

A life interest does have merit in that you can ensure that a measure of capital reaches your children. Many testators fear that their widow may remarry and that all their property would then pass to her new husband, thereby defeating the interests of their children. If you give your wife a life interest you can direct that it is to terminate on her remarriage. Also, if you have a large estate you may feel that your wife would not be able to manage your property satisfactorily, in which case you may prefer to have it managed for her by your trustees.

It is usually the best solution to give your wife a life interest and at the same time give your trustees unrestricted powers for advances and loans. There is no capital transfer tax advantage in lending capital as opposed to advancing it. The main advantage of a loan is that your trustees will know that the capital will be used in accordance with your wishes. This would not necessarily be the case if they were to advance capital to your wife which she could then deal with as she saw fit.

If you make your wife's life interest terminable on her remarriage such termination will be a transfer of value for capital transfer tax purposes. There will also be a deemed disposal for capital gains tax purposes at the time when she remarries. However, if you give your trustees an over-riding power of appointment this will ensure that they at least have a greater measure of control over the termination of the life interest.

Your children's fund

If you give your wife a life interest you may provide that on her death or remarriage your children are to take the capital of her fund. Their interest will then be contingent on their surviving both your wife and yourself. In addition you might wish to provide that they take their shares only on attaining a specified age, eg, 21 or 25 or even 30. If any one of your children fails to satisfy these conditions his or her share could then pass to his or her children in equal shares.

In addition to your wife's fund, or if you are widowed or divorced, you might wish to set aside a separate fund for your children. You would be advised to consider setting up an accumulation and maintenance settlement for your children. The main characteristics of such a settlement are:

(1)   One or more of your children will become entitled to the capital of the fund or to a life interest in the income of the fund on attaining a specified age not exceeding 25.

(2)   While any child is under age the income of its share will be accumulated so far as it is not applied for the maintenance, education or benefit of that child.

(3)   Not more than 25 years must have elapsed since the day on which you made the settlement or (if later) since the time when the settled property began to satisfy the requirements in (1) and (2) above or all the persons who are or have been beneficiaries are or were grandchildren of a common grandparent (or their widows, widowers, etc).

(4)   There will be a disposal for capital gains tax purposes as and when each child becomes entitled to his share or when an advance of capital is made but rollover relief is available (p 46).

(5)   Your trustees will be given a power of advancement or an over-riding power of appointment or of revocation.

● *An accumulation and maintenance settlement has substantial capital transfer tax advantages. A payment made to a beneficiary out of the settled property is not taxable. When a beneficiary becomes entitled to an interest in possession no tax is payable. Finally, the ten year charge (which would otherwise be levied on the property of a trust without an interest in possession) is not applicable to such a settlement (p 102).*

Discretionary trusts in a limited form

(*CTTA s144*)

● *You can provide for the rearrangement of the trusts of your will after your death without incurring capital transfer tax disadvantages. The way this is done is to provide for a discretionary trust (p 158) terminable by a power of appointment amongst a specified class of beneficiaries within two years. If the discretion is not exercised by your trustees within, say, 23 months of your death the other provisions of your will automatically take effect. These could provide for absolute interests, life interests in income or an accumulation and maintenance trust.*

The following are the advantages of such a provision:

(1)   *It enables your executors and trustees to draft your will after your death when they will be able to take account of lifetime gifts and of recent changes in tax law.*

(2)   *The termination of the discretionary trust itself will not attract a Capital Transfer Tax charge.*

(3)   *The distribution or trusts decided upon by your executors and trustees are treated for capital transfer tax purposes as having taken effect from your death.*

Precatory trusts

(*CTTA s143*)

● *You may express a wish as to the manner in which property you have left* to a beneficiary by will is to be distributed. Provided the legatee distributes the property within two years of your death, the transfer by him will not be a 'transfer of value' for capital transfer tax. Instead, the property will be treated as if you had left it to the transferee directly by your will.

Administrative clauses

Your will may include a number of technical or administrative clauses which extend the powers of your executors and trustees. The following clauses are usually inserted:

Maintenance and advancement
(TA 1925 Ss31 & 32)

Where there is a likelihood that your trustees will be administering funds for minors the statutory powers of maintenance out of income and advancement of capital will apply.

Under Section 31 your trustees have a discretion to pay income for or towards a minor's maintenance, education and benefit. They may pay only such part of the income as is reasonable having particular reference to other income available. If an interest is contingent on attaining an age greater than 18, once the child attains 18 your trustees *must* pay him the income until his interest vests. You may, as is often the case, wish to amend the terms of Section 31 by substituting age 21 for 18.

Under the power of advancement (Section 32) trustees have power to advance capital to an infant up to one half of his vested or presumptive share. Often the will provides for this statutory power to be modified to enable the trustees to advance the whole of a child's share.

Investment

You may find it convenient to give your trustees as wide a power of investment as possible. An investment clause may be included giving your trustees power to purchase freehold or leasehold property and to improve such property. The purchase of property for occupation by a beneficiary is not an investment and if you wish your trustees to have such a power you should specifically provide for it.

Borrowing

The statutory power of borrowing by trustees is restricted and it is often convenient to include a wider power of borrowing enabling trustees to borrow for investment purposes.

Nominees

Trustees have a duty to ensure that all of the trust property is brought under their control. If you wish your property to be held in the name of one trustee only or of a nominee for all of them you should make specific provision for this.

Carrying on a business

There is no general or statutory power for your trustees to carry on your business. If you would like your trustees to do so you should give them specific power. You may wish to appoint a separate set of trustees for this purpose.

Apportionments

It is usually convenient to exclude the legal apportionments required by the Apportionment Act 1870. This will apply not only on your death but at all other times. If this is not done, the Act requires that income due to your estate be considered as accruing from day to day with the result that so much of a payment relating to a period before your death will be apportioned to the capital of your estate. The exclusion of these apportionments eliminates the extra time and expense involved in making the necessary calculations which usually outweigh the advantages.

Appropriation

By Section 41 of the Administration of Estates Act 1925 your trustees are given wide powers to appropriate any part of your estate in order to satisfy any interest under your will. The power is only exercisable if the necessary consents have been obtained, usually from those adult persons who are absolutely entitled or from the person entitled to the income for life. Exercise of the power with consent gives rise to a stamp duty charge on the property distributed and it is therefore simpler to amend the terms of the Section by removing the need for consent.

Exporting trusts

If a beneficiary of a share of residue lives outside the UK you should consider giving your trustees power to appoint separate trustees of that share in a foreign country. This will facilitate the administration of your estate. This power will usually be combined with a general power enabling your trustees to carry on the general administration of your estate outside the UK.

Charging clauses

If one of your executors and trustees is a professional person, eg, a solicitor or an accountant, a standard clause is often inserted authorising him to take fees for work done in his professional capacity in connection with the administration of your estate.

It is also usual to provide that if your trustee receives remuneration from companies in which your estate has invested he may keep this for his own benefit.

Protecting trustees

It is usual to include a clause absolving your executors and trustees from liability if they have acted honestly and in good faith in the administration of your estate.

Altering and revoking your will

Your will has no effect until your death. It is therefore merely a declaration of intention and until your death it may be altered or revoked entirely.

You may alter any part of the text of your will before you sign it. If there are erasures, additions or deletions they must be signed, by both you and your witnesses. Otherwise the alteration may be invalid.

If you wish to make alterations after you have signed your will you should draw up a codicil to your will. A codicil is a supplement to your will. It sets out the amendments or additions you wish to make and confirms those parts which you wish to leave unaltered. It therefore brings your will down to the date of the codicil. A codicil must be signed and witnessed in exactly the same manner as a will.

Your will (or parts of it) may be revoked in one of the following ways:

(1)   *By destruction*
It is often customary to burn a will which it is intended to revoke. You do not, however, need to destroy your whole will in order for the revocation to take effect. If you tear off a sufficiently large or vital part of it (eg, the signatures) revocation will be effective. You must intend to revoke, as if you destroy your will by mistake it is not revoked. Someone other than yourself may destroy it on your instructions but you must be present while he does so and be aware of what he is doing.

(2)   *By making a new will or codicil (WA S20)*
The later will must either expressly revoke the earlier one or deal with all your property in such a way that previous wills are revoked by implication. A will revokes an earlier one so far as the earlier one is inconsistent with it, even if it contains no express revocation clause. It is always advisable to include an express revocation clause if you intend to revoke an earlier will.

(3)   *By your marriage (WA S18; AJA S18)*
If you marry your will is automatically revoked unless it is clear that you made your will contemplating your marriage to a particular person and that you intended your will not to be revoked by your marriage. In such a case your will will be valid provided you marry that particular person. Marriage to anyone else will automatically revoke your will. If it is clear from your will that at the time when it was made you were intending to marry a particular person and that you intended that a particular gift should not be revoked by

your marriage to that person, it is presumed that not only that gift, but all the other gifts are to take effect.

(4)   *By your divorce (AJA S18)*
        If after you have made your will, your marriage comes to an end, any appointment of your former spouse as executor will be void. Also any gift to your former spouse in the will shall be deemed to have lapsed. This rule gives way to any contrary intention which you express in your will.

Can a will be contested?

You should be satisfied with the contents of your will when you make it and ensure that its dispositions are in accordance with your wishes. Nevertheless it is possible that someone, eg, a relative or close friend, might contest your will after your death.

Your will might be contested on one of the following grounds:

(1)   That you did not have testamentary capacity at the time when you signed your will.

        A will that appears rational will be presumed valid since sanity is presumed unless the contrary is shown. Although the relevant time for testing mental capacity is when the will is signed, if you were competent when giving instructions for the will (but not at the time you signed it) the will would still be valid if at the time you signed you were aware of having given instructions and believed the will to be in accordance with them.

(2)   That you executed a later will which expressly or impliedly revoked the one it is intended to prove.

(3)   That the formalities for execution have not been complied with.

(4)   That unfair or improper pressure — 'undue influence' — was put upon you at the time when you made your will and it therefore does not reflect your true wishes. ('Undue influence' means that you were coerced into making a will you did not want to make eg, by fear, force or fraud.)

        The onus is on the person alleging undue influence, to prove it. In the first instance, the party seeking to establish the will must remove suspicion by proving that the testator knew what he was signing. Then the opponents of the will must prove fraud or undue influence.

(5)   That, as a result of a clerical error or unsatisfactory drafting, it is difficult to interpret all or part of your will and there is doubt as to

whether it carries out your true intentions. Although it is now possible to apply to the Court for rectification of a will, clear evidence that it fails to carry out the testator's intentions must be produced. As stated above, you should ensure that the wording of your will accurately reflects your intentions before signing it.

Generally, probate business is divided into 'common form' (where there is no dispute) and 'solemn form' (where there is a dispute). These are known respectively as non-contentious and contentious business and the first is dealt with by the Family Division of the High Court and the second by the Chancery Division.

Re-arranging your estate after your death

● *The terms of your will can effectively be rewritten after your death. Your beneficiaries can enter into a Deed of Family Arrangement varying the dispositions of your will. Provided such a deed is entered into within two years of your death, and the parties so elect, no capital transfer tax is payable on the variation itself. Rather, the variation is deemed to have been made by you and capital transfer tax is charged on this basis. Stamp Duty may, however, be payable (p 200).*

10 Administering the estate

Obtaining the grant

Why apply for a grant?

If a person dies leaving assets in the UK, a grant of representation must usually be obtained before the estate can be realised and distributed, unless his estate is very small.

The grant is a document issued by the Court and is the only formal authority from the Court that:

(1)   in the case of a grant of Probate, the will is valid;
(2)   the person or persons named in it are the persons entitled to administer the estate; *and*
(3)   all the assets of the deceased have been vested in the person or persons so entitled to enable them to administer the estate.

Thus the issue of the grant of representation to those entitled to it eliminates the risk of fraud in dealing with the deceased's property. Only those persons appointed by the Court will be able to obtain payment of the deceased's assets.

In England and Wales, where the deceased left a will and you have been appointed an executor, you will be entitled to apply for a grant of Probate. If the deceased has not left a will and you are entitled in priority to administer the estate under the intestacy rules (p 147) you will be entitled to apply for a grant of Letters of Administration. In Scotland, where special rules apply, the grant is known as Confirmation.

A grant of representation, whether it be Probate, Letters of Administration or Confirmation, will enable you to collect in all the assets of the estate. It will have to be produced to banks, building societies, insurance companies and other bodies in order to secure the release of funds into your name. In the case of stocks and shares, the grant is essential in order to change the name of the registered holder.

As an executor, you derive your authority from the will itself and the grant of Probate confirms your title. You can, therefore, even before the grant is issued, do various acts which do not require proof of your authority, such as paying debts, putting a house on the market or starting a Court action. An administrator has no authority until it is given to him by the Court and is therefore less able to commence administration immediately.

Small estates

Where an estate is very small it is sometimes possible for individual small amounts to be obtained without the necessity for a grant. This applies mainly to assets held by the Department for National Savings, Trustee Savings Bank and Building Societies, provided the amount involved is under £5,000. These bodies are not bound to make payment without production of a grant. They are entitled to ask for it, particularly if a complication should arise.

The above provisions do not apply to monies held by banks or insurance companies, although they may sometimes be prepared to pay over small amounts without a grant. A grant is usually required in the case of company shares or stock. However, if the holding is very small and the total estate does not exceed £5,000 individual companies may be prepared to register a transfer without sight of a grant, but against a suitable indemnity.

It is possible to obtain a letter of confirmation from the Capital Taxes Office that no CTT is payable where the estate is very small. CTT Form 22 should be completed and forwarded to the Enquiries Section, Capital Taxes Office, Rockley Road, London, W14.

Entitlement to a grant

Where there is a will
(NCPR 19)

If you are appointed sole executor you alone are primarily entitled to a grant of Probate. If you are one of two, three or four executors appointed you may apply for a grant on your own if the others are unavailable or undecided as to whether they wish to act. This is usually the best course if you wish administration to commence as soon as possible. Power will be reserved to grant what is known as 'double probate' to those executors who have not yet proved if they should wish to apply at a later stage.

If the deceased left a will but did not appoint an executor, or if an executor has been appointed but is unable or unwilling to act, the priority of entitlement to a grant is as follows:

(1)   Trustees of the residuary estate
(2)   Life-tenant of the residuary estate
(3)   Residuary beneficiaries
(4)   Specific legatees
(5)   Contingent specific legatees

In such a case the grant is known as Letters of Administration 'with will annexed'.

Where there is no will (intestacy)
(NCPR 21)

If no will can be found amongst the deceased's papers and there is no evidence that he made one it will be presumed that he died intestate. You will be entitled to share in the estate and to be one of the administrators if you are one of the next of kin of the deceased. The order of priority is as follows:

(1)   Wife or husband
(2)   Child, grandchild or great-grandchild
(3)   Parents (equally if more than one)
(4)   Brothers or sisters (equally)
(5)   Half-brothers or half-sisters
(6)   Grandparents (equally if more than one)
(7)   Uncles or aunts
(8)   Nephews or nieces

If there are a number of persons equally entitled the grant is usually issued to the first person to apply. A relative who is not within one of the above degrees of relationship is not entitled to any share of the estate. If no entitled relative can be found either in the UK or abroad the whole estate, after payment of debts, will pass to the Crown. In such a case the grant of Letters of Administration will be taken out by the Treasury Solicitor's office.

Application by a creditor

If all the executors (p 112) renounce Probate or no beneficiary wishes to apply for Letters of Administration, a grant may be issued to a creditor of the estate. This usually occurs when an estate is insolvent. The creditor will have to show in the oath that all persons beneficially entitled have either renounced or been cited (p 130). If an estate is insolvent the Court may grant Letters of Administration to any person it thinks fit.

Minors

(NCPR 31 & 32)

A minor can be appointed an executor but cannot act or take out a grant during his minority. If other adult executors have been appointed they can apply for Probate immediately. Power will then be reserved to the minor to prove the will when he reaches full age, at which time he obtains 'double probate'. If a minor has been appointed sole executor his parents may apply for a grant of Letters of Administration (with will annexed) for his use and benefit. When he reaches full age he may apply for what is known as 'cessate probate'. A cessate grant may be either of Probate or Letters of Administration and is, in effect, a renewal of the original grant.

The right of a minor who has been appointed executor to apply for a grant of Probate on attaining full age cannot be renounced by any person on his behalf. A minor's right to Letters of Administration may be renounced by a person appointed as his guardian by the registrar of the Court and authorised to renounce.

Foreign domicile

If a person dies domiciled in a foreign country and his will is valid and is in English naming executors whose duties compare with those of an English executor Probate may issue to those executors immediately. Otherwise a foreign will which deals with property in the UK may be admitted to proof if it can be established:

(1)   that the deceased was domiciled in a particular foreign country; *and*
(2)   that either the foreign Court has adopted the will or that the will is valid by the law of that country.

Evidence as to validity of the will is usually provided in the form of an affidavit of law sworn by a lawyer who has been practising in the particular country. Application for the grant in the UK is normally made by a person or persons acting under a power of attorney from the administrators of the estate in the country concerned. If no such person has been appointed, or if the deceased died abroad intestate, the affidavit of law must state who is, or would be, entitled to administer the deceased's estate in that country. The Inland Revenue Account (Form 201 — p 134), statement of domicile (p 139) and Administrators' Oath must be filed with the affidavit of law.

A person may make two wills, one dealing with his foreign property and the other with his English property, the intention being that they should take effect separately. If this is the case then, in applying for the grant of Probate in the UK, an official copy of the foreign will must also be filed. The grant will, however, issue only in respect of the English will.

Renouncing your right to a grant

You cannot be forced to act as an executor even if you have promised the deceased that you will act. Similarly, you cannot be forced to act as an administrator on an intestacy.

The right to a grant of Probate or Letters of Administration may be renounced by signing a document in standard form. The renunciation will not be final, however, until it has been filed at a Probate Registry.

Intermeddling

If you are thinking of renouncing your right to a grant of Probate you should decide as soon as possible. If you delay you risk becoming an 'executor de son tort' if you have 'intermeddled' with the estate. This means impliedly accepting the office of executor by your conduct, for example, describing yourself as executor, paying debts of the estate, or opening an executor's bank account. If you merely arrange the funeral or look after the deceased's pets, or even swear the executor's oath (p 139), this will not make you an 'executor de son tort'.

Even if you have not been appointed an executor under the will, dealing with the deceased's assets or advertising for claims may make you an 'executor de son tort'. The distinction between an executor who accepts office by implication as a result of his conduct, and the non-executor who intermeddles with the estate, is an important one. If you are appointed an executor and are held to have accepted the office by your conduct you can be compelled to take out a grant. If you have not been appointed you cannot be forced to act but you will be liable to account to the extent of the assets you have actually handled. You may also be liable to the extent of the debts you have released.

The right to a grant of Letters of Administration (with will annexed) may be renounced even though by your conduct you have impliedly accepted the office of administrator. You can never be compelled to take out such a grant. If no other person with an immediate interest in the estate is able or willing to act, a solicitor or trust corporation such as a bank may be appointed to act as administrator.

The chain of representation
(AEA S7)

If you die while acting as the sole or last surviving executor of an estate, having proved the will, your executor will become executor of that estate together with your own estate. This is called the 'chain of representation'. So long as the chain remains unbroken the last executor in the chain is the executor of every preceding testator. If any executor in the chain dies intestate or fails to appoint an executor in his will or fails to prove the will the chain is broken.

A subsequent administrator cannot act as executor of a preceding testator's estate, neither does the office of an administrator pass to his executor or administrator. If there has been a break in the chain of representation a new grant has to be taken out limited to the unadministered part of the estate. This is known as a 'grant de bonis non administratis'.

As an intending executor you should be aware of the implications of being the last link in the chain of representation. If the person who has appointed you was an accountant, solicitor or other professional person it is quite possible that he may have been acting as an executor when he died. As an executor in the chain you will have exactly the same powers and duties over the estate that you inherit as the original executor would have had. Even if you inherit an estate that has been almost completely administered you will still have to deal with any claims which may arise later. As executor of a proving executor you cannot renounce probate of the former will and only take probate of the one which specifically appoints you as executor.

Revocation of grants
(AEA Ss27 & 37)

A grant of Probate may be revoked by the Court if it has been obtained by fraud or if a later will is discovered. It may also be revoked if you become incapable of acting.

A grant of Letters of Administration may be revoked if a valid will is found. It may also be revoked if it has been granted to the wrong person, ie, where someone entitled in priority to the grantee is discovered later.

In general, acts made in good faith prior to revocation are protected so that conveyances or other transactions will not be rendered invalid. A purchaser from a personal representative is not therefore affected by a subsequent revocation of the grant.

Can the issue of a grant be stopped?

(NCPR 44)

If a person wishes to dispute a will he may enter what is known as a 'caveat' in either the Principal or any District Probate Registry. Such a person then becomes the 'caveator'.

A caveat is a stop-notice which prevents a grant of representation being issued without notice to the caveator. Once it has been entered, as executor you will have to issue a warning (this may only be done from the Principal Registry) to the caveator. The warning requests the caveator to indicate within eight days if he wishes to continue to oppose the issue of the grant. If he does so, you will have to prove the validity of the will in Court. If not, you may remove the caveat by filing an affidavit of service of the warning. A grant will then issue to you. A caveat expires automatically after six months unless renewed by the caveator.

A facility known as a 'standing search' is also available at the Principal Probate Registry only. The applicant for such a search will automatically be sent an official copy of any grant which complies with the details given in the application. Any such grant issued either not more than 12 months before the date of application or within six months thereafter will be sent to the applicant.

A citation is often used to deal with someone with a prior right to a grant. If the person cited does not enter an appearance to the citation he loses his rights to the grant. The person who issues the citation may then obtain a grant of Letters of Administration (with will annexed) or Letters of Administration if a simple intestacy is involved. Before a citation is issued a caveat must usually be entered.

How to obtain a grant in England and Wales

Personal application

You may make a personal application for a grant if you do not wish to instruct a solicitor. Personal applications may be made to the Personal

Application Department of the Probate Registry or Sub-Registry at which it is most convenient for you to attend. You will have to attend for an interview at a Registry or Sub-Registry or at a Probate Office. A list of Probate Offices together with the relevant forms may be obtained from Probate Personal Application Department, Principal Registry Family Division, 5th Floor, Golden Cross House, Duncannon Street, London, WC2N 4JF. There is no time limit within which an application must be made.

The following documents are required to be submitted:

(1)   Death certificate.
(2)   The will (if appropriate).
(3)   Return for capital transfer tax.
(4)   A guarantee (if appropriate).

The return for capital transfer tax is known as Cap Form 44. In this form you are required to give full particulars of the whole of the deceased's property. This means assets of any description such as cash, goods, investments, and arrears of salary as well as freehold and leasehold property. You are also required to answer questions in order that the Capital Taxes Office may determine whether capital transfer tax is payable on the deceased's death in respect of property other than his own. In particular you will need to know:

(1)   whether the deceased at the time of his death was entitled to an interest in any settled property whether as beneficiary or otherwise and whether he ceased to be entitled after 26 March 1974 or within ten years of his death;
(2)   whether the deceased made any gift or settlement after 26 March 1974 or within ten years of his death (details of the date of each gift, the name and address of the donee and the value of the property involved must be given);
(3)   whether an annuity becomes payable on the deceased's death under a superannuation scheme; and
(4)   whether the deceased held any property jointly with any other person (full details of the name of the other joint owner and the date of purchase, investment or deposit must be given).

The Cap Form 44 duly completed may be incorporated by the Registry in an Inland Revenue Account which you will also have to sign. In this Account you have to declare the truth and accuracy of the statements made and of the details provided in the form. Generally, in the case of small estates, the need for such an account is waived. If this is the case, the completed Cap Form 44 will be returned to you to keep.

When you attend for interview you will also have to swear (or affirm) as to the exact value of the estate.

A personal application fee (normally £1 per £1,000) is payable and also Probate Court fees, as follows:

Net value of estate	Probate Court fee
Not exceeding £10,000	Nil
£10,001–25,000	£40
£25,001–40,000	£80
over £40,000 but not exceeding £100,000	£2.50 per £1,000 or part thereof
over £100,000	£250 and for every additional £100,000 or part thereof a further £50

Capital transfer tax may be payable and all or part of this must be paid before a grant can be issued. After the grant has been issued the Capital Taxes Office will examine the account of the deceased's property. Enquiries may be sent to you and adjustments in value may be proposed. Depending on the values finally agreed additional capital transfer tax may be payable.

You may be required to obtain sureties to guarantee administration of the estate. The Registrar has power to refuse to accept a personal application, particularly if there is a dispute or the case presents special difficulties.

Application by a solicitor

You may wish to instruct a solicitor to prepare and submit the papers in application for the grant on your behalf, particularly if the estate is large and complicated. Depending on the type of grant required and the value of the estate your solicitor will need to lodge the following documents at a Probate Registry.

Inland Revenue Account

If a person is domiciled in the UK at the time of his death all of his assets wherever they may be situated form part of the gross value of his estate for capital transfer tax purposes. In the Inland Revenue Account you are required to provide a detailed inventory of all the assets and liabilities of the deceased's estate, the values being those at the date of death.

Excepted estates
An Inland Revenue Account is not required to be delivered in the estate (called an 'excepted estate') of any person who dies on or after 1 April 1983 where:

(1)   the total value of the estate is £40,000 or less;
(2)   the estate consists only of property which has passed under the deceased's will or intestacy or by nomination or survivorship;
(3)   not more than the higher of 10% of the total value or £2,000 consists of property situated outside the UK; *and*
(4)   the deceased died domiciled in the UK and has made no lifetime gifts chargeable to capital transfer tax.

Unless within 35 days of the grant the Inland Revenue issue a notice requiring completion of an account, you will at the end of that time automatically be discharged from any liability to capital transfer tax. If you obtain a grant without delivery of an account and later discover that the estate is not an 'excepted estate' you must then deliver an account of all the property in the estate. The account must be delivered within six months of the time when you discover that the estate is not an 'excepted estate'.

Non-excepted estates

In all other cases an Inland Revenue Account must be completed and, once signed by you, be delivered to the Capital Taxes Office. There are two forms in current use — CAP Form 202 and CAP Form 200.

CAP Form 202

CAP Form 202 is a short form of account. It is for use where:

(1)   the deceased died on or after 27 March 1981 domiciled in the UK;
(2)   the estate consists only of property which has passed under the deceased's will or intestacy or by nomination or beneficially by survivorship (p 148);
(3)   the whole of the deceased's property is situated in the UK and its total net value after deducting any Exemptions and Reliefs claimed does not exceed the threshold above which capital transfer tax is payable at the date of death (p 82).

CAP Form 200

The full account Form CAP 200 is used in all other cases. This is a 12 page form and is divided into three sections. In addition, on page 3 of the form you are required to answer a number of questions in order that the Capital Taxes Office may determine whether tax is payable on the deceased's death in respect of property other than his own. These questions are similar to those asked in the return (CAP Form 44) to be completed in personal application cases (p 132).

The three sections of the Form 200 are as follows:

Sections 1A and 1B

In Section 1A you must account for all movable property including stocks and shares, bank and building society accounts, premium savings bonds, pensions, life policies and personal effects. Liabilities incurred by the deceased are deductible from the gross value of the property in Section 1A. Household liabilities which are settled on a monthly or quarterly basis, eg, rates, gas and electricity, may have to be apportioned to the date of death. Reasonable funeral expenses are deductible, but not the cost of a tombstone.

Section 1A property is known as 'non-instalment option' property. This means that you are required to pay any capital transfer tax on the net value of such property in full on delivery of the Inland Revenue Account.

In Section 1B you must account for the deceased's immovable property, such as freehold or leasehold property, held in his sole name or as tenant in common with another (p 117), business interests and shares in private companies. If there are liabilities relative to Section 1B property, such as a mortgage, these are deductible in computing the net value for capital transfer tax purposes.

Section 1B property is known as 'instalment option' property for the purpose of capital transfer tax. Tax on the net value of such property, after taking into account business and other reliefs, may be elected to be paid by ten annual instalments. The first instalment (or the full amount of the tax) is due and payable 6 months following the month in which the death occurred. There is no harm in electing to pay by instalments at this stage. In the case of land or other income-producing assets there may be particularly good reasons for doing so. However, interest on unpaid CTT now runs at 6% and it may be better in the long run not to involve the estate in an extra liability. If at a later stage it is clear that there will be alternative finance available all the outstanding tax can be paid off at any time.

Section 2
In this section you must account for all other property of the deceased (whether or not subject to the instalment option) for which you are liable to pay capital transfer tax. This includes foreign property and jointly owned property which passes by survivorship (p 148). Liabilities due to persons outside the UK are normally allowed against the value of foreign property.

Section 3
Details of all other property (whether or not subject to the instalment option) in which the deceased had a beneficial interest immediately before his death are inserted in this section. If the deceased had a life interest in a will trust or settlement such an interest will terminate on his death. The capital value of the trust fund is shown in Section 3 and will be added to the deceased's free estate in order to ascertain the rate of capital transfer tax payable. The proportion of the tax liability relative to the trust fund will, however, fall on the trustees of the will or settlement concerned.

Property in Section 3 should be segregated according to whether or not the instalment option is available and whether or not capital transfer tax is to be paid on delivery of the account.

Providing valuations

In the Inland Revenue Account you must enter each item at its 'principal value'. This means the estimated price which it would fetch if sold at the date of the deceased's death.

Stocks and shares should be entered at the price at which they were quoted on the Stock Exchange at the date of death. For probate purposes, quoted securities are valued at one quarter up from the lower to the higher limit of quotation. Most stockbrokers provide valuations for probate purposes and their charges are based on a fee scale. If the deceased had only a few holdings you may wish to value the securities yourself by reference to the Stock Exchange Daily Official List. Note that if a security is quoted 'ex dividend' the whole of the net dividend (or interest payment) should be entered separately.

You should take steps to establish the open market value of any freehold or leasehold property owned by the deceased at the date of death. Very often the deceased's family or relatives are able to provide you with a figure on the basis of discussions which they have had with local estate agents. In most cases where capital transfer tax is payable the valuation (which either has been arrived at by agreement with the family or supplied by a professional valuer) will be passed to the District Valuer for his opinion after the grant has been issued.

If capital transfer tax is payable on the estate and interest has started to run you would probably wish to obtain the grant as quickly as possible. Any reasonable estimate of the value of the deceased's house or other property can be provided, particularly if there is no time to obtain a more exact figure. There would be no particular advantage in inserting a low figure since this would be subject to agreement with the Capital Taxes Office in due course. While there might be an initial saving in terms of interest on any borrowing for capital transfer tax this would be offset by further interest payable on the final figures in due course.

If the estate is not taxable, the Capital Taxes Office will not be too concerned with the valuations you have provided. In such a case, however, you should still avoid inserting a particularly low figure. The probate valuations that you provide will form the base cost in any future capital gains tax calculation on a sale and you would therefore wish to establish a reasonably high (but realistic) figure.

Raising capital transfer tax

It is usual to finance the initial payment of tax by means of a bank loan although it is also possible to obtain a loan for this purpose from a building society. This enables the whole amount to be obtained quickly from one source. Once the grant has been obtained you can then give consideration to the best way in which the borrowing is to be repaid. Interest paid within one year of the loan is deductible for income tax purposes against estate income of the same year. There is no relief for interest paid on an ordinary overdraft and it will therefore be necessary to open an executor's loan account for this purpose.

There are other ways to finance payment of capital transfer tax which could result in a substantial saving to the estate. If the estate includes a life policy the company concerned may be prepared to pay the proceeds direct to the Revenue without the necessity for sight of the grant. If there is a building society account the body concerned may be prepared to release the funds either if the balance is less than £5,000 or if payment is effected direct to the Inland Revenue.

A beneficiary may be prepared to lend money to the estate. If the deceased held a joint bank or building society account with a member of his family or a close relative, the survivor would be in a position to make cash available immediately to the estate. This would avoid borrowing from the bank and the consequent expense of high rates of interest. If the lender is in agreement the loan can be interest-free or at less than the market rate. This would not have adverse capital transfer tax consequences.

Foreign Domicile

If the deceased was domiciled outside the UK CAP Form 201 should be used to account for the UK estate. This form is similar to the Form 200 except that the country of domicile must be stated. A short statement should be submitted with the Form 201 stating the circumstances relied upon to establish the foreign domicile and giving a short history of the deceased's life movements. The completed form together with the statement of domicile should be sent to the Controller, Capital Taxes Office, Lynwood Road, Thames Ditton, Surrey, for assessment prior to submission to the Probate Registry.

Calculation of tax payable

The net values from each of the sections of the Form 200 (or 201) are carried to the section headed 'Exemptions and reliefs against capital' on p 10. Here you are required to give details of any exemptions or reliefs claimed against the property described in each section. The net values and the amounts of the exemptions claimed are both carried to the summary on page 11. A total figure for aggregate chargeable transfers on death is arrived at taking into account all transfers made prior to death.

The total amount of tax payable is calculated by reference to tables (see Example 9 — p 85). Tax in respect of non-instalment option property is payable immediately and a formula is used to calculate the amount of tax referable to this property. A similar calculation is needed to arrive at the proportion of tax payable on instalment option property. If the tax on this property is to be paid by instalments the number of instalments and the amount of tax now to be paid must be inserted. If more than six months have elapsed since the month in which the death occurred interest at the rate of 6% per annum must be calculated.

It is necessary to carry forward the totals for tax and interest to the further summary on page 12 of the Form 200 (or 201). The completed

Account once signed by you, together with a cheque for the amount of tax immediately payable, ie, tax on non-instalment option property plus those instalments which have already become due plus interest (if applicable), should be sent to the Central Accounting Office (Cashier), Barrington Road, Worthing, West Sussex, BN12 4XH. The receipted account, once returned, must be lodged with the other documents mentioned below at a Probate Registry in application for the grant.

The Executors' Oath

If you have been appointed an executor under a will and you intend to prove that will then you must swear the Oath for Executors. In the Oath you recite:

(1)   that the document now produced to you is the true will of the deceased;
(2)   the full name and address and domicile of the deceased;
(3)   the date of death of the deceased;
(4)   that you are the sole executor or one of the executors or the surviving executor named in the will;
(5)   whether there is any land which was settled before the death (and not by the will) and remains settled notwithstanding the death;
(6)   the gross and net values of the estate (if the estate is an 'excepted estate' (p 134) all that you will be required to swear is that, as the case may be, the net value of the estate does not exceed £10,000 or exceeds £25,000 but does not exceed £40,000); *and*
(7)   an affirmation that you will duly administer the estate according to the law and deliver up the grant to the High Court when required to do so.

The original will

The original will is an exhibit to the Oath and must be signed by you when you swear the Oath. At the same time it should be counter-signed by the solicitor who has taken the Oath. If the original will has been lost the Court may on application grant Probate of a will contained in a copy, but will want convincing that the original has not been revoked by destruction.

The Administrators' Oath

If you are an intending administrator under the intestacy rules you must swear the Oath for Administrators. In addition to general information about the deceased and the estate similar to that required by the Executor's Oath, the Administrators' Oath states:

(1)   that the deceased died intestate;
(2)   your relationship to the deceased, eg, lawful wife, son, brother, etc;
(3)   that all those with a prior right to a grant have been cleared off, ie, have either renounced or been cited; *and*

(4)   whether or not a minority or life interest arises under the intestacy.

The guarantee
(AEA S8; NCPR 38)

In certain cases if you are an intending administrator you may be obliged to find one or more sureties to enter into a guarantee that you will perform your obligations as administrator. Usually two sureties are required but if the proposed surety is a corporation such as an insurance company, or the gross value of the estate is less than £500, one surety is sufficient. All sureties other than a corporation must show that they are solvent up to the amount of the guarantee, which is usually the gross amount of the estate.

Probate Court fees

These are payable on the net value of the estate (p 83). The amount payable must accompany the documentation in application for the grant. Application may be made to the Principal Probate Registry at Somerset House, Strand, London WC2, or to any one of a number of district probate registries or sub-registries in England and Wales, whatever the value of the estate and the place of residence of the deceased.

Dealing with the assets

After you have established your title by obtaining a grant of representation your next duty is to collect in the assets of the estate, pay the debts and funeral expenses and thereafter distribute the estate to the beneficiaries.

Collecting the assets

Frequently the will includes a bequest of personal effects. If there are items of value they should be deposited with the bank or other agent for safekeeping. Clearly if it appears that the administration of the estate is going to be relatively simple personal effects can be released to the beneficiary entitled to them. A receipt should be obtained.

You will need to produce the grant to the deceased's bank, building society and life insurance company, among others, in order to obtain payment of monies due to the estate. Once the grant has been registered you will be sent a repayment claim form for signature. If the deceased had a life insurance or retirement annuity policy you will have to send the original policy to the company's claims department. In the case of building society or National Savings Bank accounts, if the money is not urgently required these may be left open until nearer the time of actual distribution.

If the deceased held stocks and shares the certificates are often held by the bank for safekeeping together with the title deeds for any land assets such as the family home. You will have to sign an authority to send all the securities or other documents held by the bank to you or your solicitor.

It will probably be convenient to open an executor's account in order to deal with the administration of the estate. You might already have opened such an account before the grant was obtained if there were urgent liabilities which required settlement. It is usually useful to open an executor's account as soon as possible after the grant has been obtained in order that cash, cheques and dividends can be paid in without delay. If this is not possible the bank may be prepared to accept dividends and cheques payable to the deceased for credit to the account in his name, even though all payments and direct debits will have been frozen at the date of death. Sometimes the bank is prepared to open a separate suspense account to accommodate dividends and other payments which are received prior to the grant.

Stocks and shares will continue to be registered in the name of the deceased until the grant has been received for registration. The certificates covering the deceased's holding should accompany the grant for endorsement into your name as executor or administrator. Once the grant has been registered with the company registrar dividends will be sent to you if you are sole, or first named, executor or administrator. These should continue to be paid into the estate account as income of the estate until all the liabilities (including administration expenses) have been settled.

Insurance

You should give attention to the question of insurance cover as soon as possible after death. Policies in the deceased's name should be endorsed with the names of the personal representatives and your interest noted. If the deceased possessed a car the insurers should be informed of the death as soon as possible. Unless the car is to be sold, new insurance cover should be obtained.

Dealing with land

If the deceased had a family then they will in all probability continue to occupy the family home, at least for the time being. If this is the case your administrative duties with regard to that property are minimal.

If the deceased's house or flat remains unoccupied and has not been specifically bequeathed by the will you should see that it is sufficiently secured pending sale. If possible a neighbour should be asked to keep an eye on the premises. There is nothing to prevent you putting the property on the market before the grant has been obtained, but it is as well to ensure that you take the advice of at least two estate agents in the area as to the most suitable asking price. The widest market should be aimed at since otherwise you may be open to criticism on the grounds that the property was insufficiently advertised or that the asking price was too low (or, indeed, too high). Once a suitable offer has been received there is no harm in consulting the principal residuary beneficiaries as to whether they feel it should be accepted. The ultimate decision however, is yours alone.

If the property is leasehold you will need to establish both outstanding and potential liabilities under the lease. When you come to distribute the estate you will need to be satisfied that all outstanding liabilities have been settled and that a sufficient fund has been set aside to answer any future claims under the lease. You will then be able to distribute the estate in due course without incurring any personal liability under the terms of the lease.

Carrying on a business

As personal representative you can only carry on the deceased's business if you are given express or implied authority in the deceased's will. Otherwise you may only do so for the purposes of sale or winding up or assenting to a beneficiary under the will. You can only use in the business those assets which the testator used at his death unless you have been given wider powers under the will.

You will be personally liable for any debts which you incur in carrying on the deceased's business. You will, however, be able to indemnify yourself from those assets which you have been authorised to use.

The deceased's business debts should be paid in priority to any debts which you incur in carrying on the business. If the deceased's creditors have formally consented to the carrying on of the business you have a right of indemnity against any debts which you incur out of the estate and not merely out of the business assets which you use.

Partnership

(PA 1890 Ss 33, 39, 42 & 43)

If the deceased was a partner in a firm or business you will need to consider the estate's interest in the business in the light of the partnership agreement. You should obtain a copy of the partnership agreement and the latest partnership accounts as soon as possible.

A partnership is dissolved by the death of one of the partners unless there is an agreement to the contrary. If the partnership agreement makes no provision for dealing with the death of a partner or if there is no such agreement then statute law applies.

As personal representative of a deceased partner you may apply to the Court to wind up the business. This would involve sale of the assets, payment of debts and distribution of any surplus assets among the surviving partners and the estate.

You should ensure that settlement of the deceased's share is completed within a reasonable time. When distribution does take place you are entitled to see the final partnership accounts, which should follow on from the last accounts. The deceased's estate is jointly liable with the surviving partners for the debts of the partnership outstanding at death. On distribution you should therefore ensure that all such debts have been paid, or obtain a suitable indemnity from the surviving partners. The share due to the estate of a deceased partner is deemed to be a debt due at the date of death or dissolution. If there is no final settlement of accounts then, unless otherwise agreed, you may claim either:

(1)   such share of the profits made since the dissolution as is attributable to the use of the deceased partner's share of the assets; *or*
(2)   interest at 5% per annum on that share.

You do not have this right if the continuing partners validly exercise an option to purchase the deceased's interest.

Dealing with the liabilities

The solvent estate
(AEA 1925 Sch 1, Part II)

Having obtained payment of sufficient of the estate's assets your next concern is to discharge all the liabilities as promptly as possible.

If the family home continues to be occupied early settlement of household expenses such as rates, gas and electricity is usually desirable. The family should be advised to settle such debts as soon as possible after death since reimbursement from the estate can be arranged later. Funeral expenses may also be paid straight away but if this would cause hardship they can be settled after the grant has been issued.

Once cash is available from the realisation of assets or the sale of shares you can give attention to discharging the major liabilities of the estate. The most important debt is usually the loan for capital transfer tax and you may well be under some pressure to repay this as quickly as possible. If there are sufficient funds in the bank or building societies these may be used, otherwise you may need to sell securities. You will need to obtain expert advice before completing a sale, otherwise you may be open to criticism from beneficiaries and, possibly, even personal liability if it is made without guidance as to value. Besides stockbrokers, you may need to consult accountants or other professional advisers as there may be tax or other personal considerations to be borne in mind.

Normally all debts are payable within one year of death, but in practice you should settle them as soon as is convenient. As a rule, all the property in which the deceased had an interest which did not terminate on his death may be used for the payment of debts.

In practice, the will usually provides for all debts (including testamentary and administration expenses) to be paid out of the residuary estate. From the above it follows that on an intestacy all of the deceased's property may be used for the payment of debts.

Tax liabilities

Tax liabilities usually take some time to be finalised and if they are likely to be substantial a provisional figure may be given in the Inland Revenue Account. The Revenue usually wish to see a copy of the grant and, if appropriate, the probated will. If a tax assessment had been received by the deceased shortly before death and has not been paid this should be settled as soon as possible to avoid an interest charge. Generally, an assessment in respect of the deceased's tax liabilities is payable within 30 days of the date of issue of the grant.

As personal representative you will have to sign the tax return in respect of income and capital gains for the period prior to the date of death. You are also required to complete a tax return for the administration period covering the income and, if any, capital gains of the estate. An assessment will then be issued in your name.

Finalising the capital transfer tax liability

When completing the Inland Revenue Account you may have submitted a provisional or estimated valuation of the deceased's house or personal effects. This value may have been estimated or arrived at by agreement with the beneficiaries and may not reflect the true market value of the particular asset. The Capital Taxes Office will examine the Inland Revenue Account and may raise observations and queries on particular values, particularly if the estate is taxable. In most cases values are agreed without the need to engage a professional valuer. If agreement cannot be reached you may have to instruct an estate agent, chartered surveyor or other professional valuer to negotiate with the Revenue on your behalf.

If your original estimate has to be corrected additional tax and interest may become payable. Such alterations in values, together with details of any other adjustments in the assets and liabilities of the estate, must be reported to the Capital Taxes Office in a form known as a Corrective Account (CAP Form D3). This form is used to report any changes in the estate which have come to light since the papers in application for the grant were originally lodged. Once the completed form has been considered by the Capital Taxes Office a 'corrective assessment' may become necessary if additional tax is payable. Alternatively, a refund of capital transfer tax may be due to the estate.

Your liability as personal representative

You are personally liable to an unpaid creditor or beneficiary but your liability is limited to the extent of the assets of the estate. However, if you have been guilty of wilful default or some other wrongful behaviour whereby a loss is caused to the estate by some neglect or mistake on your part you may be liable beyond the assets you have received.

Advertising for claims
(TA 1925 S27)

You are liable for all the outstanding debts of the deceased at the date of death. Even if you pay all known debts you remain at risk of a claim from an unknown creditor. The only way to protect yourself is to publish notices for claims in accordance with the provisions of the Trustee Act 1925. Provided that you delay distribution until the expiration of the period of the notices (at least two months) you will not be liable for later claims. If you have not protected yourself and are compelled to pay a debt personally you can seek an indemnity from the beneficiaries if you were not aware of the debt when you distributed the estate. You may also seek an indemnity if the debt was a contingent one, even if you did know of it.

The liability of a recipient of assets

A creditor or beneficiary has a personal claim for a refund from the recipient of wrongfully distributed assets, but only to the extent that he has no remedy against you personally. The claim does not carry interest.

Family provision claims
(IPFDA 1975; MFPA 1984)

Where a person dies domiciled in England and Wales certain persons may make application to the Court within six months of the date of the grant for reasonable financial provision out of the net estate. The following are entitled to apply:

(1)   A wife or husband of the deceased; persons whose marriages are dissolved or annulled overseas now also have the right to apply.
(2)   A former wife or husband who has not remarried; note, however, that restrictions may be imposed in divorce proceedings on any future application by either spouse for provision under the 1984 Act.
(3)   A child of the deceased (including an illegitimate or adopted child).
(4)   Any other person who has been treated as a child of the family.
(5)   Any person whom the deceased was maintaining immediately before his death.

If the Court is satisfied that the deceased's will does not make reasonable financial provision for the applicant it may order suitable provision, which may take any of the following forms:

(1)   Periodical payments.
(2)   Lump sum.
(3)   Transfer of property.
(4)   Acquisition of property out of the estate.
(5)   Variation of any ante or post nuptial settlement.

If such a claim is made against the estate, it does not mean that the validity of the will itself is being questioned. The claimant is maintaining only that he or she is entitled to financial provision out of the estate.

Thus a claim may also be made where the deceased died intestate or partially intestate.

Once such a claim has been made you should adopt an impartial position between the beneficiaries and the claimant. Your duty is to see that the interests of children are properly represented. At the same time you must provide information about the estate when required to do so. If there are minor children involved any arrangement in settlement must be referred to the Court. Otherwise a compromise can be confirmed by deed without the necessity for Court proceedings.

Once you have been put on notice of a potential claim you cannot distribute the estate until it is settled. This is because you cannot be sure that the dispositions under the will will not be altered or varied.

The insolvent estate

(AEA 1925 S34)

If the assets of the estate are insufficient to meet all the liabilities then the estate is insolvent. If this is the case then debts must be paid in the following order, whether or not the estate is administered through the Court:

(1)   Funeral, testamentary and administration expenses.
(2)   Specially preferred debts, eg, money due to a Friendly Society or to a Savings Bank from its officer.
(3)   Preferred debts, eg, rates and taxes, and contributions payable by the deceased under the National Insurance Acts.
(4)   Ordinary debts.
(5)   Deferred debts, eg, a business loan by one spouse to another.

This order cannot be varied by will. The same rules apply in the case of an insolvent estate as in bankruptcy, particularly those with regard to secured creditors.

You need not continue with the administration of an insolvent estate if you do not wish to do so. You may apply to the Court for an administration order. Alternatively, any beneficiary or creditor may take proceedings to administer such an estate.

If you do continue to administer an insolvent estate you should take particular care to ensure that you do not become personally liable. If you pay a debt of a lower degree with full knowledge of the existence of a debt of a higher degree you could be held personally liable to make good the deficit. However, you will not be liable if you pay a debt in full in good faith without knowledge of the existence of creditors of equal degree and with no reason to believe that the estate is insolvent.

The rule is that if you are not certain whether the estate is going to be solvent or not you should only pay priority debts in full, ie, testamentary and administration expenses. Once the resources of the estate are fully known you will then be in a position to pay those debts of a lower priority which qualify.

Distributing the estate

Paying legacies
(AEA 1925 S44)

A vested legacy (p 114) is normally payable one year from death, but there is nothing to prevent you paying such a legacy during this year if you consider it safe to do so. However, a legatee cannot require you to pay his legacy before the end of the year.

A contingent legacy (p 114) is payable at the time when the contingency occurs. In either case, interest at the rate of 5% per annum begins to run from the time when the legacy is payable.

Debts are paid in priority to legacies. If there are insufficient assets to pay all the debts and the legacies in full then specific legacies (such as gifts of personal chattels) must be dealt with first. Thereafter cash legacies diminish rateably according to their value — this is known as abatement. If there are a number of debts and it is uncertain whether there is likely to be any residue you should pay legacies with caution. If you overpay a beneficiary you have no right of recovery unless you can show that you made the payment without knowledge of a subsequent claim against the estate.

Specific legacies (p 113) carry with them any income accrued since the testator's death. If there is a specific gift of land in the will the beneficiary will have to pay any administrative costs which may accrue. This would also be the case if there is a specific gift of valuables which have to be stored in a secure place such as a safe deposit.

If the will includes a legacy to a minor you will probably be given authority to pay the money to the child's parent or guardian and to get a good discharge for doing so. If you have no such authority it will be necessary for the legacy to be held for the child until he reaches 18, since he cannot give a valid receipt for it. You may, if you wish, appoint separate trustees of the legacy and you would then have no further responsibility for it. If a legacy to a child is contingent on his attaining a specific age you will have to set aside a fund from which the legacy can be paid when the contingency is satisfied. Once the administration of the estate has been completed it will be possible for new trustees of the legacy to be appointed.

Distribution on intestacy
(AEA 1925; IEA 1952; FPA 1966)

All the property of a person who dies intestate is held by his administrators upon trust for sale. There is power to postpone sale and the administrators may appropriate property in kind in satisfaction of a beneficiary's share. The rules for distributing an estate on an intestacy are as follows:

(a)   *Where the deceased left a widow or widower and surviving children*
As widow or widower you take all the personal effects absolutely and a statutory legacy of £40,000. In addition you are entitled to the income for life from one half of the rest of the estate, which on your death reverts to your children. The other half of the residue passes to your children on what is known as the 'statutory trusts' (p 148). 'Children' includes illegitimate or adopted children.

(b)   *Where the deceased left a widow or widower and no surviving children but also left parents or brothers and sisters*
As widow or widower you take all the personal effects, a statutory legacy of £85,000 and one half of the rest of the estate. The other half goes to the deceased's parents or, if they have not survived, to the deceased's brothers or sisters on the statutory trusts (p 148).

(c)   *Where the deceased left a widow or widower but no children, no parents and no brothers or sisters*
As widow or widower you take the whole estate absolutely.

It follows that other more distant relatives only take an interest in the event of the deceased not being survived by a husband or wife, children, parents or brothers or sisters.

The surviving spouse's rights

(AEA 1925 S47)

Capitalization of a life interest
As surviving spouse you have the right to demand a capital sum in lieu of your life interest. You must exercise your right within 12 months of the date of the grant. The amount of the lump sum payable must be calculated in accordance with rules laid down by statute. If all the children are over 18 and of full capacity, agreement may be reached as to the capital sum to be distributed without the necessity for a calculation.

The family home
If you were living in the family home at the date of death and the house was owned by the deceased you have the right to demand that the house be appropriated towards all or part of any absolute interest you may have under the intestacy. Election to this effect must be made within 12 months of the grant. You do not have this right if the deceased's interest was a tenancy which would expire or could by notice be terminated within two years from death. The value at which appropriation takes effect is the value at the date of appropriation, not the value at the date of death.

The statutory trusts

(AEA 1925 S47(1); FLRA 1969 S3(2))

Where property passes on an intestacy to children, brothers or sisters or uncles or aunts it is held on the statutory trusts. This means that the property is held in trust in equal shares for those members of the class who attain 18 or marry before then. If any members die before the deceased, leaving children living at the date of his or her death, those children take the share which their parent would have taken had he or she survived (provided they in turn attain 18 or marry).

Partial intestacy

(AEA 1925 S49)

If the deceased left a will but it only disposes of part of his property then a partial intestacy arises. If this is the case, any benefit which you receive as surviving spouse under the will must be brought into account against the statutory legacy of £40,000 or £85,000 as the case may be. Similarly, any gifts by will to children must be brought into account against their share.

Vesting assets in beneficiaries

(AEA 1925 S36)

Having settled the liabilities of the estate you are now in a position to distribute it by transferring property into the names of the beneficiaries. If the majority of actual and prospective liabilities are ascertained early in the course of administration interim distributions may be made. These will be shown in the administration accounts which set out the assets and liabilities of the estate and the transactions which have taken place since the grant was received.

Property is vested in a beneficiary by means of an assent. In the case of personalty, ie, cash or movable property, an assent can generally be informal. Stocks and shares are transferred by means of a standard share transfer form. A legal estate in land will not pass out of your hands as personal representative unless you execute a written assent in favour of a beneficiary. The assent must be signed by you and name the person in whose favour it is given. The significance of an assent is that until the property is transferred it remains at your disposal for administration purposes. You continue to be responsible for its security. Once the transfer has taken place the property belongs in law to the beneficiary and you are no longer responsible for it. You may, however, retain out of a legacy or a share of residue a debt due to the estate from the beneficiary.

Accounts

If the estate is relatively small, it is advisable to prepare a simple administration and distribution account on a single sheet of paper. If you are dealing with a complex estate you may wish to instruct accountants to prepare full and comprehensive accounts.

You are entitled to ask beneficiaries to approve the accounts. Until approval is received you may withhold final distribution of the residuary estate since you cannot be sure that there will be no further administration expenses.

If it is subsequently alleged that a loss to the estate has been caused by neglect or mistake on your part an administration action may follow. You would then be entitled to an indemnity from the estate in respect of proper expenses incurred in connection with such an action. These would fall to be included in the estate's administration expenses.

Discharge and trusteeship

Once all the capital transfer tax liabilities of the estate have been finalised you may apply for a certificate of discharge from the Capital Taxes Office. The certificate in Form CAP 30, known as 'clearance', discharges you from any further claims for capital transfer tax in respect of those assets which you have disclosed in the Inland Revenue Account and any subsequent Corrective Account. You are not, of course, covered by this certificate in respect of assets which come to light at a later stage. Usually, the date of the clearance certificate is taken as the date on which administration ceases. If a trust has been created by the will or if property is to be administered for a minor the duties of the trustees commence on this date.

The position of personal representatives is very similar to that of trustees and their rights and duties are, except where a contrary intention appears, governed by the same statute law. There are some important differences, however, as follows:

(1)   The primary function of personal representatives is to distribute the estate, while that of trustees is to hold it.
(2)   The authority of trustees is always joint, whereas that of personal representatives is joint and several (p 144) over personal property and joint in respect of land. Thus one of several personal representatives may validly dispose of personal property, but not land.
(3)   The provisions of the Trustee Act 1925 with regard to the appointment of new trustees and retirement do not apply to personal representatives (p 144).
(4)   The period of limitation in respect of actions against personal representatives by beneficiaries is 12 years where claims to the personal estate of a deceased person are concerned. The period in respect of actions against trustees is 6 years.

11 Income tax — Trusts and estates

Trusts

A trust is brought into existence when a person (the settlor) transfers assets to trustees for the benefit of third parties (the beneficiaries). Another word for a trust is a settlement. A trust may also be created under a will when a person (the testator) sets aside the whole or a portion of his estate to be administered (by trustees) for the benefit of his heirs or other beneficiaries. Because trusts are important capital tax planning tools, their legal aspects are considered in Chapter 12 (p 158) and their CGT aspects in Chapter 5 (p 50). CTT aspects are dealt with in Chapter 8 (p 101) and this chapter covers certain income tax points of which you should be aware, if considering creating a settlement.

Income tax rates

Income tax is chargeable at basic and higher rates as shown in Table 9 below. There is also a 15% additional rate on investment income. This applied to the investment income of individuals above a threshold (£7,100 for 1983–84) but has been removed for their income arising after 5 April 1984. The higher rates do not normally apply to trusts but the basic rate (30%) is so applicable. The additional rate still applies to all the investment income of discretionary trusts and accumulation ones.

The basic rate band and five higher rate bands for future years will be increased in line with the retail price index. The index comparison will be made for the previous December each year and the figures will be rounded up to the next £100. (Parliament has the power to modify the effects of indexing the income tax bands.)

Table 9: Basic and higher rates for 1984-85

Slice of income	Rate	Total income (after allowances)	Total tax
£15,400 (£0-15,400)	30%	£15,400	£4,620
£2,800 (£15,400-18,200)	40%	£18,200	£5,740
£4,900 (£18,200-23,100)	45%	£23,100	£7,945
£7,500 (£23,100-30,600)	50%	£30,600	£11,695
£7,500 (£30,600-38,100)	55%	£38,100	£15,820
Remainder	60%		

Note The 15% investment income surcharge (additional rate) no longer applies for *individuals*.

● *The ending of the investment income surcharge for individuals makes it more attractive to distribute income to them from discretionary settlements (p155). The respective beneficiaries will be able to reclaim their share of the 15% additional rate suffered by the settlement (subject to any extra higher rate tax).*

Trusts where the settlor or testator is deceased

Where the settlor or testator has died, the taxation of trusts normally follows simple rules. The trust is assessed to basic rate income tax and sometimes additional rate (p 151) on its income. Some of this tax will have been deducted at the source (eg taxed interest). Capital gains tax is charged on any capital gains of the trust (p 101).

The tax assessments are normally made in the joint names of the trustees who pay the tax out of the trust funds.

No higher rate tax is paid by the trustees but when the income is distributed to any of the beneficiaries this income is added to the beneficiaries' total income for tax purposes. The income distributions are normally treated as being net of income tax at the basic rate (30%). Thus they carry a corresponding tax credit. In the case of discretionary trusts, etc (p 155), the additional rate (15%) further increases the tax credit. If part of the underlying income of the trust is building society interest, however, the appropriate portion of each income distribution must be allocated to this interest which will be taxed in the beneficiary's hands in the same way as any income on his own building society investments. (This 'see-through' rule does not apply to any UK resident with an absolute interest in the residue of an estate who can reclaim tax on the entire income distributions).

For example, suppose A has a life interest in a trust and receives from it income for 1984-85 made up as follows:

	Total	Building society income	Other income
Gross	£1,350	£350	£1,000
Income tax at 30% (tax credit)	£300	—	£300
Actual payment to A	£1,050	£350	£700

A will include in his total income £1,500 (ie, £1,000 distribution from other income plus £350 × 100/70 grossed equivalent of building society income). If A is able to make an income tax repayment claim he will have £300 income tax credit from the trust available for repayment (but not the notional £150 in relation to the building society interest which might have been available if A had an absolute interest in the residue).

The trustees should issue with each payment a form R185E which sets out the amount paid and the relevant tax credit.

Trusts where the settlor is still living
(Ss434–459)

The taxation of trusts where the settlor is still living follows the general rules outlined above except that in certain circumstances the settlor himself will be assessed to tax on the income of the trust. This can be avoided by observing various rules, including the following:

(a) *Period (S434)*
    The settlement must be set up for a period which is capable of exceeding six years.

(b) *The settlor must not have an interest (Ss447 & 457)*
    In the event that the settlor has retained an interest in the income or assets of the trust, he will be assessed to income tax on the income of the settlement to the extent that it remains undistributed. (The settlor has retained an interest in the trust if he or his wife can obtain some benefit from it.) Furthermore, if the income is distributed to others, subject to certain exceptions, the settlor and not the recipient will be charged to the excess of higher rate tax over the basic rate on the distribution.

(c) *The settlement must be irrevocable (Ss445 & 446)*
    If the settlor or his wife has power to revoke the settlement or partially revoke it, he is assessed to income tax on its income.

(d) *Discretionary settlements (S448)*
    Discretionary settlements are those under which the application of the income and/or capital of the trust is left to the discretion of the trustees. Under such a trust the settlor or his wife must not be able to benefit from the income, or else he will be assessed to income tax on that income, whether or not any of it is actually paid to him. This does not apply if only the widow of the settlor may benefit.

(e) *Settlements for benefit of own children (Ss437–444)*
    Under a trust created by the settlor, his own minor children (under 18 years of age) must not receive any income nor must it be

used for their upkeep or education. Otherwise the settlor will be assessed to income tax on such income. This does not apply to accumulation settlements, however (p 155), provided the income is in fact accumulated.

(f)   *Capital sums paid to settlor (S451; FA 1981 Ss42-43 & FA 1982 S63)*
Where 'capital sums' from a settlement (including loans and loan repayments) are paid to the settlor, he is assessable to income tax. The assessments are limited to the undistributed trust income and the balances carried forward for matching against future income. After 5 April 1981, the carry forward period is limited to 11 years from the 'capital sum' payment and no income is assessable for any period subsequent to the repayment by the settlor of a loan from the settlement.

The rules extend to companies connected to the settlement (normally where the trustees are participators and the company is close). A 'capital payment' from the company to the settlor before 6 April 1981 gave rise to the assessment of trust income on the settlor. After 5 April 1981, this only applies if there is an associated capital payment or asset transfer within five years from the trust to the company.

Note: In all of the above cases there are rules to prevent the double taxation of the trust income so it will not be assessed both on the settlor and the beneficiaries. Usually, basic rate income tax is paid by the trust or it has already been deducted at the source as in the case of, for example, interest on government securities. Dividends received by the trust carry with them tax credits which are effectively transferred to beneficiaries who are given income distributions. Also, if the trust is subject to investment income surcharge correspondingly higher tax credits attach to income distributions to beneficiaries (see below).

(g)   *Deeds of covenant*
These provide an effective method of tax saving in certain circumstances. Unless made to charities, they must be capable of exceeding six annual payments and running for more than 6 years. They should not be made by you to your minor children (see (e) above). Another relative such as a grandparent or uncle could execute deeds of covenant in favour of your minor children; but note that the Revenue have powers to block the tax-effectiveness of reciprocal arrangements.

● *Once your children have reached age 18, if they are still studying or otherwise are likely to have little or no income, you might usefully execute deeds of covenant in their favour.*

The covenantor who makes the payments deducts basic rate income tax (30%) and pays the net amount to the beneficiary. If the latter is not liable for income tax because his income is less than his tax allowances, he reclaims the income tax deducted by the covenantor.

- *If you wish to pay income regularly to elderly relatives with low incomes, this may be done profitably by means of deeds of covenant, so that the relatives may reclaim basic rate income tax in respect of any unused tax reliefs and allowances.*

- *Payments under deed of covenant to approved charities are of benefit to them since they reclaim the basic rate income tax which you deduct on payment. Furthermore, from 6 April 1980 charitable covenants qualify if they are capable of exceeding three years; and after 5 April 1981 you obtain higher rate tax relief for any such payments up to £3,000 gross in total each year. From 6 April 1983, this limit is £5,000.*

The deed must be property drawn up — most charities have prepared forms for covenanted donations — otherwise seek professional advice.

Accumulation settlements for the benefit of the settlor's children

If you wish to create a trust for the benefit of your minor children without being assessed to income tax on its income (p 155) this can be done by means of an accumulation settlement. The income of the settlement should be accumulated for each child until at least the age of 18 and no payments should be made for their benefit until that age. (The trust deed must state that the trustees are empowered to accumulate income.) If it is wished to distribute income to adult beneficiaries this can be done, but the income shares of the settlor's minor children must be accumulated, or else the settlor is liable to higher rate income tax on such income. When the income accumulations are paid to the beneficiary they are treated as capital in his hands and not subjected to higher rate income tax.

Income of discretionary trusts, etc
(FA 1973 Ss16–18)

After deducting certain expenses, the income of discretionary and accumulating trusts assessable after 5 April 1973 is subject to the additional rate (15%). Thus if a discretionary trust receives dividends of £700 during 1982-83 these will be imputed with £300 tax to make a total of £1,000 on which additional tax of £150 will be payable by the trustees. If, however, allowable expenses of say £200 are incurred then only £1,000 – £200 = £800 is liable to the additional tax and so £800 × 15% = £120 is payable.

The above applies to trusts where the income is accumulated or is payable at the discretion of the trustees but not where the income is treated for tax purposes as being that of the settlor; nor where a person is absolutely entitled to the income.

Where income distributions are made to beneficiaries, the amounts received by the latter are treated as being net of tax at 45% (30% basic rate plus 15% additional rate). The recipients can reclaim part or all of this tax if their incomes are low enough. For example, if a discretionary trust pays £275 to your child (or for his maintenance) and he has no other income, there is a tax credit of £275 × 45/55 = £225 which is all reclaimable.

Beneficiaries can reclaim tax on distributions of income made to them after 5 April 1973 even if the trust received the income before that date and thus only paid tax on it at the standard rate of income tax (38.75% or previously 41.25%). If, however, the tax attributable to such distributions exceeds notional tax of two thirds of the total net accumulations at 5 April 1973, the balance is assessed on the trustees.

● *Trustees of discretionary settlements should consider the tax positions of potential recipients of income distributions. If their other income is low then substantial repayments of tax can result. On the other hand, distributions of income to higher rate income tax payers should be avoided.*

Foreign trusts
(CGTA S17)

For taxation purposes a trust is generally treated as being resident abroad if a majority of the trustees are so resident and its administration and management are carried out overseas. Such foreign trusts are exempt from CGT on realisations of assets in the UK and elsewhere, subject to the detailed rules and stringent anti-avoidance provisions (p 52).

UK income of foreign trusts is charged to income tax here along roughly the same lines as non-resident individuals are so charged. There is no higher rate liability, however, unless distributions are made to beneficiaries resident in this country or if the anti-avoidance provisions apply regarding transfers of assets abroad. In the latter event, in certain circumstances, the Revenue may charge any beneficiaries who are resident in this country with basic and higher rate income tax on the trust income.

● *In view of the tax advantages of foreign trusts, if you are concerned with a UK one, in appropriate circumstances you should consider exporting it. This is discussed in more detail later (p 177).*

Estates of deceased persons

The income tax liability of the deceased
(TMA 1970 Ss40, 74 & 77)

When a person dies, income tax and other taxes must be settled on all his income, etc, up to the date of his death. Any of this tax that is not paid during his lifetime must be settled by his executors or administrators out of his estate.

If the deceased has not been assessed to tax on all his income prior to his death, the Revenue are allowed to make assessments on such income within three years after the end of the tax year in which death occurred. The Revenue may make assessments in this way in respect of any tax years ending within six years before the date of death in cases of fraud, wilful default or neglect of the deceased but no earlier years can be assessed.

Income tax during the administration period
(Ss426–433)

During the administration period of an estate (p 147), the executors or administrators pay any basic rate income tax assessments that arise on the income for that period. The tax paid by direct assessment or deduction at source is subtracted from the amounts of income paid to those entitled to the income of the estate. The latter include the income that they receive in their tax returns when the payments are made to them. They must return the gross equivalents allowing for income tax at the basic rate (30%). Once the total income payable to each beneficiary has been ascertained, it is allocated to the respective tax years for which it arose and they pay (if applicable) higher rate tax on that basis.

12   The legal aspects of trusts

What is a trust?

A trust is the relationship that is created when a person ('the settlor') transfers assets ('the trust fund') to trustees, either for the benefit of third parties ('the beneficiaries') or for the benefit of some object, eg charity. The benefit of the trust assets is enjoyed by the beneficiaries, not the settlor or the trustees, although one of the beneficiaries may be the settlor himself or a trustee. Another word for a trust is a settlement.

A trust may be created by a settlor during his lifetime (a trust *'inter vivos'*) or incorporated in a will, in which case it will take effect only when the testator dies.

Types of trusts

Trusts may be classified according to the nature of the duties undertaken by the trustees, according to their purpose or according to the way in which they have been created. The following is merely a brief outline of the main types of trust.

'Strict' or fixed-interest trusts

In a strict trust one or more beneficiaries are entitled as of right to the income from the trust fund during their lifetime. These beneficiaries are said to enjoy a life interest in the trust fund and are referred to as life tenants. After their death the capital passes to some other person or persons (called 'the remainderman') or to charity. Such persons or bodies are said to have a 'reversionary interest' in the trust fund. The trustees are often given power to distribute all or part of the capital of the trust fund to the life tenant.

Discretionary trusts

In a discretionary trust the trustees are given power to distribute both capital and income or either amongst a class of beneficiaries as they, in their sole discretion, think fit. A trust period is usually defined, at the end of which there is an ultimate destination for capital or income not distributed. The trustees are therefore given a far greater element of judgement and initiative than in a strict trust. They also have the added responsibility of considering the competing interests of the members of the specified class. The discretionary trust has suffered a decline in popularity in recent years because of its CTT disadvantages (p 104).

Protective trusts

(TA 1925 S33)

This type of trust is designed to protect a beneficiary from his own irresponsibility or the consequences of his own financial mismanagement. The terms of a protective trust are governed by statute law, although they may be modified by the terms of the trust deed itself. As a general rule, such trusts last for the life of a principal beneficiary until a particular event occurs which has the effect of depriving this beneficiary of his right to receive the income. Such a determining event may be the bankruptcy of the beneficiary or his conviction for a criminal offence or if he gives up his right to part of the income. Whether the beneficiary's interest has been terminated by the events which have happened is a question of construction of the relevant clause in the trust deed.

If the Court is satisfied that the principal beneficiary has forfeited his right to the income a discretionary trust will be held to arise automatically for the benefit of a class of beneficiaries usually comprising the principal beneficiary, his or her spouse and their children.

Accumulation and maintenance trusts

These trusts are particularly useful as a way of providing for your children. The trust fund can be used for the maintenance, education or benefit of your children but they do not have to be entitled to a share of the income until they are 25. The advantages of this arrangement are more fully set out at p 120 in Chapter 9.

Implied, resulting and constructive trusts

In some circumstances, where there is no trust as such, the law demands that a person becomes a trustee, and when this occurs, implied, resulting or constructive trusts are created.

Implied and resulting trusts

The law will imply a trust where it considers that it was intended by the parties to a particular transaction. As an example, where two persons agree to make wills in a certain form and put this into effect, on the death of the first person, the survivor, if he accepts the benefits given to him under the deceased's will, is bound by an implied trust to give effect to their agreement.

Nearly all implied trusts are also resulting trusts in that the beneficial interest goes back or 'results' to the settlor. The most common examples are where trusts fail or are only partially achieved in which case the trust property, or the surplus reverts to the settlor.

Another example of an implied and resulting trust is where a purchaser buys property in the name of another. The nominal purchaser is regarded as holding the property on trust for the true purchaser. However if the true purchaser is the father, husband or fiancé of the nominal purchaser the presumption is that the purchase in the other's name was intended to be a gift.

Constructive trusts

These arise independently of any express or presumed intention of the parties normally where there has been misconduct on the part of an existing trustee, or interference by an outsider with trust property. Some examples are:

(a)   a trustee who makes a profit from his trust becomes a constructive trustee of the benefit received for his beneficiaries (p 172);

(b)   if a stranger acquires trust property, knowing (or later discovering) its transfer to be in breach of trust, he becomes a constructive trustee of that property for the existing beneficiaries. However, a bona fide purchaser will not become a constructive trustee even if he discovers the true nature of his property.

(c)   A vendor of land becomes a constructive trustee of the property for the purchaser from the date of exchange of contracts.

Charitable trusts

A trust can only be charitable if it is for certain specified purposes:

(1)   the relief of poverty,
(2)   the promotion of education,
(3)   the promotion of religion, or for
(4)   other purposes of benefit to the community.

Trusts for the promotion of education or religion must, in order to be charitable trusts, show an element of public benefit.

A trust is not charitable unless the objects are exclusively charitable, ie, the words 'for benevolent purposes' or 'charitable or benevolent purposes' will not do. Such phrases are too vague to imply an exclusively charitable trust.

Charitable trusts have numerous advantages, the principal ones being:

(1)   A charitable trust will not fail because the trust objects are uncertain, provided it is clear that the settlor intended the property to go to charity exclusively. (For a non-charitable trust to be valid the interest to be taken by the beneficiaries must be certain).

(2)   Charitable trusts enjoy freedom from income tax, investment income surcharge and CGT, provided that any profits from trade or any capital gains are applied solely for charitable purposes.

(3)   Capital transfer tax does not apply to gifts to charities.

(4)   Charities obtain rate relief on land held by them.
(5)   A non-charitable trust is void if under its terms, trustees are bound
       to hold property beyond what is called 'the perpetuity period',
       usually 80 years. The objects of a charity may last indefinitely
       without affecting its validity.

Charitable trusts are administered and supervised by the Charities
Commission. In particular, the Commissioners maintain a register of
charities and all charities with a permanent endowment are required to
register. Promoters of new charities must submit details of their
proposed objects for approval to the Charity Commissioners.

Setting up a trust

A trust may be created by anyone over the age of 18 with full capacity to
manage his or her affairs. A minor can make a valid trust but this is
voidable by him when he comes of age.

You may set up a trust either by means of a formal declaration of trust or
by transferring property to your trustees.

Thus, for a trust to be validly constituted, you must ensure that not only
are the required formalities with regard to writing or evidence in writing
satisfied but that the trust property itself has been vested in the trustees.

The legal formalities
(LPA 1925 S53)

No particular form of documentation is required for a declaration of
trust *inter vivos* of cash, stocks and shares and other movable assets.
Such a trust may be declared orally or even inferred from conduct. Any
words expressing the settlor's intention are sufficient, although, as a
general rule, no conditions must attach to them. For such a trust to be
completely constituted, however, the property must be transferred into
the names of the trustees.

In general, in order to pass legal ownership to the trustees the forms of
legal documentation necessary to transfer the particular type of
property settled must be used. You will therefore have to sign a
conveyance or transfer if freehold land is to be put into the trust,
leasehold land must be assigned by deed and if stocks and shares are to
be put into trust then the standard form of transfer must be signed and
forwarded for registration.

A declaration of trust of land or of any interest in land must be in writing
and must be signed by the settlor himself. Such writing need not take
any particular form and a letter or memorandum is sufficient, provided
all the requisite terms of the trust are set out.

A declaration of trust of any property, whether it be cash, shares or land, that is to come into existence on the donor's death must be set out in a will which complies with the formalities for execution (p 119).

A beneficiary under an existing trust may set up a further trust of his beneficial interest for the benefit of someone else. Such a trust must be in writing (not merely evidenced by writing) and must be signed by the person creating it or by his agent. If these requisites are not complied with the trust will be void.

A completely constituted trust can be enforced by any beneficiary whether or not he has given anything of value in return for the benefits he receives under the trust. In practice, most beneficiaries are 'volunteers' in the sense that they have not provided any value in return for their beneficial interests. If a beneficiary has given value for his interest it does not matter whether the trust is completely constituted. He can enforce the trust. If a trust is incompletely constituted it cannot be enforced by a volunteer.

In general, an ineffectual attempt to transfer property to trustees will not be construed as a declaration of trust. However, if you are able to show that you have done everything reasonably within your power to transfer ownership to trustees the trust will be effective. This will be the case even if the trustees still have to do something further to perfect their own legal title.

The costs

If you are planning to set up a trust you should be aware that the legal fees and disbursements incurred are your responsibility as settlor. You may, however, expressly authorise the trustees to take them out of the trust fund once the trust has been set up.

Besides solicitors' costs, stamp duty, CGT and CTT may also be payable. You are primarily responsible for tax liabilities but if you do not pay them the Revenue may call upon the trustees to do so. Your trustees may therefore ask for confirmation that all the tax liabilities arising on the creation of the trust have been assessed and paid before they accept the trusts.

Trustees

Anyone over 18 years of age may act as a trustee. The appointment of a minor as trustee is void but another person can be appointed to act instead. A minor may, however, hold property on an implied, resulting or constructive trust.

Trust corporations

Certain companies may act either as a sole or a co-trustee. They are known as trust corporations, and are usually subsidiary companies of banks or insurance companies, charging a fee for their services. They must be authorised to act as trustee and apart from companies incorporated by special Act or Royal Charter, they must have very substantial issued share capital. This of course means that in practice only the larger companies can act in this capacity, thus offering an effective guarantee that, in the event of any improper conduct, the corporation will be of sufficient substance to reimburse the beneficiaries for any loss.

The position of a trust corporation is largely the same as that of private trustees, except that whereas two trustees must act together in transactions involving land which forms part of the trust fund, a trust corporation can act on its own.

The conditions under which a bank or insurance company will accept trusteeship are published in booklets available from them and always include the requirement that a charging clause (ensuring payment to the corporation for its services) be included in the will or trust deed.

The Public Trustee
(PTA 1906)

The Public Trustee is a trust corporation and was established by statute at the beginning of this century. The Public Trustee himself is appointed by the Lord Chancellor.

The Public Trustee is authorised to charge for acting as executor, administrator or trustee. He cannot act for a charitable trust, although he has a discretion as to whether to accept any other particular trusteeship but he may not refuse to undertake any work merely because the value involved is too low. He may act as a Custodian Trustee (below).

Generally, the Public Trustee does not have any particular status over and above ordinary trustees. He is authorised to obtain professional advice particularly on legal matters and his powers to manage a business which forms part of a trust are limited.

Custodian Trustees
(S4 PTA 1906)

The office of Custodian Trustee was also created by Statute Law. The Public Trustee, other trust corporations and various other bodies may act as Custodian Trustees. The settlor himself may appoint a Custodian Trustee or such an appointment may be made by order of the Court.

If a Custodian Trustee does act, the exercise of the administration of the trust is placed in the hands of managing trustees. The trust property is transferred into the name of the Custodian Trustee who has custody of all securities and documents of title.

The main advantage of appointing a Custodian Trustee is that changes in the managing trustees can take place without the need to transfer the trust property into the names of the new trustees. The Custodian Trustee arrangement has never been popular. It does however form the basis of many pension funds where a corporate trustee holds the trust fund while individual trustees manage the fund itself.

Number

If the trust fund consists entirely of assets other than freehold or leasehold land (cash or stocks and shares are the most common) only one trustee is necessary. There is no maximum to the number that may be appointed.

If the trust fund comprises or includes land at least two trustees must be appointed, unless a trust corporation is acting as sole trustee. Otherwise a sole trustee cannot give a valid receipt for the proceeds of sale of property, even if so authorised by the trust instrument. The number of trustees must not exceed four and if more than four are appointed only the first four able and willing to act may do so. This restriction does not apply to charitable trustees.

Accepting trusteeship

If you are setting up a trust you will need to inform your prospective trustees of your intentions and of the terms of the intended trust. If one of your trustees is a professional person he will probably wish to see a copy of the draft trust deed. A prospective trustee would wish to ensure that the proposed trusts are capable of implementation and that the wording of the deed is clear and unambiguous.

No one can be compelled to act as trustee if he does not wish to do so. Acceptance is usually evidenced by the trustee signing the trust deed. A trustee need not accept the office and may disclaim before he does any act which shows that he has assumed the office. Disclaimer of office may be in any form. It may be inferred from a trustee's conduct, eg, by not acting as trustee for a long period. If a trustee does not expressly accept the trust acceptance may be presumed by his subsequent conduct and even small acts may be construed as acceptance.

The mechanics of appointment and retirement

As settlor, you usually appoint the original trustees on creation of the trust. Once the trust is in existence you cannot appoint new trustees unless you have reserved such a power for yourself in the trust deed. Subsequent trustees may be appointed under powers given by statute law or, in certain circumstances, by the Court. In the case of charitable trusts the Charity Commissioners have the power to appoint new trustees if the circumstances warrant it.

Appointment under the statutory power
(TA 1925 Ss36 & 37)

Statute law authorises the appointment of a new trustee in a number of circumstances:
(1)   on the death of a trustee;
(2)   on the retirement of a trustee;
(3)   if a trustee refuses to act or is unfit or incapable of acting; or
(4)   if a trusteee remains out of the country for more than 12 months (in which case he can be removed against his wishes).

The appointment may be made by:
(1)   the persons nominated in the will or trust instrument or, if none,
(2)   the surviving or continuing trustees or, if none,
(3)   the personal representatives of the last surviving or continuing trustee; or
(4)   if none of these methods is possible, the Court.

There is also power to appoint an additional trustee provided that a trust corporation is not acting and the number of trustees is not increased above four. Separate trustees up to a maximum of four may be appointed of any part of the trust property to be held on trusts separate from those of the rest of the trust property.

Appointment by the Court
(TA 1925 S41)

The Court may appoint a new or additional trustee on the application of a trustee or beneficiary if it would be difficult to do so by any other method. The Court does not have power to appoint a new trustee against the wishes of a sole trustee who intends to exercise his statutory power of appointment. Neither will the Court normally interfere if a trustee has been appointed under the statutory power, even though it feels that some other appointment may have been more suitable.

Retirement
(TA 1925 S39)

Once accepted, trusteeship cannot be disclaimed. A trustee may retire by deed provided the following conditions are fulfilled:

(1)   a trust corporation or at least two individual trustees should remain to carry out the terms of the trust;
(2)   the continuing trustees and the person entitled to appoint new trustees consent; and
(3)   the retiring trustee has done everything necessary to vest the trust property in any new trustee and the continuing trustees.

Usually the retiring trustee and the continuing trustees are made parties to the deed of retirement. A declaration vesting the trust property in a new trustee appointed by the same deed may be included but is not strictly necessary (p 164).

A retiring trustee would normally wish to ensure that all debts incurred prior to his retirement are settled before it becomes effective. He may seek an indemnity from the continuing trustees but is only entitled to one for costs and expenses properly incurred. A former trustee cannot be held liable for taxation or other liabilities which have been incurred after his retirement.

Removal of trustees

(TA 1925 S36)

It is possible for you to give yourself a power to remove trustees in the trust deed. Such a provision is considered undesirable since it gives the settlor too great a degree of control over the trust. It may be strictly construed by the Court.

A trustee may be removed by the Court in the following circumstances:

(1)   if he remains out of the country for more than 12 months;
(2)   if he refuses to act;
(3)   if he is unfit to act; or
(4)   if he is incapable of acting.

In addition, the Court has a general power to remove a trustee and appoint a new one if the circumstances warrant it.

Remuneration and indemnity

(TA 1925 S30)

A trustee is not entitled to any remuneration for his duties unless such a power is given in the trust instrument. On the whole, such clauses are strictly construed by the Courts.

If a professional person is acting as trustee it is usual to include a professional charging clause. Such charges must be reasonable. A power to charge must be widely drawn if a professional person is to be permitted to charge for services that do not require professional expertise.

Trustees may come to a separate agreement with the beneficiaries on the question of payment, provided the latter are all of full age and absolutely entitled to the trust fund. The Court may authorise remuneration of trustees in special circumstances where the trust has become particularly difficult to administer.

If a trust corporation is appointed (p 162), a power to charge is usually given in the trust deed. The Public Trustee and a Custodian Trustee (p 163) may also charge.

Trustees may, however, reimburse themselves in respect of their out of pocket expenses from the trust fund. Reimbursement comes primarily from the capital of the trust fund but is a charge on all of the trust property, both capital and income.

The duties and powers of trustees

Securing control over the trust fund
(TA 1925 S40)

Trustees have a duty to ensure that they have full control over the trust assets by having them transferred into their names as soon as possible. However, a deed of appointment of new trustees is deemed to include a vesting declaration whereby the trust property is automatically placed in the names of the new trustees. Nevertheless, in the case of the following forms of property such an implied vesting declaration will not operate:

(1) mortgages of land;
(2) stocks and shares (which should be transferred and re-registered); and
(3) leasehold property (where a transfer into the names of new trustees would be a breach of the covenant against assignment in the lease).

On taking up his appointment a trustee should familiarise himself with the terms of the trust and the nature and extent of the trust property. If, in the course of his enquiries, he discovers that a breach of trust has been committed in the past it is his duty to correct the situation. An examination of the trust accounts should reveal the changes which have taken place in the trust assets. If accounts are not available a new trustee will have to study the trust's documents in order to satisfy himself as to its history.

Accounts
(TA 1925 S22)

Trustees are under a duty to keep accounts and produce them to any beneficiary when required to do so. Trust accounts should be audited by an independent accountant not more than once every three years unless the nature of the trust necessitates a more frequent audit.

Trustees must provide beneficiaries with reasonable information as to the manner in which they have dealt with the trust property. Beneficiaries should be given an opportunity to inspect title deeds and any other documents relating to the trust fund.

Delegation
(TA 1925 Ss23 & 30)

The trust assets should be placed under the joint control of all the trustees. The trust deed may authorise one trustee to have sole control of certain assets and this is the case where a trust corporation is appointed. In certain circumstances during the course of administration (such as the signing of trust tax returns) only one trustee need act. As a general rule, however, trustees have a duty to act jointly and they should keep records in the form of minutes or resolutions of the joint decisions which they have taken.

Trustees have a duty to act personally. They are expected to take basic decisions themselves and to administer the trust fund themselves.

The trust instrument may, however, include an express power of delegation. Most modern trust deeds include a power to delegate investment management and to place investments in the names of nominees.

Trustees may employ the services of professional agents, such as solicitors and accountants, to deal with routine administration of the trust. In the absence of an express authority in the trust deed, agents may only carry out the decisions of the trustees. They cannot take decisions themselves.

Trustees are not liable for the negligence of an agent provided he was employed in good faith. They are also not liable for any loss to the trust estate unless this was caused through their own 'wilful default'.

Nevertheless, trustees should exercise care over the choice of their agents and should supervise them where necessary. Professional trustees, in particular, have a higher duty of care. Trustees should not allow funds to be left in the hands of an agent for longer than is necessary. They will be accountable if an agent with whom trust money or securities are deposited defaults as a result of their own negligence or neglect.

Special delegation
(TA 1925 S25; & PAA 1971 S9)

A trustee may, by Power of Attorney, delegate for a maximum period of 12 months all his powers and duties as trustee. The donee of the Power of Attorney may be a trust corporation but not the donor's only other co-trustee. Within 7 days of the appointment the donor must give written notice to the persons having power to appoint new trustees and to the other trustees. The donor of the power is liable for the acts and defaults of the donee as if they were his own.

Investment of trust funds

Trustees have a duty to invest the trust fund. They may only invest the trust property in those investments which are authorised by the terms of the trust deed or by law.

In most modern trusts very wide powers of investment are given to the trustees. These are called 'beneficial owner' powers since they give trustees the same powers of investment as those which a person who beneficially owned the property might have. As trustees cannot invest in land unless they are specifically authorised to do so, the investment clause should include power to buy land and buildings and to improve them. It is also useful to give trustees power to invest in foreign assets.

● *If the trust deed does give trustees power to invest in land, the investment must yield income. For example, a power to invest in land does not allow trustees to purchase a house for a beneficiary to live in. This is because part of the purchase price is paid for vacant possession and is not laid out in an income-producing asset. Therefore, it is useful to include a power both to invest in non-income-producing assets and for beneficiaries to occupy land or buildings rent-free.*

Trustee Investments Act 1961

This Act applies to all trusts (including those arising under a will or on an intestacy) which grant investment powers less than those conferred by the Act itself. Thus the powers contained in the Act are in addition to the powers set out in the trust deed. The trust deed may narrow or broaden the scope of the Act and it is usual for this to be done. The application of the Act has therefore become somewhat limited.

The Act lays down general guidelines on the appropriateness and diversification of investments (S6). These principles are intended to apply to all trusts regardless of whether the other provisions of the Act are applicable to them or not.

Trustees are under a duty to have regard for the need to diversify the investments of the trust 'insofar as is appropriate to the circumstances of the trust'. The suitability of an investment to the trust itself, rather than merely for its own sake, is emphasised.

When considering an investment trustees must have regard to the particular requirements of the beneficiaries. Thus if the trust is a fixed-interest trust the rival claims of the life-tenant and the person ultimately entitled to capital (the remainderman, p 158) have to be considered. Trustees must ensure that they maintain a balance between capital growth and possible loss of income which would be to the detriment of the life-tenant.

Mortgages
(TA 1925 S8)

Trustees may lend money on mortgage subject to the following conditions:

(1)   the security mortgaged must be either freehold property or leasehold property where the lease has not less than 60 years to run;
(2)   the loan must not exceed two-thirds of the value of the property; and
(3)   the property must be valued by a surveyor believed to be competent by the trustees.

Provided that the surveyor states the value and advises the loan to be made and the above conditions are complied with, the trustees cannot be held liable on the grounds that they have lent too much. If trustees do lend too much on a security which is authorised (as above) they will be liable only for the excess over the proper amount. If the security is unauthorised they will be liable for the whole loss.

Maintenance and advancement

Maintenance out of income
(TA 1925 S31)

Where property is held by trustees in trust for any person who is a minor (or is under a disability) then subject to any prior interests in the property, the trustees can use any part of the income towards that person's maintenance, education or benefit during his or her minority. The statutory power applies regardless of whether the interest is dependent on the beneficiary attaining a particular age or on the happening of a particular event, but it must carry the right to intermediate income.

The power of maintenance may be expressly excluded or varied in the trust deed or may not apply at all if a contrary intention is shown. If a minor's interest is contingent on his attaining the age of majority, and there is a direction that the income be accumulated, then there is no power to maintain.

If an interest is contingent on attaining a greater age than that of majority (ie, more than 18 years of age) and it does carry the right to intermediate income then the trustees may maintain the beneficiary out of income during his minority. However, once he attains 18 he must be paid the income until he either attains a vested interest and becomes entitled to capital or he dies.

Where there is surplus income after the power has been exercised this is added to capital and invested. However, at any time during a beneficiary's minority the trustees may use such accumulations as income.

Advancement of capital
(TA 1925 S32)

Trustees have the power to use the capital of the trust fund for the 'advancement or benefit' of both infant and adult beneficiaries. Advancement means helping a beneficiary to establish himself at an early stage in his life or his career. It does not cover merely casual payments to him or paying his debts.

Benefit has a wide meaning and covers a payment to a parent or guardian on behalf of a beneficiary as well as a payment direct to the beneficiary himself. It may also cover a loan to set up a beneficiary's husband or wife in business or payments to a beneficiary's dependants who are in financial need. Most trust deeds specify that the receipt of a beneficiary's parent or guardian will be a good discharge to the trustees. The power applies even though the beneficiary's interest may be dependent on the happening of a particular event and despite the fact that the size of his or her share may be reduced by an increase in the class of beneficiaries of which he or she is a member. The statutory power may be varied or excluded by an express provision for advancement given in the trust instrument. It may also be excluded by implication if a power has been granted to accumulate the income of capital during the settlor's lifetime.

There are a number of limits on the statutory power, as follows:

(1) the maximum that can be advanced is one half of the beneficiary's vested or presumed share;
(2) the owners of prior interests in the property must be alive, of full age and give their written consent; and
(3) if the beneficiary becomes absolutely entitled to trust property at some time after an advance of capital has been made, the advance already received must be accounted for as part of the share.

The effect of the power

The effect of the exercise of the power in most cases is that money is taken out of the trust fund and handed to the beneficiary. However, it is sometimes possible for the power to be exercised so as to create new trusts quite independent of the original trust. The original trustees may continue as trustees of the new trust or they may retire in favour of new trustees. Such an appointment may however have capital gains tax consequences (p 50).

Insurance
(TA 1925 S19)

Trustees may insure up to three-quarters of the value of the property insured. Premiums are payable out of the income of the property insured or of the other property held on the same trusts.

Trustees may not insure trust property for its full value unless specifically authorised to do so by the trust deed.

Breach of trust

The relationship between trustees and beneficiaries is based on 'utmost good faith'. Trustees must preserve the trust fund and act honestly and fairly at all times. If they do not do so they may find themselves under a personal liability to make good any loss suffered.

Liability for acts of co-trustees

A trustee is personally liable for any breach of trust he commits. He is not liable for breaches by his co-trustees unless they acted with his knowledge in which case he may be liable as well.

Since trustees are under a duty to act jointly it follows that they are jointly and severally liable for a breach of trust. This means that if two or more trustees are liable each may be sued for the whole loss but if one trustee pays more than his share he can seek a contribution from the others since all trustees must bear liability for the breach in equal shares in the absence of any contrary agreement between themselves.

Trustees should ensure that the trust property is placed within the control of all of them. In particular property should not be left in the sole control of one trustee for an unreasonable period of time. If this does happen and the trustee defaults they will be liable for any loss suffered.

A retiring trustee remains liable for breaches of trust committed while he was a trustee. He is not liable for a breach committed after his retirement unless he retired in order that a breach be committed.

Making a profit from the trust

A trustee must not take advantage of his position and his knowledge of the trust fund in order to obtain an advantage or profit for himself. If he does acquire a profit he is accountable as a constructive trustee (p 160) to the beneficiaries.

If a trustee uses the trust assets in a commercial venture or in his own business then he is personally liable for any losses suffered. Any gain accrues to the beneficiaries.

A trustee must act with prudence. Trust assets should not be the subject of reckless speculation in land or shares.

Purchase of the trust estate

If a trustee buys the trust property for himself the transaction may be set aside by the beneficiaries. It makes no difference that the sale was fair and honest and that a fair price was obtained. The trust deed may however authorise such a transaction.

A trustee cannot retire expressly in order to purchase trust property. If he does so the transaction is voidable unless it is shown that his retirement took place several years before the date of the transaction.

A sale by a trustee of trust property which he has purchased can be adopted by the beneficiaries. The trustee may be required to account for the profit he has made. If there has been no sale the Court may order the property to be offered for resale. If a greater price is offered than that paid by the trustee the sale to the trustee will be set aside.

In certain circumstances the Court may give permission for such a sale. Provided the beneficiaries do not object, the transaction will be valid.

Overpayment

If trustees by mistake overpay a beneficiary they are entitled to recover the excess by adjusting future payments. If the wrong person is paid the trustee is personally liable to the beneficiary entitled to the payment. He can however claim against the person wrongly paid.

It may happen that after the trust fund has been distributed a claim is made against it of which the trustees had no previous knowledge. They can then ask the beneficiaries to refund the property to the extent necessary to satisfy the claim.

Tracing

If by mistake trust property is handed to the wrong person then the beneficiary who is entitled to the property may try to trace his property to the recipient and reclaim it. The recipient, being a stranger to the trust, becomes a constructive trustee of the property he has received for the true beneficiary (p 174) The property does not become part of the recipient's estate.

Unauthorised investments

A trustee who makes unauthorised investments (p 168) may be required to sell them and make good any loss suffered or account for any profit made. It is open to the adult beneficiaries to adopt an unauthorised investment.

Trustees have a duty to invest the trust fund and are absolutely liable for failure to carry out this duty. Thus if trustees do not invest at all they will be liable for loss of profit.

If trustees do make authorised investments and a loss occurs because they retain these investments they will not be liable if they have acted honestly and with reasonable prudence in the exercise of their discretion. However trustees must obtain advice before making investments and they must seek advice from time to time on the continuing suitability of their investments (p 168).

Remedies of beneficiaries

If beneficiaries discover that a breach of trust has been committed they may bring proceedings against the trustees personally. The measure of liability is the loss caused to the trust estate. Beneficiaries may claim any profit made. If there have been several breaches a trustee cannot set off a loss against any profit made. If a trustee is required to replace trust money interest is payable at a rate determined by the Court.

Beneficiaries may follow trust property into the hands of a recipient and recover it provided the recipient was aware that it was trust property (p 172), even if he gave value for it.

If a trustee in breach of trust is also a beneficiary his interest may be impounded to make good the breach as far as is necessary.

If a beneficiary has in any way consented to a breach of trust he cannot complain of this breach unless he was under some disability at the time. Other beneficiaries who have not so agreed may compel a trustee to make good the breach. In such a case the Court may grant the trustee an indemnity against the beneficiary who has instigated the breach.

An adult beneficiary who is aware of the facts may preclude himself from further action against a trustee by giving a formal release. A trustee is not however entitled to a formal release as of right on the termination of his duties.

Release by the Court
(TA 1925 S61)

The Court may, at its discretion, relieve a trustee from liability if he has acted 'honestly and reasonably and ought fairly to be excused'.

A trustee who is seeking to escape liability must prove that he has acted in such a manner.

The Court has a discretion in such cases and is not bound to excuse a trustee.

Trustees should not view this provision as a general indemnity clause. They should at all times exercise a high degree of care in the execution of their duties. They may however only be prepared to accept office if the trust deed contains a blanket indemnity clause.

Changing the terms of a trust

Action by beneficiaries

Beneficiaries cannot interfere with the way a trustee administers the trust, although they can intervene to prevent a breach of trust.

If all the beneficiaries are of full age and capable of consenting they can reach agreement on a variation of the terms of the trust with the trustees without referring the matter to the Court. The arrangement will then be set out in a deed of family arrangement executed under seal by all the parties. The deed will contain an indemnity by the beneficiaries in favour of the trustees. The costs of the exercise are payable from the trust fund.

In a simple trust where all the beneficiaries are of full age, not under any disability and between them absolutely entitled to the trust property they may terminate the trust. They can ask the trustees to transfer the trust property to them or as they direct, regardless of the wishes of the settlor. This is known as 'the rule in *Saunders* v *Vautier*'.

Beneficiaries may be able to remodel or terminate a trust by a number of other methods. A life tenant (p 158) may surrender his life interest to the remainderman (p 158) bringing the trust to an end. An elderly person entitled to an interest in reversion (p 158) may assign all or part of his interest to younger relatives or to the life tenant. The trust property may be divided between the life tenant and the remainderman thereby also terminating the trust. A life interest may also be disclaimed.

All the above transactions are capital transactions and may involve a liability for CTT and CGT and, in addition, stamp duty. Reversionary interests may be assigned or surrendered without a charge to CTT provided they are regarded as 'excluded property' (p 78). (Income tax may be involved under S 437 if the recipient is the minor child of the reversioner.)

Statutory provisions

In more complex situations trustees may need to obtain the Court's approval to any proposed change in the terms of the trust. There are a number of statutory provisions which can be used and in some circumstances trustees do not even have to make the application themselves. The following are two of the most important provisions.

Management and administration
(TA 1925 S57)

The Court has power to sanction a particular transaction which it considers to be 'expedient' in the management or administration of trust property. The Court can authorise specific dealings with trust property but cannot alter the beneficial interests under the trust. Trustees make the application and the costs of all the parties are usually met from the trust fund.

Variation of Trusts Act 1958

The Court has a general statutory power under the Variation of Trusts Act to vary trust terms on behalf of persons who lack the ability to do it themselves. Adult beneficiaries who are not under any disability must reach a decision on their own.

Where property is held on trusts arising before or after the passing of the Act and contained in a Will, settlement or other disposition the Court may at its discretion approve any arrangement which either:

(1)   varies or revokes all or any of the trusts; or
(2)   enlarges the powers of the trustees in relation to the trusts on behalf of the following persons:
    (a)   a minor beneficiary or someone who is under a disability and therefore incapable of assenting;
    (b)   persons who might become entitled to an interest at a future date;
    (c)   unborn persons; and
    (d)   persons who may be granted a benefit under a discretionary trust arising under the provisions of a protective trust where the interest of the principal beneficiary has not failed.

The consent of the trustees to the proposed arrangement is not required and the application is often made by the beneficiaries themselves. Application can also be made by the settlor who should in any case be consulted on the proposed variation and be given an opportunity to express his views. In practice proposals for a variation are usually discussed between trustees and beneficiaries although the details should be formulated by the beneficiaries themselves. Separate representation is usually insisted on by the Court.

The Court will not approve the proposed arrangement unless it is satisfied that it will be for the benefit of all interested persons. Neither will the Court override objections or a refusal of consent from an adult beneficiary no matter how unreasonable such objections might be.

The Act has frequently been used to vary investment clauses where the settlor's wishes limit the scope of the Trustee Investments Act (p 168) to the disadvantage of the trust interests. Many other applications have had as their object the avoidance of tax. This has been regarded as a legitimate use of the Act's powers provided it is clear that the arrangement is for the benefit of all interested persons under the trust.

The importance of a flexible trust deed

● *The general law and the statutory provisions outlined above provide a limited means of varying the terms of a trust. Application to the Court is both expensive and time consuming and inevitably involves delay. It is most important that the trust deed itself is made as flexible as possible. This will enable your trustees to take advantage of changes in tax law as well as your own and the beneficiaries' financial circumstances without recourse to the Court.*

If the trust deed contains an express power of variation it may be possible to effect a variation of the trust terms without the need for a formal deed. Alternatively there may be power to appoint the trust property on entirely new trusts. These powers may be exercisable with or without the consent of the settlor. Section 32 of the Trustee Act may also be used to release or resettle capital on entirely new trusts.

Discretionary trusts

Discretionary trusts, the majority of which were created before 1974 have suffered from numerous CTT disadvantages (p 104). It has often been found desirable to terminate them altogether under an overriding power of appointment in the trust deed or to reconstruct them so that they cease to be discretionary in nature. Following the 1982 Finance Act, however, smaller discretionary settlements have become more popular.

Reconstruction of a discretionary trust is usually effected by means of a deed of appointment executed by the trustees. The deed is usually drafted so that the new settlement or trust is part of the old settlement which remains in existence. Many of the administrative provisions of the old trust are expressed to apply to the new sub-trust. This is to avoid a possible CGT charge. Such a charge may arise if it can be shown that the trustees of the new trust have become absolutely entitled to the trust assets as against the trustees of the old trust.

The main aim behind the reconstruction of a discretionary trust is to remove the trustees' discretion as to which beneficiaries are to benefit under the trust. To this end particular individuals are given the right to property or at least to the income of trust assets. Usually provision is made for those persons who were members of the 'specified' or 'appointed' class of beneficiaries in the old discretionary trust to receive a benefit. Frequently the reconstruction is designed to benefit the settlor's children or grandchildren. This is accomplished by means of the accumulation and maintenance trust (p 159) because of its tax advantages.

Exporting trusts

An English trust is a trust made in conformity with English law and where the trustees are subject to the jurisdiction of the English Courts. An overseas trust is one which is controlled and managed outside the UK. For tax purposes the UK does not include the Channel Islands or the Isle of Man.

Provisions can be inserted in an English trust whereby it can be removed to another country. This can be done by substituting for the English trust a new trust in another country and then transferring the trust fund to that new trust. It is desirable to appoint new foreign trustees at the same time.

If there is no power in the trust deed to export the trust, it may be necessary to apply to the Court under the Variation of Trusts Act.

Alternatively, UK trustees may merely retire in favour of foreign trustees. The trust will then become resident outside the UK as it will be controlled and managed abroad notwithstanding that the trust assets are situated here. This will have certain income tax consequences (p 157).

There is nothing in law to prevent the appointment of non-resident trustees. However it seems that any such appointment against the wishes of a beneficiary is voidable by that beneficiary particularly if it would not be sanctioned by the Court. If all the beneficiaries approve a non-resident appointment it cannot later be set aside. It would appear that it is also unlikely that the Revenue could interfere with such an appointment. If all the beneficiaries of an English trust are resident in another country the Court is likely to approve the appointment of non-resident trustees.

Indemnities will in all probability be required by the retiring trustees. Trustees retiring in favour of non-residents will have to ensure that all liabilities to the date of retirement have been settled. It will be more difficult for creditors (and the Revenue) to recover debts in another country and the former trustees may well find themselves personally liable for them.

Exporting a trust could have substantial CGT advantages. However unless the settlor was domiciled abroad at the time when the settlement was made it will not produce any CTT advantage (p 101).

13 Capital taxes and life assurance
by KEN BULGIN

This chapter is concerned with the impact of capital taxes on:

(1) life policies (whole-life policies, endowment policies, term assurance, etc);
(2) privately purchased general annuities (immediate and deferred); and
(3) pension policies (occupational pension schemes and private Retirement Annuity policies).

Capital gains tax is dealt with first, briefly because its impact on life assurance is not great. The greater part of the chapter is devoted to CTT, because virtually all aspects of life assurance have CTT implications.

Life assurance companies are liable to development land tax (DLT) and this tax applies also to pension funds, which are exempt from most other taxes, but in the usual case the deemed disposal at material development will have taken place before the property is purchased by the life office and the consequent DLT will merely be an element in the price; the subject is therefore not considered further.

For the stamp duty payable on policies and on the various documents involved in setting up and administering a policy trust, see p 200.

Capital gains tax and life assurance

The company's tax position
(FA 1972 S93(2); & FA 1974 S26)

Capital gains tax on policyholders' funds in respect of life assurance and general annuities is charged at the lower of the rate for individuals (currently 30%) and 37.5%, except in the case of exempt gilts (p 79). As life companies are generally able to defer realisations of assets for a long period, they usually pass on this benefit in the form of a lower rate of deduction for CGT on the benefits offered under their policies. This is seen most directly in the case of unit-linked policies, where unit prices are commonly adjusted to reflect potential CGT liability at a rate lower than 30%.

Insurance companies' pension funds are exempt from CGT (TA 1970 S314).

The tax treatment of policies

(CGTA 1979 S143)

In the ordinary way, life assurance policies are exempt from CGT under S143. You will only be liable to CGT on the gain on a life policy if it was taken out in the first place for someone else's benefit *and* you bought it for money or money's worth. 'Buying' here means buying from the owner — not buying from the insurance company by paying premiums (though your base cost on a disposal would be the price you paid for the policy plus the aggregate of the premiums you paid subsequently to keep it in force).

- *The market in life policies, which are sold mainly by specialist firms of auctioneers, is much diminished since the introduction of CGT but still exists, because if you are liable to pay tax on your income at 60% the alternative of a capital gain on a life policy taxed at only 30% is clearly attractive. This is especially so as you would normally keep up such a policy until the death of the life assured and so receive the sum assured, which is usually much larger than the cash value of the policy, ie the return on your investment reflects not simply the insurance company's investment yield but also a mortality profit.*

- *Because buying the policy introduces a CGT liability it is particularly important when you give a policy away that the document recording the transaction (referred to as a voluntary assignment) does not introduce a nominal price of, eg, £1. To do so makes what was always intended to be a gift technically a sale — even though the price is nominal — and so makes the recipient potentially liable to CGT when he or she subsequently disposes of the policy.*

If you have an immediate annuity, this is exempt from CGT (S144(*b*)). Deferred annuities are not exempt and are treated in the same way as life policies, but liability to CGT does not often arise as deferred annuities are not usually bought and sold.

The benefits under pension policies are generally non-assignable, ie, personal to you. The exception to this is term assurance under S226A (p 197), which is assignable. But again, while you might well mortgage such a policy as security for a loan, you would never buy one because:

(1)   if the life assured survived till the end of the term you would get no return on your investment at all; and

(2)   in any case, the Retirement Annuity legislation effectively prevents you from continuing to pay premiums and so keep the policy in force.

So a S226A term assurance policy will also not give rise to a CGT liability in practice.

Capital transfer tax and life assurance

Domicile

The usual rules as to domicile apply, including deemed domicile (p 69); if you are domiciled in the UK any life policies, wherever they were effected, are potentially liable to CTT but if you are not domiciled here you will not be liable in respect of any policies which are not UK assets for CTT purposes.

- *So if you are not domiciled or deemed domiciled in the UK your life policies will not be liable to CTT, provided they are either:*

    (1)   off-shore policies, ie, ones issued abroad (by a foreign insurance company or an overseas branch of certain UK companies) and expressed to be payable outside the UK; or
    (2)   issued under seal and kept physically out of the UK. A UK policy issued under seal is legally considered to be payable in the place the policy itself is when the claim is made, so if the policy is outside the UK on your death it will not be liable to CTT if you are not domiciled here when you die.

Own-life policies
(FA 1975 Ss20(2) & 22(1) & Sch10)

When you pay premiums on a policy effected on your life for your own benefit you are not decreasing your estate and there are no CTT implications.

On your death the sum assured is taxable as part of your net estate (Sch 10, paras 1 and 2).

If you make a lifetime gift of the policy this constitutes a potentially taxable transfer. For the purpose of lifetime transfers a policy is generally valued at the higher of its cash value and the aggregate premiums paid under it (Sch 10, para 11), except for term assurance and pension policies (p 197).

Joint-life policies

There are two kinds of joint-life policy: the sum assured can be payable on the first death or payable on the second death.

If you take out a joint-life policy the second life will usually be your wife's or husband's. So there will be no liability on the death of whichever of you dies first because of the spouse exemption (unless your policy is written as a tenancy in common and the first to die leaves his or her share to someone other than the survivor), and the rest of this section only applies if the second life on your joint-life policy is not your wife's or husband's. In those circumstances there are two occasions on which CTT may be payable:

(1)   As premiums are paid, if the joint premiums are in fact coming from the resources of only one of you, as the one providing the money is effectively making a gift to the other of his or her share of the premium. This applies particularly to joint-life single-premium investment bonds, because the normal expenditure exemption cannot apply to one-off gifts and the £3,000 pa capital exemption is unlikely to be adequate, whereas one of these two exemptions will usually apply to gifts of annual premiums.

(2)   On the death of the first to die under a first-death policy. You can usually avoid this possibility by splitting your joint policy into two, so that you each pay a premium on a policy which pays only if the other dies before you. You need documentary evidence of the split, ie, there should actually be two separate premiums payable under two separate policies.

If you are the second to die on a second-death policy then the sum assured will form part of your taxable estate in the usual way, unless the policy is written in trust (p 184).

Whether or not you will have any CTT liability on a joint-life policy therefore depends on:

(a)   whether you hold the policy as joint tenants or as tenants in common (see p 117 for an explanation of these terms), which will depend on the exact wording of the policy;
(b)   who provided the premiums; and
(c)   which of you dies first.

So the tax consequences of arranging a joint policy with someone other than your wife or husband can be complicated and you should seek specialist advice.

Life-of-another policies

If you take a policy on someone else's life then you are making payments on a policy from which you expect to benefit yourself. You are therefore not decreasing your estate by paying premiums, nor is there a transfer on the death of the life assured — you are merely collecting the proceeds of a policy you already own — so neither aspect has CTT consequences.

On the other hand, because you own the policy, if you die before the life assured then the market value of the policy (which usually equates roughly to the cash value) forms part of your taxable estate like any other asset.

If you indirectly fund a policy on your life owned by someone else by making them a gift of each premium as it falls due, such gifted premiums are potentially liable to CTT but will usually escape liability under one or other of the annual exemptions (p 74). The treatment of the life-of-another policy itself is unaffected.

Annuities

If you buy an ordinary lifetime annuity instalments will stop on your death and there is therefore nothing to be transferred and no CTT liability.

If, however, your annuity is guaranteed for a minimum period and you die before the guarantee runs off, then there is a CTT transfer on your death of the discounted value of the remaining instalments under the guarantee. If, for example, your annuity is for life but guaranteed for five years in any event and you die after three years, the discounted value of the remaining two years' guaranteed payments will be part of your net taxable estate for CTT purposes, though there will be no liability if you leave your residual estate (p 72) to your wife.

Similarly, if you buy a joint annuity then when one of you dies there is a potential CTT liability on the discounted value of his or her share in the annuity. Joint annuities are nearly always husband and wife contracts but if the second life is not your wife's or husband's then, as in the case of joint-life policies, the CTT position will depend on whether the annuity is written as a joint tenancy or a tenancy in common, whether there is one annuity policy or two, which of you provided the purchase money and who dies first.

Trust policies — domicile

As far as trusts are concerned, the CTT domicile rule is that there is no liability if:

(1)   the settlor is not domiciled in the UK at the time he made the settlement; *and*
(2)   the trust property is outside the UK when the event occurs which would otherwise have given rise to a CTT liability.

The *residence*, whether of the settlor, the trustees or the beneficiaries (which is crucial for CGT) is irrelevant for CTT.

● *So, if you are not domiciled in the UK and your trust policy is either off-shore or issued under seal and physically outside the UK when the claim arises (p 86), you can disregard the following section because your trust policy will be excluded property for CTT purposes (p 78).*

Trust policies — Married Women's Property Act (MWPA)

You can set up a trust for your beneficiaries of any ordinary life policy — whole-life, endowment, term assurance and including joint-life policies (for pension policies see p 196). If the beneficiaries of your 'own life' policy are limited to your wife or husband and children (which normally includes illegitimate and adopted children but not stepchildren or grandchildren) your policy will be issued under the special trusts of the MWPA; you can set up a trust policy for beneficiaries outside this small class but the special provisions of the MWPA will not apply. If, after setting up a trust policy, you go bankrupt a policy under the MWPA enjoys greater protection against your creditors than one not under the Act. As far as the CTT implications are concerned, however, the principles set out below apply regardless of whether the policy is under the Act or not.

The use of trust policies

Trust policies are widely used to provide for CTT because:

(1)   death is the main occasion of paying CTT and a life policy is the only savings vehicle guaranteed to produce the money exactly when it is needed;

(2)   the proceeds of a trust policy are normally themselves free of CTT; and

(3)   provision is manageable from income: if you are 45 and in normal health you can provide the sum you need to pay the CTT bill on your death for about 1½% pa; and if your wife is 40, also in normal health, and your arrangements for the disposition of your estate are such that you will not need the sum until the second of you dies, you can provide it for about ½% pa of the sum required.

One clear example of CTT provision is covering the extra CTT payable if you die within three years of making a life-time gift (p 70) by means of a three-year term assurance, ie, one which pays only on your death within three years of effecting the policy.

Policy trustees

You will probably want to be a trustee of your trust policy, though you need not be. You need at least one other trustee so that the insurance company can pay the surviving trustee(s) with the minimum of delay after your death. If you are the only trustee the trusteeship passes to your personal representatives (p 112) and payment cannot be made until probate or letters of administration (p 132) have been granted.

It is usually convenient to appoint your wife as trustee, especially if she is a beneficiary. If you have a joint-life policy payable on the second death you will, of course, need at least one trustee apart from you and your wife if probate delay is to be avoided.

There is no bar in principle to beneficiaries also being trustees and if your policy is for the benefit of your adult children you may think that they (or some of them) will make the most suitable trustees. Minor children, however, cannot act as trustees (p 162).

The insurance company can generally deal only with all the trustees acting together, so you should not appoint more trustees than is necessary since otherwise administration of the policy trust can be unwieldy. Further trustees can always be appointed later if necessary.

Trustees' powers

(see also pp 167-169)

The powers that trustees are allowed automatically by law are somewhat restricted and it is therefore usual to give your trustees specific powers in the document setting up the trust. Standard printed policy trusts vary to some extent according to the insurance company supplying them but they usually include power to:

(a)   make the policy paid-up, borrow on it, sell it or surrender it;

(b)   invest in a wider range of investments than is allowed by the general law, including non-income-producing assets such as investment bonds (p 192); and

(c)   where income is to be accumulated during a beneficiary's minority, pay income and/or capital for the minor beneficiary's benefit; it is usually provided that the trustees can get a good receipt for such advances from the minor beneficiary's parent or guardian. There may also be a specific power to pay CTT.

You can, of course, have your solicitor draft wider powers than those given in the standard form if you wish.

Life policy trusts

Within the limits the law allows you can set up a trust of a policy for any beneficiaries you choose and subject to whatever conditions you like. The legal effect will depend on the way your trust document is worded, ie, a combination of the wording of the gift (examples of which are set out below) and the trustees' powers discussed above. The general law of trusts will also apply whenever a question arises which your trust document does not cover specifically.

The following sections outline the main kinds of trust available, some of their applications and the CTT consequences of using them. A comprehensive treatment is not appropriate in a Guide of this nature and it is emphasized that what follows is only an outline. You should in any case *never set up a policy trust without taking specialist advice*.

There are, broadly, three types of life policy trust, which may for convenience be labelled:

(1)   an *absolute* trust, eg, 'for the absolute benefit of my wife Mary and my children John and Joan in equal shares'. You would use this kind of simple trust on a modest policy which you took out primarily to protect your dependants against the financial loss which your early death would otherwise involve. The beneficiary is often just your wife, in which case there would be no CTT liability on the policy even if it were not in trust because of the spouse exemption, and the main trust benefit is speedy payment. The surviving trustee (frequently your widow) has only to produce the policy and death certificate to the insurance company, comply with the company's usual claims procedures and payment can be

made very quickly without waiting for probate (p 132).

(2)   a *class* trust, eg, 'for such of my sons Thomas, Richard and Henry, and any other children of mine whenever born, as survive me and attain age 25, if more than one in equal shares and if none so survive then for the benefit of the last to die'. This is a simple example of the sort of trust you can set up if you feel able to decide at the outset who the beneficiaries are to be and what share of the policy proceeds they are to get. You can set out what is to happen if various events occur — the most usual 'contingencies', as they are called, are that the beneficiaries must survive you and must reach a particular age if they are to benefit. But this is an area in which you will need specialist advice, because if your wording is not sufficiently precise its effect according to trust law may not be what you intended.

(3)   a *flexible* trust, eg, 'for such of my children Albert, Brenda, Charles and Dorothy as I appoint and to the extent that I make no appointment then for Dorothy'. *(NB this is an abbreviated wording given purely for illustrative purposes: for a full wording you must take professional advice).* This is the kind of trust you would use when you are not absolutely clear as to the destination of the policy at the time you set up the trust. It leaves you free to change the beneficiaries, or the shares of the policy they are to have, at a later date when the situation is clearer. The class of possible beneficiaries can be much larger than in the abbreviated wording given above and you may include yourself, so that the trustees can effectively dismantle the trust by reverting the policy back to you if circumstances make this necessary at a later date. You can also word this kind of trust so as to enable your trustees to switch beneficiaries after your death. This power may be limited to the two years following your death to restrict the duration of the trust after your death. The two-year period also corresponds with that in which the policy can be reverted to your widow or widower free of CTT (p 126).

A longer appointment period, however, offers greater flexibility and more protection to the surviving spouse should he or she need the policy proceeds further in the future.

Notice that both class trusts and flexible trusts must finish by saying who is to get the benefit as a last resort, ie, if none of the events set out in the class gift happens (in the example, if none of your children both survives you and reaches age 25 or no appointment is made under a flexible trust. This person is called 'the default beneficiary' and is the estate of the last of your children to die (in the class trust example) or Dorothy (in the flexible trust example).

● *Whether you choose a class trust or a flexible trust depends on whether you want to set up an apparatus which is virtually self-driven — all you have to do is continue to pay premiums; or whether you prefer an arrangement which you can, to a large extent, adapt to changing circumstances. A flexible trust needs 'servicing' — considering from* time to time whether the beneficiaries/shares should be changed and, if so, making the necessary appointments — but ideally you should in any case consider your CTT arrangements periodically to ensure that they fit your current circumstances.

If the facility of having the policy appointed back to you if necessary is of overriding importance you will choose a flexible trust. If your beneficiaries are all minors (and especially if you may have further children whom you would want to include) you may decide on a class trust because this will save you the trouble of appointing a share to each child as it is born. In general, where the beneficiaries are adult, the CTT consequences of a change of beneficiary are the same whether the switch occurs automatically, because of the failure of a contingency under a class trust, or as the result of an appointment under a flexible trust.

Some natural applications of the flexible trust are:

(1)   You can arrange your policy trust in conjunction with the dispositions in your will: you can arrange for the recipient of, eg, shares in your family company to benefit under the policy so as to put them in funds with which to pay the CTT on the shares. Alternatively, you can leave the shares to one beneficiary and appoint another as beneficiary under the policy by way of compensation for not benefiting them under your will. Because of the beneficiary-switching facility you can set up the policy while you are in normal health and young enough for life assurance to be cheap, but postpone such decisions until you can see clearly which way you want to go.

(2)   Partnership assurance — arrangements between partners to enable the survivor(s) to buy the share of a deceased partner. If you effect a policy for the benefit of your partner but in fact survive to retiring age the life cover will no longer be needed for its original purpose and it is very useful to be able at that stage to have the policy appointed back to you. You can then declare new trusts of the policy (for the benefit of, say, your family) or surrender it, according to your circumstances at the time. The same applies to co-director insurance.

(3)   You can arrange your trust policy to operate in parallel with your will trusts. You may want to take advantage of being able to leave your property on two-year discretionary trusts (p 177) so that your trustees can decide in the two years following your death how your property should be distributed. In that case it is convenient to have the same facility in your trust policy, even though a benefit switch after your death (unless to your widow/widower within two years of your death) will involve a CTT charge on the sum assured.

CTT implications of trust policies — premiums

When you pay a premium on a trust policy you are in principle making a transfer of value. But in practice, in the great majority of cases, the transfer will be exempt either as normal expenditure (p 75) or as being within the £3,000 pa exemption (p 74). Small premiums may fall within the £250 pa per donee exemption (p 75), but these 'small gifts' have to be outright gifts, ie, with no conditions attached, so this exemption only applies to premiums where the policy is written under an absolute trust for a single beneficiary.

Since April 1979 most life assurance premiums have been paid net of life assurance relief, but whenever the premium does not qualify for relief (or there is some doubt as to whether or not it qualifies) it must be paid gross. The transfer for CTT purposes is the premium you actually pay, ie, net if you pay net, otherwise gross. So if yours is a doubtful case where the Inland Revenue have directed the insurance company that premiums must be collected gross, the transfer is the gross premium, and this applies even if you subsequently get a tax refund so that the effective cost to you is only the net premium.

Life assurance relief is no longer available in respect of insurances made after 13 March 1984.

● *If your estate is large enough it may pay you to pay premiums of more than £3,000 pa from capital. You would then be accepting that to the extent that the premium exceeded £3,000 pa you would be eroding your £64,000 nil rate band and, eventually, actually paying CTT on premiums, because this would be worthwhile in relation to the very large and normally CTT-free sum assured (see below) which the policy would produce.*

CTT implications — proceeds

When your trustees collect the proceeds of your policy and pass them to your beneficiaries (under an absolute trust) or the beneficiaries entitled at the time the claim arises (under a class trust or a flexible trust), there is no CTT liability. The policy was already held for the benefit of those beneficiaries and there is no transfer of value involved in the insurance company paying the claim. The principle is the same as when a life-of-another policy becomes a claim (p 182). This applies whether the policy becomes a claim on your death or is surrendered during your life.

CTT implications — changing beneficiaries/altering shares

Because the absolute/default beneficiary is already entitled to the policy it follows that there is a potential liability whenever there is a transfer of his entitlement, which can occur if the beneficiary dies or if another beneficiary is appointed so that the existing default beneficiary loses his • share, or part of it. For example, if you put your policy in trust for whoever you appoint from Albert, Brenda, Charles and Dorothy, with Dorothy as the default beneficiary, and at a later stage decide to appoint Albert instead, then your appointment has effectively transferred the benefit of the policy from Dorothy to Albert. If you decided instead to appoint to all four children equally then, after the appointment,

Dorothy has the benefit of one quarter of the policy, whereas before she had the whole of it, ie, she has effectively lost the benefit of three quarters of the policy. In both these cases the loss of benefit is treated as a transfer for CTT purposes.

The events giving rise to such notional transfers usually take place during your life and the value of the policy (or share in it if the default beneficiary is losing only part of the value of the policy) therefore relates not to the sum assured (because you are still alive) but to the market value of the policy, which is usually the cash value but with a minimum of the aggregate premiums paid.

Note that:

(1)   the calculation of the CTT liability is made with reference to the personal 'meter' of the beneficiary whose benefit is being reduced (Dorothy in the example above) and, with his/her permission, the losing beneficiary's £3,000 pa annual exemption (but *not* the beneficiary's normal expenditure exemption) can be set against the liability;

(2)   it is the policy trustees on whom the liability to pay the tax falls in the first instance; and

(3)   the notional amount transferred disappears from the losing beneficiary's 'meter' after ten years (p 71).

There is one very important exception to the beneficiary-switching charge: there is no liability if the appointment switches the benefit of your trust policy back to you or your spouse. The exemption for switches to your spouse extends for two years after your death, which is particularly useful because after your death the value of the policy is the sum assured and without the exemption switching the benefit to your widow/widower could give rise to a substantial CTT charge.

● *As a general rule, purely from the point of view of tax-efficiency and disregarding other factors, it is better to have your children as default beneficiaries rather than your spouse. This is because the trustee(s) can always appoint back to your widow within two years of your death with no CTT liability (see above), whereas an appointment from your widow to the children would involve CTT on the sum assured. If your children are the default beneficiaries no action need be taken if your widow is otherwise well provided for and it is appropriate for the benefit to go to them; but if, for instance, you die early and your widow is left with young children the benefits can be appointed back to her. If she is the sole surviving trustee of a policy on your life she can appoint back to herself. (References in this note to 'widow' include references to 'widower').*

CTT implications — accumulation and maintenance trusts

Under a *class* trust (but not usually a *flexible* trust) the beneficiaries may all be minors and, provided that the other requirements of the legislation are met (p 161), such a policy trust will be an accumulation and maintenance trust for CTT purposes. The legislation requires that minor beneficiaries of an accumulation and maintenance trust must become entitled to *income* at not later than age 25 (entitlement to capital may be postponed to any later age). In practice, the income entitlement age is usually 18, as in the following examples.

There are special rules when the potential share of an accumulation and maintenance trust beneficiary changes:

(1)   While all of the beneficiaries are under age neither the death of a beneficiary (which increases the potential share of all the other beneficiaries, where they are sharing equally) nor the birth of a further beneficiary where the class includes unborn children (which decreases the potential share of all the other beneficiaries) gives rise to any liability.
So if your sons Thomas, Richard and Henry in the example above are all under 18 they are potentially each going to get one third of the policy proceeds. If Thomas dies he will lose his potential one third (and Richard's and Henry's potential entitlements will go up to one half each); and if you have another child he or she will automatically be potentially entitled to one quarter of the proceeds and Thomas, Richard and Henry will each lose one twelfth (one third minus one quarter). But because of the special accumulation and maintenance trust rules there will be no liability in either case.

(2)   Where any of the beneficiaries have reached age 18, however, their share will have 'vested', as it is called technically, and any change to such a share will give rise to a CTT liability.
To return to the example, once Thomas has reached 18 his prospective entitlement to one third of the policy vests. So if at that stage Thomas dies, or his entitlement is reduced from one third to one quarter by the birth of another child, there will in either case be a potential CTT charge.

Where liability arises under (2) above the policy will be valued at its market value with a minimum of the aggregate premiums paid. The minimum does not apply when liability arises on the death of the losing beneficiary (Thomas in the example in (2) above).

Declaring a trust of an existing policy

If you decide to put an existing own-life policy in trust for beneficiaries, setting up the trust is a gift of the policy, which is usually valued at the higher of its cash value and the aggregate premiums paid. Thereafter the CTT treatment of premiums and proceeds is the same as if the policy had been written in trust from inception. Bear in mind that the document setting up the trust bears stamp duty on the market value of the policy.

Life policies as investments of existing trusts

If you are an income beneficiary of an existing trust, and you are thinking of effecting a substantial policy to provide for the CTT on your estate, you may be attracted to the idea of having your trustees pay the premiums from the trust income. This may be possible but, even assuming that the trustees' powers are wide enough for them to effect a policy on your life, this is an area in which you have to be very careful because:

(1)   the Revenue may argue that effecting a policy in this way constitutes a reduction in your income entitlement (because the trustees would be effectively accumulating income which they would otherwise pay to you) with a consequent charge to CTT on the fund to the extent of the reduction; and

(2)   it will be highly desirable to arrange for the trustees to hold the policy in a separate trust (although for the same beneficiaries), as otherwise the proceeds on your death will simply fall into the main trust. This will provide the trustees with substantial cash, which is of course very useful if the rest of the trust assets are not so liquid, but it does mean that the proceeds will themselves go to swell the trust fund and so increase the CTT payable.

A more promising area is that of accumulation and maintenance trusts, where single-premium investment bonds can often be an attractive investment. If you are the trustee of such a settlement then you will have to consider whether your investment powers are wide enough to put trust funds in investment bonds and the insurance company will need to satisfy itself that the trustees have an insurable interest in the beneficiary on whose life the bond is effected, although insurable interest is not usually a problem if a minor beneficiary who is potentially entitled to the capital represented by the bond is chosen as the life assured.

Provided that these potential problems are satisfactorily resolved an investment bond offers trustees:

(a)   an easily managed investment with an attractive spread of risk;

(b)   the insurance company's income tax rate of not more than $37\frac{1}{2}\%$, instead of the 45% they would otherwise pay on accumulated income; and

(c)   the choice, when the beneficiary comes of age, of realising the investment and paying him the money or passing him the bond and letting him realise it. In either case the CGT liability which normally arises when trust assets pass from trustees to the absolute ownership of the beneficiary (p 51) would be avoided, because of the exemption from CGT of life policies (p 15).

If, when the beneficiary attains his majority, he is likely not to be liable to higher rates of tax for some years he may prefer to take over the bond himself, whereupon he will be able to take advantage of the 'cumulative 5% per annum' system of taking withdrawals from it (see Chapter 21 of the *Allied Hambro Tax Guide*).

A bond (as a non-qualifying policy) can always give rise to a charge to higher rates of income tax on partial or total encashment. In the case of a settled bond this liability falls on the settlor, who has the right to recover from the trustees any tax he pays as a result. Therefore, while the settlor of the main trust (being a higher rate tax payer) is still alive withdrawals should not exceed 5% pa of the bond purchase price and, if he is still alive when the minor beneficiary comes of age, it will probably be essential to assign the bond out of the trust and let the beneficiary cash it in, as otherwise a substantial charge is likely to fall on the settlor.

An even more attractive result can sometimes be obtained by using withdrawals from the bond to pay premiums on a 'Maximum Investment Plan' on the life of the same beneficiary. If ten years' premiums have been paid on the MIP when the beneficiary comes of age, and it is assigned to him, he can then take withdrawals from it (at any level) completely free of tax. If the settlor is still alive the withdrawals from the bond to pay premiums must not exceed 5% pa of the bond purchase price if a charge to higher rates of income tax on the settlor is to be avoided (see above).

'Back-to-back' arrangements
(FA 1975 Ss42 & 44)

It was common during the estate duty era for estate holders to effect at the same time a whole-life policy in trust and a life annuity on their life. The instalments of annuity then effectively funded the premiums on the whole-life policy, the proceeds of which were normally free of estate duty. To avoid the Revenue invoking the estate duty 'associated operations' provisions it was necessary for the two contracts to be issued on independent terms, ie, it was not acceptable for the life policy to be issued at ordinary rates (in consideration of the purchase of the annuity) when your state of health was such that you would in the ordinary way have been charged an extra premium.

The 'associated operations' provisions have been carried over into the CTT legislation (FA 1975 S44) and the position continues that the Revenue will not invoke them against 'back-to-back' arrangements if the life policy is underwritten independently of the annuity. However, the annuity instalments are normally dissected for income tax purposes into capital and interest and the capital part is tax-free, only the interest part being taxable (S230); and FA 1975 S42 provides that only the (taxable) interest part of each instalment is eligible to be exempt as normal expenditure (p 75). You can, therefore, still set up a 'back-to-back' arrangement if you wish but if the life policy is substantial you may well have to use your £3,000 pa annual exemption (p 74) as well as the normal expenditure exemption in order to escape CTT on the premiums as you pay them.

Investment bonds and CTT

There are a number of plans on the market for mitigating CTT liability on investment capital by the use of single-premium investment bonds in trust.

'Inheritance Plans'

There are basically two types of inheritance plans. With one version you apply for a bond for a purchase price of £1,000, issued in a flexible trust, and then lend the trustees the balance of the sum to be invested, which sum they in turn invest in bonds, in small denominations for flexibility. The trustees then agree to repay you the loan, usually at 5% pa so as not to attract higher rate tax immediately (see *Allied Hambro Tax Guide*, Chapter 21).

The effect of this is to provide you with an 'income' (the loan repayments). Once the loan is repaid the trustees can provide further 'income' by cashing in a bond and appointing it back to you from time to time or, as a further refinement, making loans to you. The latter method has the advantage that on your death the outstanding loans are debts in your estate and, on the assumption that you have in fact spent them, this will reduce your estate for CTT purposes.

On your death the outstanding loan to the trustees is part of your estate but may be balanced by loans from the trustees to you and the value of the bond (value at death, less outstanding loan repayments made) passes to the beneficiary free of CTT.

The second version is a plan which combines gifts from the settlor with the prospect of loans being made by the trustees, as briefly referred to above. A trust is established with a large initial gift (which is invested in bonds), for example to make use of the settlor's nil rate band. The trustees are empowered to make loans to any of the trust beneficiaries and, should they decide to exercise this power, use the withdrawal facility on the bonds to obtain the necessary cash

Both types of inheritance plan ensure that the growth on the money transferred to the trust accrues outside the settlor's estate. The second version also makes use of the ten-year cumulation rules and the fact that any loans made to a beneficiary (for example, the settlor) are debts against his or her estate.

Of course, larger gifts could be made by the settlor to take advantage of the lower lifetime rates of CTT and a combination of gifts and loans is also possible.

Endowment bond schemes ('Peta' Plans)

Under these schemes you invest in a bond which is technically an endowment, but with a maturity date (commonly your 100th birthday) to which you are unlikely to survive. The bond usually has no value before maturity date (apart from the withdrawals at a pre-determined rate) but you also effect, again in a flexible trust, a term assurance running to the same term as the endowment bond and with a sum assured which is always equal to the value of the bond, ie it reflects unit growth and/or withdrawals.

The result is that you get 'income' from the endowment bond by way of withdrawals, as with the 'Inheritance Plan', and the capital passes to the beneficiary free of CTT on your death.

Setting up the arrangement is in itself a chargeable transfer of the difference between the capital invested and the actuarial value of the endowment bond. This actuarial value depends on your age and state of health and the rate of withdrawals you choose. The discounting inherent in this actuarial valuation means that you can usually invest considerably more than £64,000 with no CTT liability, because the CTT transfer still falls within the £64,000 nil-rate band, eg, at age 65 an investment of £100,000 can give rise to a transfer of about £45,000.

There are further elaborations of this approach, involving artificial endowment bonds, which rely on highly technical arguments of the kind which have recently come under attack both in the courts and by legislation. You should not contemplate investing in such plans without taking professional advice but in the end it is a personal decision as to whether you think the potential tax advantages, which can be considerable, are so attractive as to outweigh the possibility of the plan being effectively negatived by the Inland Revenue successfully challenging it in the courts.

Occupational pension schemes

(FA 1975 Sch 5 para 16; FA 1976 S89; SPs 20/1975 & 7/1976; & IR Notes, 7 May 1976)

Contributions

The larger part of an occupational scheme contribution is usually paid by the *employer* and is not a CTT transfer (FA 1976 S89).

Any contribution paid by the *employee* is usually expended primarily to provide pension and on this basis is normally ignored for CTT purposes by the Capital Taxes Office. Any contribution made to death benefit is treated as incidental to the main (pension) purpose and disregarded.

Pensions

Exempt approved occupational pension schemes are almost invariably set up in trust and if the ordinary CTT treatment of trust property applied (p 101) then every pensioner would be treated as having an interest in possession in the trust fund to the extent needed to support his pension and the scheme trustees would consequently be liable to tax every time a pensioner died. Para 16 therefore provides that the death of a pensioner is not to be treated as the coming to an end of an interest in possession in the trust fund.

If, however, your pension continues after your death, either because you die before the end of a guaranteed period or because the pension has been set up to continue to your widow or widower, then the same principles apply as to privately purchased non-pension annuities (p 183) and there will be a potential CTT charge, although there is in practice usually no liability because of the spouse exemption.

Pension schemes often give you the option, when you retire, of having the available funds applied so as to produce a smaller pension for you than you would otherwise have been entitled to in exchange for a pension (or larger pension) payable to your widow or dependant on your death. In this case, unless the dependant is your wife and the spouse exemption applies, the potential CTT liability arises not on your death but when you make the arrangements just before you retire, when you will be treated as having made a gift of the funds necessary to provide the pension payable after your death.

The rules of your scheme may provide that the balance of guaranteed payments of your pension (where the guarantee is for not longer than 5 years) are to be paid as a lump sum, and this will then usually be subject to the same treatment as other lump-sum benefits payable under the scheme (p 195).

Lump-sum payments on death

Pension schemes nearly always provide for the payment (if you die before reaching retiring age) of a lump sum which, under Inland Revenue regulations, must not exceed four times your salary at the date of death plus a return of your personal contributions, if any. It was at one time common for such payments to be freely disposable at the direction of the member, ie, you completed a nomination form when you joined the scheme (and could of course change your nomination later if circumstances changed) and on your death the trustees were required to pay to the person you nominated. This sort of arrangement is practically indistinguishable from being able to dispose of the benefit by will and it was consequently treated for CTT purposes in the same way, ie, it formed part of your net taxable estate.

Nowadays, however, most pension scheme rules provide for what is known as *discretionary disposal*. Under this system you indicate to the trustees the beneficiary to whom you would like them to pay the benefit and in all ordinary cases they will follow your preference, but they are not *required* to do so — they have complete discretion as to which beneficiary (from a large class of potential beneficiaries) they will pay the benefit — and this ensures that the death benefit is free of CTT. The class invariably includes all members of your family. Note that:

(1)   It does not matter whether the lump-sum death benefit comes from the fund which was being accumulated to provide your

pension or from a specially arranged term assurance on your life, as long as it does not exceed four times your salary.

(2)   It may also include, in *addition* to four times your salary, the return of your personal contributions.

(3)   If you are already drawing your pension when you die then the remaining instalments under a guarantee (provided the guarantee is not more than five years) can also be paid as a lump sum under the same discretionary disposal rule and will then also be free of CTT.

The lump-sum death benefit is normally paid direct to an adult beneficiary but if it is paid to outside trustees (or held by the pension scheme trustees, if the rules provide for this) then the usual CTT rules applicable to trusts apply (p 101). In practice, the usual reason for holding death benefits on trust is that the beneficiaries are under age, in which case the special exemptions for accumulation and maintenance trusts (p 102) can apply.

● *Because lump-sum death benefits can be paid free of CTT you may wish to take the opportunity of putting funds in the hands of the second generation by expressing a preference to the scheme trustees for the benefit to be paid to your children, as long as your wife is otherwise well provided for. In particular, if your family company has set up a pension scheme of which you are a member you may wish to use the scheme death benefit as a tax-efficient aid to passing shares in the company to the second generation. If, for instance, your son is going to follow you in the business you will probably want to leave him your shares, or most of them, but if you do this in your will there will be a CTT liability. If, instead, you leave the shares to your wife (free of CTT under the spouse exemption) and the scheme trustees pay the death benefit to your son, then he will receive this free of tax and can use it to buy shares from his mother. (It is essential that he buys the shares at the same sort of price at which they would change hands in an arm's-length sale, ie, a sale between unconnected persons.) By this method:*

(1)   *The shares pass to your widow free of CTT under the spouse exemption and any CGT liability is cancelled by your death.*

(2)   *The death benefit passes to your son free of CTT under the pension scheme discretionary-disposal exemption.*

(3)   *The purchase of shares by your son from his mother is free of CTT as a sale and it will take place too soon after your death for any significant CGT liability to have arisen.*

● *When setting up a family company scheme you can maximise the CTT-free lump-sum benefit by having your salary increased by 17.65% and then making a 15% contribution. It makes no difference to your company whether the extra money is paid as a pension scheme contribution or to you as salary — it is normally deductible for corporation tax purposes in either case — and as the 15% contribution of the increased salary (which is tax-deductible) exactly matches the 17.65% increase in salary your tax position is also unchanged. But:*

(1)   *a lump-sum benefit can now be paid on your death of up to four times your increased salary; and*

(2)   *your personal 15% pa contributions will build up over the years and these can also be returned on your death free of CTT.*

● *If your family company has set up a pension scheme then the company is usually itself the trustee of the scheme. This means that the disposal of the lump-sum benefit after your death will be at the discretion of the company, which in turn means that any decision will effectively be taken by whoever is in control of the company at that stage. In this situation the company acts as trustee and is therefore legally required to make decisions in good faith and consider only the interests of the beneficiaries. If you nevertheless prefer not to leave such a decision in the hands of your company you can arrange for the company to retire as trustee and for outside trustees, such as your solicitor or accountant, to be appointed instead.*

Retirement annuities and S226A term assurance policies

(FA 1975 Sch 2, para 5 & Sch 5, para 16; & IR Notes, 7 May 1976)

Pensions

If you have a retirement annuity and payments continue after your death the CTT treatment is exactly the same as that of an occupational pension in the same circumstances (p 194). This applies whether payments continue to your widow or for the unexpired balance of a guaranteed period.

The position is also the same if you exercise the option, just before retiring, of re-allocating the fund so as to provide a smaller pension for you in exchange for a larger one for your widow (p 195).

Death benefits

If you take out a retirement annuity (ICTA 1970 S226) the contract may include a return on premature death; and you can effect a term assurance policy under S226A specifically to provide a lump-sum death benefit if you die before pension age. Until 1980 both types of policy had to be written so as to pay the death benefit to your estate and the CTT consequences were the same as taking an ordinary life assurance policy on your own life (p 94): no liability on paying the premiums and the proceeds formed part of your net taxable estate.

There was a variation as far as the proceeds are concerned in that you could nominate a dependant and the proceeds on death would then be applied to provide a pension for that dependant instead of being returned to your estate as a lump sum. Such nominations were revocable but this did not give rise to any CTT liability (Sch 7, para 2). The nomination method was a survivor of the estate duty era and was not much used after the introduction of CTT, because the dependant was usually the policyholder's wife and it was more beneficial to leave her the lump-sum return (which would in any case be free of CTT under the spouse exemption) than to provide for a pension. This would be especially true if you were to die young, because the return would not have had time to build up to a substantial figure and the pension rate available to a young widow with an expectation of life of many years is unattractive. The nomination method has now been virtually superseded by the trust method (see below).

S226/S226A policies in trust

It has been possible since FA 1980 to write S226A term assurance in trust and also the *death benefit* of a retirement annuity (but not the pension which remains personal to you).

Premiums

Under retirement annuity contracts, regular premiums on which tax relief is obtained are ignored for CTT purposes on the principle that they are paid primarily to provide the policyholder with a personal benefit (his pension) and that the death benefit, which is being gifted to the trust beneficiaries, is incidental. One-off contributions are treated differently (see *Putting existing policies in trust,* p 199).

Under S226A life assurance contracts, regular premiums are not ignored (because, by definition, they are paid not to provide a personal benefit but to provide the in-trust death benefit) but they will in virtually every case be exempt as normal expenditure out of income (p 75). Again, one-off contributions are treated differently (see *Putting existing policies in trust,* p 199).

Proceeds on death

The trust may take various forms but whether it is an absolute trust, a class trust or a flexible trust (p 185) or a discretionary trust similar to the discretionary disposal clauses used in occupational pension schemes (p 195), no liability to CTT arises on the death of the policyholder.

Switching beneficiaries

If you decide on a flexible trust for your policy then the position is in principle the same as with a life policy (p 194): every appointment of a beneficiary means the loss or reduction of the existing default beneficiary's share, with a consequent potential liability to CTT. There is, however, a significant difference in the valuation of the benefits switched, because the 'minimum of the aggregate premiums paid' basis which applies in the case of ordinary life policies does *not* apply to either retirement annuities or S226A term assurance policies.

On lifetime appointments the value switched is the (notional) market value of the death benefit, and this will usually be too small to attract

CTT. The value would only be significant if you switched beneficiaries at a time when you were in such poor health as to have a very short expectation of life. If, for instance, you were at the time of the switch only likely to live about a year then the notional market value of the death benefit would be something approaching its face value discounted for 12 months. The £3,000 annual capital exemption (p 74) is also available, so unless the beneficiary from whom the benefit was switched has already himself made sufficient CTT transfers to have both used his annual capital exemption and used up or seriously depleted his nil-rate band, there will very rarely be any CTT actually payable on lifetime transfers.

If appointments under a flexible trust are made in the two years after your death the value switched will be the actual death benefit paid, in which case there may well be CTT payable (unless the appointment is to your widow or widower).

Putting existing policies in trust

Since it has only recently become possible to put retirement annuities and S226A term assurance policies in trust, there are inevitably thousands of existing cases where the policyholder will now wish to take the death benefit outside his estate for CTT purposes by declaring a trust of it. Declaring a trust of an existing policy is in principle a gift for CTT purposes (p 190), the value transferred being the market value of the death benefit, unless the immediate beneficiary is your wife, in which case the spouse exemption will apply. Non-regular contributions to both retirement annuities and S226A life assurance policies are treated in the same way.

The transfer involved in your making such a declaration of trust, however, is in practice likely to be treated as negligible unless you die from natural causes within two years of making it. In such cases the Capital Taxes Office may (retrospectively) treat the market value at the time of the transfer, calculated on medical/actuarial principles, as a transfer made at the time of the declaration. Under the 'transfers within three years of death' rule (p 71) CTT would be payable at the death rates.

● *If you have an existing retirement annuity or S226A contract and are considering whether to declare a trust of the death benefit it is worth bearing in mind that if you leave it as it is the entire fund value (not its market value at the date of declaration) will fall into your estate on death and be chargeable at the death rates. So even if you cannot be sure whether a declaration will be liable to precipitate a (retrospective) CTT charge, and at what level, as a general rule it is true to say that you have something to gain from putting the death benefit in trust (CTT-free proceeds to the immediate beneficiaries and exempt further input) and very little to lose. However, every case must be considered on its own merits.*

Once the trust has been declared future premiums, proceeds and beneficiary-switches will be treated as set out above.

14 Stamp duty

Introduction

Stamp Duty is imposed by the Stamp Act 1891 (SA), as amended by sub-sequent Finance Acts, whilst the Stamp Duties Management Act 1891 gives many of the administration provisions. The detailed rules of Stamp Duty are very involved and the following is only a broad outline of particular points with which you may be concerned regarding your capital transactions.

There are two kinds of stamp duties, *fixed duties* and *ad valorem duties*. *Fixed duties* do not change, regardless of the money involved (eg, the duty of 50p on a deed). On the other hand, *ad valorem* duties are charged according to the value of the transaction (eg, the duty on the conveyance of a house).

The payment of Stamp Duty is confirmed by a stamp being impressed on the document (adhesive stamps may also be used but only for contract notes). The stamps are impressed on the documents at the local stamp office. First a marking clerk indicates the duty and then, on payment, the stamp is impressed. It may be either necessary or desirable for the document first to be *adjudicated* by the stamp office, which involves supplying them with the necessary particulars. They will then determine the duty to be paid. This applies particularly to voluntary dispositions and company reconstructions, for example.

Basic rules

The following are some general guide-lines:

(1) Stamp Duty is essentially a charge on instruments (documents): it is not charged on the transactions.

● *If you carry out a transaction without documenting it, as when you make an oral contract, no duty will be chargeable. Of course, this may not be desirable commercially.*

(2) Although the duty is charged on instruments, the exact category of the charge, and hence its amount, depends on the nature of the transaction, not only the form of the document.

(3) No duty is chargeable on an instrument which is ineffective for the purpose for which it was executed.

(4) No duty is chargeable regarding a transaction which is effected orally. This follows from (1) above, since stamp duty falls on instruments and not transactions.

● *If you later make a separate written record of an oral contract, this will not normally require stamp duty to be paid.*

(5)   If a document covers several different matters all ancillary to its main purpose it only bears duty according to the latter. However, if several separate instruments are embodied in one document, they are all individually stampable. This also normally applies to several distinct matters covered by one instrument (SA Ss3 & 4).

(6)   Under a contract, the sum finally payable may depend on future events; eg, the final price might depend on results. In these circumstances, the *ad valorem* duty on this instrument is calculated on the maximum possibly payable. However, if only the minimum can be calculated in advance, this must be used.

(7)   If more than one head of charge applies to an instrument duty can only be charged under one of them, but the Revenue can choose which.

(8)   Sometimes it is necessary for one transaction to be effected by two or more instruments. An example might be the settlement of land. Provided it is at least 50p, *ad valorem* duty cannot be charged more than once in these circumstances.

Unstamped instruments

If you do not stamp a document, in general you will not be open to any action against you by the Revenue. However, whilst the instrument remains unstamped it will not be admitted in evidence and will generally be of no value. Exceptionally, the Revenue can recover by action in the High Court certain duties, including particularly capital duties on companies and loan capital duty. Note that when a document is presented for stamping out of time in practice after 30 days from when the instruments are first executed, or brought into the UK, the Revenue may, at their discretion, charge penalties. These comprise £10 together with 5% per annum on the duty and also, for certain categories, the amount of the original duty in addition. The categories where more than twice the duty can become payable on late stamping include gifts, leases and conveyances on sale.

Overseas aspects
(SA S14(4) & FA 1984 S109)

Stamp duty applies to instruments executed anywhere within the UK and those, wherever executed, relating to any property in this country or anything being done here. Thus an instrument executed in the UK must be stamped, even if it takes effect abroad. Furthermore, there is normally no double taxation relief in respect of stamp duty suffered abroad, except in Ireland.

A reduced rate of *ad valorem* duty was applied on sales of shares, etc, to overseas residents. Broadly speaking, the rate was approximately 1%

instead of 2%. However, instruments executed after 19 March 1984 only bear 1% duty (p 204) and this rate also applies to overseas residents.

Exemptions

Certain documents are exempted from stamp duty by the Stamp Act 1891 and subsequent legislation. The following table lists some of the more important exemptions.

Table 10: Exemptions

Transfers of Government Stocks ('Gilts')
Transfers of certain fixed rate non-convertible loan stocks
Conveyances, transfers or leases to approved *charities* (FA 1982 S129)*
Conveyances, transfers or leases to the National Heritage Memorial Fund*
Transactions effected by the actual operation of law
Documents regarding transfers of ships (or interests in them)
Transfers brought about by wills (testaments and testamentary instruments)
Articles of apprenticeship and of clerkship
Customs bonds, etc
Certain legal aid documents
Contracts of employment
Certain National Savings documents
Deeds of Covenant and bonds
Policies of insurance and related documents (excluding life assurance)
One life assurance policy which is substituted for another according to the rules (FA 1982 S130)
Transfers (and issue) of certain EEC Loan Stocks
Transfers of Treasury guaranteed stock (eg, British Electricity 3% 1968–73)

Not treated as duly stamped unless having a stamp denoting not chargeable to duty.

Ad valorem duties

The most important Stamp Duties with which you may be involved are those which increase according to the consideration involved. These are known as *ad valorem* duties. Normally, *ad valorem* duties are charged at a fixed percentage but this is sometimes expressed in bands, so that the 1% charge on share transfers, etc, is £1 for every £100 or part thereof (with 50p per £50 up to £500). Also, for some duties, sliding scales apply for small transactions. The following table gives the basic percentage rates of various *ad valorem* duties, which were largely reduced for documents executed after 19 March 1984 (or executed after 12 March 1984 and stamped after 19 March 1984). For stock exchange securities, the reduced rate applies to transactions after 11 March 1984 for settlement after 12 March 1984.

Table 11: Ad Valorem Duties	Instrument Executed	
	Before 20 March 1984	After 19 March 1984
Capital Duty (p 203)	1%	1%
Conveyance or transfer on sale (p 204) (includes share transfers, land, etc)	2%	1%
Exchanges or partitions of freehold land	2%	1%
Inland bearer instruments	6%	3%
Overseas bearer instruments	4%	2%
Lease premiums	2%	1%
Leases — duty based on rent (p 206)	up to 24%	up to 24%
Voluntary dispositions (gifts etc)	2%	1%

Capital duty

(FA 1973 Ss47 & 48 & Sch 19)

Capital duty applies to 'chargeable transactions' (see below) carried out by 'capital companies' (see below). The companies must be effectively managed in Great Britain; or managed outside the EEC with their registered office in Great Britain.

'Capital companies' include UK limited companies, limited partnerships (formed under Limited Partnerships Act 1907) and EEC companies. 'Chargeable transactions' which you should particularly note are the formation of a capital company and an increase in its capital by the contribution of assets, including the capitalisation of a debt. Other examples of chargeable transactions include the changing of a member's liability regarding his capital from unlimited to limited and certain transfers of the registered office or place of management back to the UK from abroad.

Rate of capital duty

Duty is charged at £1 on every £100 of the amount on which duty is chargeable. Parts of £100 count as £100: thus if the amount is £101, the duty is £2. The amount on which duty is charged on the formation of a company or the increase of its capital is the consideration contributed by the members. This is normally cash but could be other assets taken at open market value. Where the registered office, etc, is transferred from abroad, the duty is charged on the net asset value of the company.

Exemptions from capital duty

The following transactions do not normally attract capital duty:

(1)   Capitalisation of reserves by bonus issues etc.

(2)   Company reconstructions, etc (p 205).
(3)   Increases in capital following reductions.
(4)   Company demergers (FA 1980 Sch 18).
(5)   Share issues following preference share redemptions.

(Items (2), (3) and (4) above require adjudication — p 200.)

Conveyance or transfer duty
(SA Ss54–61 & Sch 1 etc & FA 1984 Ss109 & 110)

In essence, duty is charged at £1 for every £100 (or part) of the value comprised in a conveyance or sale of any property, subject to an exempt portion for most assets (p 205). (Broadly, prior to 20 March 1984, the rate was 2%.) Certain *voluntary dispositions* are charged to full *ad valorem* duty, so you should bear this in mind regarding any gifts of property which you make. (There are various exclusions such as marriage settlements.) The property will need valuing and duty will be charged as if it had been a sale. (This assumes that an instrument was involved in the gift on which stamp duty could be charged.) Other conveyances or transfers not subjected to the *ad valorem* duty bear a fixed 50p duty.

House purchases at discounted prices by public sector tenants and discounted sub-sales by housing associations carry duty on the discounted rather than the full market value.

Reduced rates of duty

Prior to (broadly) 20 March 1984 (p 204), duty was charged at a reduced rate of only 50p for every £50 (or part) for transfers at full value of stock or marketable securities to a non-resident. Subsequently, however, no such relief is given from the general 1% rate. An exemption applies for bearer securities. The duty (at the time of issue) is now 2% for overseas and 3% for British bearer securities.

Prior to 20 March 1984, reduced rates applied where property other than stock and marketable securities was transferred (FA 1982 S128). In order to qualify, you included in the instrument a *Certificate of Value* that the transaction effected by the instrument did not form part of a larger transaction or series of transactions, in respect of which the amount or value of the consideration exceeded a stated limit. The limits were £25,000, £30,000, £35,000 or £40,000 which respectively reduced your duty rate to nil, 25p, 50p and 75p for every £50 (or part). (Below £300, special rates applied, as shown in the following table.) From broadly 20 March 1984, the relief has been simplified so that transactions not exceeding £30,000 are free of duty (apart from stock, etc) and others carry 1%.

Table 12: Conveyance or transfer — rates of ad valorem duty

Before 20 March 1984 Consideration	Reduced rates — instruments certified at:				Ordinary Rate
	£25,000	£30,000	£35,000	£40,000	
Up to £5	Nil	5p	5p	10p	10p
£5·01 — £100 for each £10 or part	Nil	5p	10p	15p	20p
£100·01 — £300 for each £20 or part	Nil	10p	20p	30p	40p
Over £300 for each £50 or part	Nil	25p	50p	75p	£1
From 20 March 1984					
Up to £500 for each £50 or part	Nil	Nil	50p	50p	50p
Over £500 for each £100 or part	Nil	Nil	£1	£1	£1

Reliefs on company reconstructions and amalgamations, etc

Provided certain conditions are satisfied, company reconstructions and amalgamations are afforded relief from capital duty and duty on conveyance or transfer. Also, transfers of assets between associated companies are relieved from duty on conveyance or transfer, provided one company owns at least 90% of the issued share capital of the other or both are owned to the same extent by a third company (FA 1930 S42).

Relief from capital duty
(FA 1973 Sch 19; & FA 1976 S128)

Relief from capital duty (p 203) applies where an existing capital company (p 203), or one being formed, acquires share capital of another capital company so that it owns 75% of it. Relief also applies if the whole or part of one capital company's undertaking is acquired by another.

In order to obtain the relief, the consideration must consist of no more than 10% cash and the rest must consist of shares in the acquiring company. The relief is normally lost if within five years the shareholding in the acquired company falls below 75%.

Relief from conveyance or transfer duty
(FA 1927 S55; & FA 1928 S31)

Similar (though more stringent) rules apply to those for capital duty relief (see above). For example the shareholding requirement which must actually be comprised in the transaction is at least 90% of the shares in both the acquiring and the acquired company. Similarly, where the undertaking of one company is acquired by another, the consideration must be at least 90% of the shares in the latter. However, the relief can only be lost within two years.

Leases

(SA Sch 1; FA 1974 Sch 11; FA 1980 S95; FA 1982 S128; & FA 1984 S111)

Stamp duty at the 1% *ad valorem* rate applies to premiums on leases. The special scale in the following table applies to the rent element in a lease of land and buildings but not chattels, etc. Also excluded are licences.

Table 13: Leases — ad valorem duty on rents		
Term	Annual Rent	Duty for every £50 or part thereof
Not exceeding 7 years or indefinite	not exceeding £500 exceeding £500	Nil 50p
7–35 years	—	£1
35–100 years	—	£6
over 100 years	—	£12
(Where the rent does not exceed £500, a sliding scale applies.)		

From 20 March 1984 an *agreement for a lease* is subjected to stamp duty as if it were a lease. This blocks a previous avoidance device.

Fixed duties

These duties are paid at the same rate regardless of the size of the consideration involved in the transaction. The rate of duty is normally 50p which applies, for example, to miscellaneous deeds, miscellaneous conveyances or transfers not covered by *ad valorem* duty, appointments, declarations of trust, letters of attorney, revocations of trust and surrenders. A rate of £1 applies to leases of small furnished lettings and £2 to miscellaneous leases (eg, leases with uncertain rent or none at all).

15 Capital tax planning signposts

Tax planning points have been interspersed throughout this book and generally appear in italics to distinguish them. Thus, CGT planning regarding your main residence appears in the section of the book which deals with that subject. However, other facets of capital tax planning regarding your home appear elsewhere in the book, such as joint ownership with your wife for CTT purposes and DLT on a second home. The purpose of this chapter is to group together references to the various tax planning points under various different headings and circumstances. Thus, page references are given together to various different planning points concerning houses.

As a general point, you should remember that, as with all other tax planning, capital tax planning should under no circumstances involve tax evasion. Evasion is completely illegal and could result in your paying substantially more to the Inland Revenue, including penalties and interest.

Tax avoidance, on the other hand, is completely legal and consists of arranging your affairs in such a way that they attract the lowest possible tax charge. It must be said, however, that very comprehensive anti-avoidance provisions are to be found in the Taxes Acts, some of which are described in outline in this Guide. In addition, a number of case decisions have been decided in favour of the Inland Revenue which increase their powers, with regard to blocking artificial tax avoidance schemes.

A fairly recent example was the decision in the House of Lords early in 1981 in two jointly considered CGT avoidance cases (*W T Ramsay* v *IRC* and *Eilbeck* v *Rawling*). This far-reaching decision decided, among other things, that the effect of an artificial tax avoidance scheme had to be considered as a whole if it had no commercial result other than the saving of tax. More recently, *Furniss* v *Dawson* has held this to mean that stages in a chain can be disregarded if they have no effect but to save tax.

The tax planning points throughout this Guide are not of an artificial nature. On the whole, they indicate various ways in which advantage can be taken of the legislation without exploiting it.

Put in a nutshell, capital tax planning consists of the art of maximising your wealth, for the enjoyment of your wife, yourself and your children. Enjoyment is one of the key factors and if the measures which you have to take, such as going abroad to a country which you do not like, detract from your quality of life then the tax advantages probably would not justify the upheaval. Similarly, the gain of tax advantages at the risk of leaving your wife insufficient to live on is not to be recommended.

A particular point to remember regarding capital tax planning is that, especially regarding CTT, the projected savings are not likely to take place for many years. Within that period of time, the law could be completely altered and so it is most desirable to have a degree of flexibility in your arrangements.

Remember that the following 'signposts' usually only relate to the planning points in the text and so it will normally be advisable also to refer to the basic rules shown nearby. Furthermore, the 'signposts' are not exhaustive and so reference to the contents and index may be necessary. The main headings are as follows:

Page	**Business assets**
44	Replacing business assets – CGT relief
46	Gifts – CGT relief
47	CGT retirement relief
47	awaiting required age
47	wife obtaining relief
47	chargeable business assets
56	Inter group transfers – using up CGT losses

	Buying and selling assets in general including shares
13	Using annual CGT exemption — 'bed and breakfast' — minor children

Index